Albert Stickney

State Control of Trade And Commerce by National or State

Authority

Albert Stickney

State Control of Trade And Commerce by National or State Authority

ISBN/EAN: 9783744733731

Printed in Europe, USA, Canada, Australia, Japan

Cover: Foto ©ninafisch / pixelio.de

More available books at **www.hansebooks.com**

STATE CONTROL

OF

TRADE AND COMMERCE

BY

NATIONAL OR STATE AUTHORITY

BY

ALBERT STICKNEY
OF THE NEW YORK BAR

NEW YORK
BAKER, VOORHIS & COMPANY
1897

TABLE OF CONTENTS.

PAGE

INTRODUCTORY..1–8
Recent decisions at variance with tendencies of the law.
Early stages of English law.
Numerous attempts to control prices by statute.
In time all such attempts abandoned.
Experience of this country.
Recent growth of alarm over trusts.
Distinction between public and private employments.

CHAPTER I.

THE COURSE OF THE ENGLISH LAW AS TO STATE CONTROL OF PRIVATE EMPLOYMENTS............................9–83
Early English statutes regulating trade, labor and prices.
Same as to forestalling, regrating and engrossing.
Same as to combinations to raise prices.
This statute nearly a dead letter.
Rex v. *Journeymen Taylors of Cambridge.*
No other conviction reported.
Statutes against forestalling, etc., repealed.
Rex v. *Waddington.*
Offenses abolished.
English law as to combinations to raise prices as finally established.
Mogul Steamship Co. v. *McGregor.*

CHAPTER II.

THE COURSE OF THE ENGLISH LAW AS TO PUBLIC EMPLOYMENTS 84–88
No distinction at first between public and private employments.
That distinction now well established.
Munn v. *People of Illinois.*
Instances of public employments.
Innkeepers.
Common carriers.
Statutes relating to carriers.

CHAPTER III.

THE COURSE OF THE AMERICAN LAW AS TO PRIVATE EMPLOYMENTS UNTIL CERTAIN RECENT DECISIONS........89–116

> The course of the law down to the statutes against conspiracies in restraint of trade.
> No such crime at common law.
> Blackstone's "Offences against Public Trade."
> Forestalling, Regrating, Engrossing and Monopolies.
> Monopolies not properly so classified.
> All these offenses created by statute.
> Such English statutes never a part of our law.
> *Commonwealth* v. *Hunt*.
> Our own experience with statutes regulating prices.
> Resolutions of Continental Congress.
> Early New York statute.
> Early New England statutes.
> New York Revised Statutes as to Conspiracy.
> *People* v. *Fisher*.
> Other cases.
> The situation of the New York law as it was prior to 1893 stated.

CHAPTER IV.

THE COURSE OF THE AMERICAN LAW AS TO PUBLIC EMPLOYMENTS 117–134

> Great increase in degree of control of such employments.
> Reasons therefor.
> Railroad companies.
> *People* v. *New York Central etc. R. R. Co.*
> *Munn* v. *People of Illinois*.
> Examples of statutes regulating public employments.

CHAPTER V.

RECENT DECISIONS AS TO CONTRACTS IN RESTRAINT OF TRADE OR COMMERCE 135–178

> *People* v. *Sheldon*.
> *U. S.* v. *Trans-Missouri Freight Association*.
> The decisions in these cases stated.
> Preceding positions re-stated.
> Unsoundness of interpretation of Revised Statutes in *People* v. *Sheldon*.
> Authorities as to interpretation of statutes which change the common law.

People v. *Sheldon* quoted. PAGE
Attempted limitation of its doctrine to articles of necessity.
This point examined.
Elements of crimes in general.
The crime of conspiracy.
Unconstitutional to fix prices by statute.
Taylor v. *Porter.*
Owner's right to freedom of contract.
And to fix prices either individually or in combination with others.
As to combinations of laborers.
Commonwealth v. *Hunt.*
Conspiracy defined.
Necessity of element of legal injury to others.
Raising of prices not such an injury.
The rights of the public.
Instances of enforcement of contracts in restraint of trade.
Diamond Match Co. v. *Roeber.*
Other cases.
Impossibility of reconciling *People* v. *Sheldon* with these.
U. S. v. *Trans-Missouri Freight Association.*
Interstate Commerce Act.
Anti-Trust Act.
Applicability of foregoing argument to this case.

CHAPTER VI.

SOME GENERAL CONSIDERATIONS....................179–193

Economic questions involved.
Whether any public damage from contracts to prevent competition.
The answer from experience.
The best regulation of prices.
Groundlessness of fears of "trusts."
The increased concentration of capital.
Relations of labor thereto.
Needlessness of attempts at statutory control.
And futility of such attempts.
Summary of positions reached.
Latest proposed legislation.

TABLE OF STATUTES.

ENGLISH :
                                                     PAGE

23 Edw. III. (1349)..9–14
    "Statute of Labourers ;" also regulating prices of victuals.
25 Edw. III. Stat. 1 (1350)...15–20
    "Statute of Labourers."
25 Edw. III. Stat. 4 (1350)... 38
    Prescribing the penalty of him that doth forestal wares, merchandise or victual.
37 Edw. III., c. III., V., VI., VII., VIII., XV. (1362)..................21–24
    Regulating prices, forbidding engrossing, forbidding artisans to follow more than one craft, regulating quality of goldsmiths' work, and the diet and clothing of servants and others.
14 Rich. II., c. IV. (1390).. 42
    "To keep the price of wools the better."
14 Rich. II., c. V. (1390).. 43
    Prohibiting the export of certain staples.
14 Rich. II., c. VI. (1390)... 42
    Providing that English merchants shall freight only in English ships.
14 Rich. II., c. VII. (1390).. 43
    Prohibiting the export of tin except out of Dartmouth.
4 Edw. IV., c. 1 (1465).. 35
    Regulating the length and breadth of cloths to be sold, and providing that no cloths wrought beyond sea shall be brought into England.
7 Edw. IV., c. 1 (1468).. 36
    Regulating the making of worsteds.
2 and 3 Edw. VI., c. 15 (1549)...............................2, 43–45
    The bill of conspiracies of victuallers and craftsmen.
3 and 4 Edw. VI., c. 21 (1550)..................................... 38
    "An Act for the buying and selling of butter and cheese."
5 and 6 Edw. VI., c. 14 (1552)..................................39, 40
    "An Act against Regrators, Forestallers and Engrossers."
5 and 6 Edw. VI , c. 15 (1552)..................................... 41
    "An Act against Regrators and Engrossers of Tanned Leather."
5 Eliz., c. 4 (1563)...24–34
    "An Act containing divers orders for artificers, labourers, servants of husbandry and apprentices."
1 Jac. I., c. 6 (1603).. 35
    Amending the 5 Eliz., c. 4.

	PAGE
21 Jac. I., c. 3 (1624)...	95
As to monopolies.	
3 Wm. and Mary, c. 12 (1691)...	86
Regulating carriers of goods.	
12 Geo. III., c. 71 (1772)...	48
Repealing statutes against forestalling, regrating and engrossing.	
5 Geo. IV., c. 95 (1825)...	45, 47
Repealing the 2 and 3 Edw. VI., c. 15.	
2 and 3 Wm. IV., c. 120 (1833)...	86
Regulating stage carriers.	
2 and 3 Vict., c. 66 (1839)...	86
Amending the preceding.	
7 and 8 Vict., c. 24 (1844)...	48
Abolishing the offenses of forestalling, regrating and engrossing.	
17 and 18 Vict., c. 31 (1854)...	86
Railway and Canal Traffic Act.	
36 and 37 Vict., c. 48 (1873)...	88
Regulation of Railways Act.	
38 and 39 Vict., c. 86 (1875)...	85
"Conspiracy and Protection of Property Act;" repealing 5 Eliz., c. 4.	

UNITED STATES:

24 Stat. at Large (c. 104 of 1887)......................................	171
Interstate Commerce Act.	
26 Stat. at Large (c. 647 of 1890)......................................	172
"An Act to protect trade and commerce against unlawful restraints and monopolies."	

NEW YORK:

Constitution of 1777..	137
As to application of English law and statutes.	
Laws of 1778, c. 34..	100
"An Act to regulate the wages of mechanicks and labourers, the prices of goods and commodities, and the charges of inn-holders within this State, and for other purposes therein mentioned."	
Laws of 1788, c. 46..	137
Providing that none of the Statutes of England shall be considered as law of this State.	
2 Revised Statutes, 691 (1830)...	100
Defining offense of conspiracy.	
Laws of 1870, c. 19..	114
Amending the preceding.	
Laws of 1890, c. 566...	133
Transportation corporations law.	

TABLE OF STATUTES. ix

	PAGE
Laws of 1892, c. 617	133

Amending the preceding.
Laws of 1892, Vol. 2, p. 2120.................................... 130
Defining powers of Board of Railroad Commissioners.

MASSACHUSETTS :

Province Laws of 1776, 1777, c. 14.................................... 101
" An Act to prevent Monopoly and Oppression."
Province Laws of 1776, 1777, c. 46.................................... 105
Amending and " more effectually carrying into execution" the preceding.
Province Laws of 1777, 1778, c. 6.................................... 108
Repealing the two preceding.
Province Laws of 1778-1779, c. 31.................................... 108
" An Act against monopoly and forestalling."

TABLE OF CASES.

A.
PAGE
Abbott v. Johnstown R. R. Co., 80 N. Y. 31............................ 124
Alger v. Thacher, 19 Pick. 51.. 161

B.
Bloodgood v. Mohawk & H. R. R. R. Co., 18 Wend. 9................. 120
Bolt v. Stennett, 8 T. R. 606... 127
Bowen v. Hall, 6 Q. B D. 333..54, 58
Bridgewater Case (unreported)... 52
Bromage v. Prosser, 4 B. & C. 247... 57

C.
Capital & Counties Bank v. Henty, 7 App. Cas. 741..................... 57
Carrington v. Taylor, 11 East. 571.....................................58-65
Chappell v. Brockway, 21 Wend. 157....................................... 161
Chasemore v. Richards, 7 H. L. C. 348..................................... 57
Chic. & N. W. R. R. Co. v. People, 56 Ill. 365............................ 123
Clifford v. Brandon, 2 Camp. 358.. 58
Commonwealth v. Boynton, 3 Law Reporter, 295......................... 96
Commonwealth v. Carlisle, Brightly, 36..................................... 97
Commonwealth v. Hunt, 4 Metc. 111.................................96, 153
Commonwealth v. Judd, 2 Mass. 329... 96
Commonwealth v. Pierpont, 3 Law Reporter, 296......................... 96
Commonwealth v. Tibbetts, 2 Mass. 536.................................... 96
Commonwealth v. Ward, 1 Mass. 473.. 96
Commonwealth v. Warren, 6 Mass. 74....................................... 96
Cousins v. Smith, 13 Ves. 542..62, 70

D.
Diamond Match Co. v. Roeber, 106 N. Y. 473............ 159, 165, 166, 167
Dunlop v. Gregory, 10 N. Y. 241... 161

F.
Farmers' L. & T. Co. v. Heming, 17 Am. Law Reg. (N. S.) 266......... 123
Farrer v. Close, L. R. 4 Q. B. 602.. 66

G.

	PAGE
Garrett v. Taylor, Cro. Jac. 567	65
Gregory v. Brunswick, 6 Man. & G. 205	58

H.

Hilton v. Eckersley, 6 E. & B. 47	62, 66, 71, 76, 80
Hodge v. Neill, 107 N. Y. 244	167
Hornby v. Close, L. R. 2 Q. B. 153	60
Homer t. Graves, 7 Bing. 735	162
Hutchins v. Hutchins, 7 Hill, 104	59

I.

Ind. R. R. Co. v. State, 37 Ind. 489	123

J.

Johnston Harvester Co. v. Meinhardt, 9 Abb. N. C. 395	114

K.

Keble v. Hickringill, 11 Mod. 74	53, 58, 65

L.

Leslie v. Lorillard, 110 N. Y. 519	164, 167
Lough v. Outerbridge, 143 N. Y. 271	169
Lumley v. Gye, 2 E. & B. 216	54, 55, 58

M.

Master Stevedores' Association v. Walsh, 2 Daly, 1	113
Matthews v. Associated Press, 136 N. Y. 333	166
Messenger v. Pa. R. R. Co., 36 N. J. 407	121
Mirams, *In re*, L. R. 1 Q. B. 595 (1891)	76
Mitchel v. Reynolds, 1 P. Wms. 181	65, 66, 160, 161
Mogul Steamship Co. v. McGregor, L. R. 21 Q. B. Div. 544	50, 51–57
Mogul Steamship Co. v. McGregor, L. R. 23 Q. B. Div. 613	57–71
Mogul Steamship Co. v. McGregor, App. Cas. 1892, p. 35	71–82, 89, 90, 135, 170
Mulcahy v Regina, L. R. 3 H. L. 306	63
Munn v. People of Illinois, 4 Otto, 123	84, 124

N.

New Brunswick, etc. R. R. Co., *In re*, 1 P. & B. 667	123
N. J. Nav. Co. v. Mer. Bank, 6 How. 382	127
N. Y. C. & H. R. R. R. Co. v. People, 12 Hun, 195; 74 N. Y. 302	123
Noble v. Bates, 7 Cow. 307	161

O.

O'Connell v. The Queen, 11 Cl. & F. 155..................................59–62
Olcott v. Supervisors, 16 Wall. 678.. 120

P.

People v. A. & V. R. R. Co., 24 N. Y. 261................................. 123
People v. Bush, 4 Hill, 133.. 148
People v. Collins, 19 Wend. 56...118–123
People v. Comrs. of Salem, 1 Cow. 23.. 123
People v. Fanshawe, 137 N. Y. 68... 138
People v. Halsey, 37 N. Y. 344.. 118
People v. N. Y. C. etc. R. R. Co., 28 Hun, 543......................... 118
People v. North River Sugar Refining Co., 121 N. Y. 582............. 168
People v. North River Sugar Refining Co., 54 Hun, 354................ 169
People v. Palmer, 109 N. Y. 110.. 138
People v. Richards, 108 N. Y. 137... 138
People v. Sheldon, 139 N. Y. 251 ....135, 140, 146, 157, 169, 170, 178, 188
People el rel. v. B. & A. R. R. Co., 70 N. Y. 569. 123
People ex rel. v. D. & C. R. Co., 58 N. Y. 152......................... 123
People ex rel. v. Rochester State Line R. R. Co., 14 Hun, 373 ; 76 N. Y. 294.. 123
Pettibone v. United States, 148 U. S. 203................................... 156
Price v. Green, 16 M. & W. 346... 66
Printing Co. v. Sampson, 19 Eq. Cas. 462.................................. 163

R.

Regina v. Daniell, 6 Mod. 99... 70
Regina v. Druitt, 10 Cox. C. C. 592......................................53, 73
Regina v. Parnell, 14 Cox. C. C. 508.. 59
Regina v. Rowlands, 17 Q. B. 671 ....54, 61, 64
Rex v. De Berenger, 3 M. & S. 67... 52
Rex v. Eccles, 1 Leach C. C. 274 ....54, 70
Rex v. Ivens, 7 C. & P. 213... 85
Rex v. Journeymen Taylors of Cambridge, 8 Mod. 11.........46, 47, 54, 97
Rex v. Kimberty, 1 Levinz, 62... 69
Rex v. Norris, 2 Ld. Keny. 300...46, 49
Rex v. Severn & Wye Ry. Co., 2 Barn. & Ald. 646..................... 123
Rex v. Sterling, 1 Levinz, 126.. 69
Rex v. Turner, 13 East. 228..53, 54, 70
Rex v. Waddington, 1 East. 167..48, 61
Richardson v. Mellish, 2 Bing. 252... 76
Rogers v. Rajendro Dutt, 13 Moore, P. C. 209........................... 57
Rousillon v. Rousillon, 14 L. R. & L. Div. 351........................... 162

S.

	PAGE
Skinner v. Gunton, 1 Wms. Saund. 229..	59
State v. H & N. H. Ry. Co., 28 Conn. 538...	123
State v. N. E. R. R. Co., 9 Richardson, 247	123
State v. R. R. Co., 37 Conn. 154	123
Stowell v. Zouche	139

T.

Talcott v. Township of Pine Grove, 1 Flippin, U. S C. C. 144	121, 123
Tarleton v. M'Gawley, Peak, N. P. C. 270	58, 65
Taylor v. Porter, 4 Hill, 140	150, 188
Tex. & P. R Co. v. Interstate Com. Comsn. 162 U. S. 197	191
Tode v. Gross, 127 N. Y. 480	166

U.

U. P. R R. Co. v. Hall, 91 U. S 343	123
U. S. v. E C. Knight Company, 156 U. S. 1..	174
U. S. v. Trans-Missouri Freight Association, 166 U. S. 290	135, 170, 176, 188

W.

White v. Wager, 32 Barb. 250 ; 25 N. Y. 328	138
Wickens v. Evans, 3 Y. & J. 318	67
Wilkinson v. Leland, 2 Pet. 657	151
Winsmore v. Greenbank, Willes, 577	54

STATE CONTROL

OF

TRADE AND COMMERCE

INTRODUCTORY.

RECENT decisions of our highest legal tribunals, especially the United States Supreme Court and the New York Court of Appeals, holding that a mere combination of common carriers, or of private property owners, providing for the fixing of rates and prices for their own property, by one common authority for all, constitutes a crime, are, in my opinion, so far at variance with the tendencies and growth of English and American law, and are so hopelessly in conflict with the fundamental principles of the law of property under a modern constitutional government, that an unusual degree of interest attaches at the present time to an examination of the law applicable to such combinations.

It will be found that much light will be thrown on the questions involved, by a short review of the history of the English and American law relating to state control of trade and commerce. Careful investigation will show, that the recent statutes under which the decisions alluded to have been made, are not novelties; that they are merely revivals of old attempts to protect the community —by statute—against dangers of the imagination; and we shall find the strongest reason for believing that here again history will repeat itself, and that the legislation and judicial interpretation of the present will follow the same course with the legislation and judicial interpretation of the past.

The rudimentary stages of the growth of the English law abounded in attempts to restrict and control trade and commerce by statute. Those attempts took various forms. The most frequent consisted in the passage of statutes regulating prices, of labor and merchandise. Other statutes, as to trade and commerce of specific classes, were completely prohibitory. Such were the statutes prohibiting the export of gold and silver, of wheat and other grains, of wool, of tools and machinery; and forbidding the departure of artificers from the kingdom to work in foreign countries. Violations of these statutes were made crimes, and were punishable by fine and imprisonment.

One class of these statutes, while not fixing specific prices, for specific classes of merchandise, endeavored to prevent any attempts to raise prices, whether by single individuals, or by combinations of individuals. "Engrossing," as it was termed in the old statutes, which consisted only in buying and holding in quantity, with a view to a subsequent sale at an advance in price—the object of nearly all wholesale buying—was made a crime; whether on the part of a single individual, or of individuals in combination, was immaterial. The old English statutes on this branch of the law, if they had been enforced, would have abolished the occupation of wholesale merchant or middleman, and would have virtually compelled every producer to be his own salesman. Trade and commerce, as they exist to-day, and as they necessarily must exist to supply the needs of any large community, would have been made impossible.

In connection with the statutes of the classes already mentioned are to be considered statutes against conspiracies, or combinations, to raise prices, of both labor and merchandise. The earliest of these was the Statute 2 & 3 Edw. VI., c. 15, which made it a crime, for certain classes of tradesmen to combine to raise the prices of the commodities in which they dealt, or for workmen to combine to raise the prices, or limit the hours, of their labor. These statutes were part of the general scheme of state control, of labor, trade, and commerce.

In time all these attempts to control prices and labor were abandoned. From the earliest date, the reported cases of indictments for mere combinations to raise the prices of the combiners' own property, whether of their labor or their merchandise, are very few. Where their purpose was the doing of legal injuries to others, the law was frequently invoked to punish such combinations. But where the purpose of single individuals, or of combinations of individuals, was limited to the mere raising of the price of their own property, either their labor or their merchandise, the reports of cases in the English courts show an almost entire absence of even so much as an attempt to enforce those old statutes. In time, by common consent, the statutes making such combinations criminal became obsolete. It was found by experience, that they could not be enforced, and that their mere existence, with occasional sporadic attempts at enforcement, did more harm than good. The only effect of such attempts was to cause temporary annoyance to that part of the community which had an especial regard for the law. In the end, the statutes were repealed. The final outcome has been, in England, that it is to-day the law, as worked out by the courts and the legislature together, that there is virtually no limitation or restriction, directly or indirectly, on the right of every individual and corporation, either singly or in combination with others, to dispose of their own labor and merchandise at their own free will. In England to-day the law is well established, that the ownership of property, of all ordinary kinds, comprises not only the right of free use (always subject to the proviso that its use is to be in such manner as not to interfere with the rights of others), but also the right of free sale, at the will of the owner, whether the property be labor or merchandise, and whether the owner's will be exercised separately or in combination with other individuals.

The experience of this country has been somewhat different from that of England. In our early colonial legal history there is an almost entire absence of attempts to fix prices, of either labor or merchandise, or to interfere in any degree with the full freedom of the citizen in the exercise of his lawful right to sell his own labor, and his own merchandise, on his own terms, or to refuse to sell it at all. Such attempts, so far as they have come under my notice, were first made, at least to any considerable extent, during the war of the revolution, when the depreciation of the continental and state paper currencies, in connection with the severe burden of public expenditures, caused such widespread distress, that, by a common impulse, resort was had to legislation, in different forms, in the attempt to alleviate that distress. In the year 1777, we find action taken in the Continental Congress, and in several of the state legislatures, looking to a protection of the community by legislation, against the advance in the prices of labor and merchandise, and the fall in the prices of the different kinds of paper money. That action took different forms. But those forms, substantially all of them, consisted in attempts to regulate prices by statute. Very speedily they were found to be, not only ineffectual to good, but, on the contrary, effectual only to evil. For that reason, the greater number of them were promptly repealed. Such as were not repealed, if any such there were, were by common consent ignored.

Thereafter there was in this country virtually an entire abandonment of all attempts by statute, or by the action of government in any form, to interfere with the freedom of contract in private employments. That condition continued until a recent period, when there has grown up a widely spread alarm over the modern large combinations of capital, called "trusts," which have been at times stigmatized as "monopolies." These large combinations of capital have revived the vague dread, felt in antique rudimentary times, of an oppression of the entire community by an excessive raising of the prices of merchandise at the hands of large capitalists. As matter of historical fact, even in early times, in both England and this country, notwithstanding the extremely imperfect development of the machinery of transportation which then existed, no substantial practical evil ever resulted from any attempt to merely raise prices, of labor or merchandise, on the part of either single individuals or combinations of individuals. Such attempts soon found their own levels, and their own limitations. But to-day, with our vast modern development of the science and machinery of transportation, when the markets of the whole world have largely become one, when a rise in the price of any kind of merchandise immediately causes an increase in supply, with a decrease in demand, and when the prospect of large profits invariably draws large amounts of fresh capital to paying investments, there is no longer any danger, from any attempt to enhance the prices of merchandise, whether by single individuals, or by individuals in combination, whether to single individuals, or to that combination of individuals which we term the community. Any attempt to raise the price of any article of merchandise immediately impels purchasers to curtail their consumption ; consequently it immediately curtails the demand; and inevitably it soon brings a return to prices that are reasonable. Experience shows, in times recent as well as ancient, that any attempt to interfere by legislation, or by the arm of the law, with the citizen's full freedom of contract, in fixing the price of his own labor or merchandise, either singly or in combination with others, is wholly needless, and is productive only of evil.

This fact it is, which, in times past, both here and in England, has been the real cause of the virtual abandonment, until recently, of attempts to interfere with the freedom of contract, by the processes of law.

This same fact will—in time—put an end to the present series of such attempts.

Meantime, in view of the revival in this country of legislation of like character with the old English statutes, it becomes important to ascertain the precise condition of the law regulating such attempts, not merely for the purposes of practising lawyers, but for legislators, and students of political science.

In order to fully comprehend the law of to-day on this subject, it will be necessary to some extent to examine its previous history, through the different stages of its development, in England and in this country.

Before, however, beginning such an examination, it is well to call attention to one fundamental distinction. That distinction is the one which exists between private property and private employments, on the one hand, and a class of property and employments which are correctly termed public, on the other, although the title to that property be not vested in the state, and the employments be not those of ordinary public officials. Reference is here had, of course, to railroads, to all classes of public highways, and to all classes of common carriers, innkeepers, and the keepers of public resorts. From a very early period, the state has exercised control, in one form or another, over innkeepers and common carriers, from the necessities of the situation, without reference to any other fact than that their employments were quasi-public, and that state control, to some extent, was necessary for the full protection of the ordinary citizen. Such control did not rest on the fact that innkeepers and common carriers held any franchise, or any property, derived from the state, or, so far as my reading goes, from any fact other than those just stated. In later years, common carriers by steam and rail have found it necessary, in order to construct their roads, to use the right of eminent domain, with other special rights and privileges conferred by the state. This fact has furnished an additional reason, in their case, for holding that they are subject to state control, in the use of their rights, privileges, and property. But in cases where there is an entire absence of any grant, or franchise, or other property, directly conferred by the state, we still find that these properties and employments have for a long time been subject to some form of state control, by virtue of their public nature. Such common carriers are virtually public servants, occupying and operating the people's highways. For every reason, therefore, it becomes necessary that they should be subject to state control. The same reasons generally apply to telephone and telegraph companies, to gas and electric light companies, to ferry companies, to turnpike, plank road, and bridge companies, to the owners of elevators, to companies for owning and operating tramways, pipe lines for oil and gas, and waterworks. They are all public, in their nature and uses; and nearly all of them exist, and get their property, or part of it, by some form of grant from the state.

As to property and employments of this public nature the tendencies and growth of the law are in a precisely opposite direction from those which apply to ordinary private property and employments. In early times, the interests of these common carriers were of comparatively slight importance. In recent times they have increased to an enormous extent. The railroad employees alone in this country number upwards of a million of men. The number of individuals engaged in other employments of the same general nature is very large. Public control, of these properties and employments, has become a greater necessity than ever, in the face of their intimate connection at every point with the daily life of the community.

Public control, with these properties, has taken the form of control, both of the use of the properties, and of the prices of such use. Such control is a necessity. It is recognized as such by all competent judges. It has its legitimate province, and its legitimate limitations. It appears to be increasing, rather than decreasing. The reason is, that the public necessities demand such increase.

This distinction, between public and private properties and employments, will be found to be fundamental. It lies at the bottom of all sound legislation for the regulation of properties and employments of all kinds. Especially it will be found to constitute the essential and conclusive reason in favor of state control of all public employments, and in opposition to state control, and all attempts to interfere with the fullest freedom of contract, as to all private property and private employments.

CHAPTER I.

THE COURSE OF THE ENGLISH LAW AS TO STATE CONTROL OF PRIVATE EMPLOYMENTS.

In the early stages of English parliamentary government, we find a large number of statutes which put restrictions of many kinds on the freedom of the individual citizen, but especially on his right to choose his own field of labor, and his right to make his own price for his own labor and merchandise. In time, as has been stated, all these restrictions came to be practically ignored; and most of them were formally abolished by a repeal of the statutes in question. The intention, as evidenced by the later statutes, was to repeal all. But many of the ancient statutes creating those restrictions remained unrepealed until a very recent date.

In order to get an adequate idea of the progress of the English law in this respect, it will be necessary to go into some degree of detail. And in order to get a complete idea of the character of such legislation, it is important to examine those statutes with some thoroughness.

The Statute of Labourers is the first one which calls for our attention. It will be necessary, in order to present satisfactorily the quality of the legislation embraced therein, to give it *verbatim*. It is as follows:

" The Statute of Labourers, made 23 Edw. III. and Anno Dom. 1349.(*a*)

(*a*) 2 Pickering's Statutes, 26. All the English statutes here quoted are from Pickering's edition.

"EDWARD by the grace of God, &c. to the reverend father in Christ, William, by the same grace archbishop of Canterbury, primate of all England, greeting. Because a great part of the people, and especially of workmen and servants, late died of the pestilence, many seeing the necessity of masters, and great scarcity of servants, will not serve unless they may receive excessive wages, (2) and some rather willing to beg in idleness, than by labour to get their living; we, considering the grievous incommodities, which of the lack especially of ploughmen and such labourers may hereafter come, have upon deliberation and treaty with the prelates and the nobles, and learned men assisting us, of their mutual counsel, ordained:

"CAP. I.

"Every person able in body under the age of sixty years, not having to live on, *being required*, shall be *bound to serve him that doth require him*, or else *committed to the gaol* until he find surety to serve.

"That every man and woman of our realm of England, of what condition he be, free or bond, able in body, and within the age of threescore years, not living in merchandize, nor exercising any craft, nor having of his own whereof he may live, nor proper land, about whose tillage he may himself occupy, and not serving any other, *if he in convenient service (his Estate considered) be required to serve*, he *shall be bounden to serve him which so shall him require*. And *take only the wages, livery, meed, or salary, which were accustomed to be given in the places where he oweth to serve, the XX. year of our reign of England, or five or six other common years next before*. Provided always, That the lords be preferred before other in their bondmen or their land tenants, so in their service to be retained: so that nevertheless the said lords shall retain no more than be necessary for them. And *if any such man or woman, being so required to serve, will not the same do*, that proved by two true men before the sheriff or the bailiffs of our sovereign lord the King, or the constables of the town where the same shall happen to be done, *he shall anon be taken by them or any of them, and committed to the next gaol*, there to remain under strait keeping, till he find surety to serve in the form aforesaid.

"CAP. II.

"If a workman or servant *depart from service before the time agreed upon*, he shall be *imprisoned*.

PRIVATE EMPLOYMENTS. 11

"ITEM, If any reaper, mower, or other workman or servant, of what estate or condition that he be, retained in any man's service, do *depart from the said service without reasonable cause or licence, before the term agreed, he shall have pain of imprisonment.* And that none under the same pain presume to receive or to retain any such in his service.

"CAP. III.

" The *old wages, and no more,* shall be *given to servants.*

" ITEM, That *no man pay, or promise to pay,* any servant any *more wages, liveries, meed, or salary than was wont, as afore is said.* Nor that any in other manner shall demand or receive the same, upon pain of doubling of that, that so shall be paid, promised, required, or received, to him which thereof shall feel himself grieved, pursuing for the same. And if none such will pursue, then the same to be applied to any of the people that will pursue. And such pursuit shall be in the court of the lord of the place where such case shall happen.

"CAP. IV.

" If the lord of a town or manor do offend against this statute in any point, he shall forfeit the treble value.

" ITEM, if the lords of the towns or manors presume in any point to come against this present ordinance either by them, or by their servants, then pursuit shall be made against them in the counties, wapentakes, tithings, or such other courts, for the treble pain paid or promised by them or their servants in the form aforesaid. And if any before this present ordinance hath covenanted with any so to serve for more wages, he shall not be bound by reason of the same covenant, to pay more than at another time was wont to be paid to such person. Nor upon the said pain shall presume any more to pay.

"CAP. V.

" *If any artificer or workman take more wages than were wont to be paid, he shall be committed to the gaol.*

" ITEM, That sadlers, skinners, white-tawers, cord-wainers, taylors, smiths, carpenters, masons, tilers, shipwrights, carters, and all other artificers and workmen, *shall not take for their labour and workmanship above the same that was wont to be paid to such persons the said twentieth year, and other common years next before,* as afore is said, in the place where they shall happen to work. And *if any man take more, he shall be committed to the next gaol, in manner as afore is said.*

"CAP. VI.

"*Victuals shall be sold at reasonable prices.*

"Item, That butchers, fishmongers, regrators, hostelers, brewers, bakers, pulters, and *all other sellers of all manner of victual,* shall be bound to sell the same victual for a *reasonable price,* having respect to the price that such victual be sold at in the places adjoining, so that the same sellers have *moderate gains, and not excessive,* reasonably to be required according to the distance of the place from whence the said victuals be carried. (2) And if any sell such victuals in any other manner, and thereof be convict in the manner and form aforesaid, he shall pay the double of the same that he so received, to the party damnified, or, in default of him, to any other that will pursue in this behalf. (3) And the mayors and bailiffs of cities, boroughs, merchant-towns, and others, and of the ports of the sea, and other places, shall have power to inquire of all and singular which shall in any thing offend the same, and to levy the said pain to the use of them at whose suit such offenders shall be convict. (4) And in case that the same mayors and bailiffs be negligent in doing execution of the premises, and thereof be convict before our justices, by us to be assigned, then the same mayors and bailiffs shall be compelled by the same justices to pay the treble of the thing so sold to the party damnified, or to any other in default of him that will pursue; and nevertheless towards us they shall be grievously punished.

"CAP. VII.

"*No person shall give any thing to a beggar that is able to labour.*

"Item, because that many valiant beggars, as long as they may live of begging, do refuse to labour, giving themselves to idleness and vice, and sometime to theft and other abominations; none upon the said pain of imprisonment shall, under the colour of pity or alms, give any thing to such, which may labour, or presume to favour them towards their desires, so that thereby they may be compelled to labour for their necessary living. Wherefore our said sovereign lord the King, the xiiii. day of June, the xxiii. year of his reign, hath commanded to all sheriffs of England by divers writs, that they shall do openly to be proclaimed and holden, all and singular the premises in the counties, boroughs, merchant-towns, seaports, and other places in their bailiwicks, where to them shall seem expedient : and that they do thereof due execution, as afore is said.

"CAP. VIII.

"He that taketh more wages than is accustomably given, shall pay the surplusage to the town where he dwelleth, towards a payment to the King of a tenth and fifteenth granted to him.

"Subsequently our sovereign lord the King, perceiving by the common complaint, that his people, for such excessive stipend, liveries, and prices, which to such servants, labourers, and workmen were constrainedly paid, be oppressed, and that the disme and quinzime to him attaining might not be paid, unless remedy were therefore provided : regarding also the coactions and manifest extortions, and that there was no man, which against such offenders, did pursue for the said commodity so ordained to be obtained : wherefore it was consonant, that that thing which was ordained to be applied to singular uses, seeing that the same persons did not, nor would not, pursue, should be converted to a publick and common profit, by the advice of his counsel, Hath ordained, That all and singular workmen, servants and artificers, as well men as women, of whatsoever estate or condition they be, taking more for their labours, services, and workmanship, than they were wont to take the said XX. year, and other years aforesaid, should be assessed to the same sum, which they shall receive over and above, with other sums as well for the time past, when the stipend, wages, liveries, and prices were augmented, as for the time then to come. And that the said whole sum received over and above, should be levied of every of them, and gathered to the King's use, in alleviation of every of the towns, whereof the said artificers, servants, and labourers be, towards the payments of the sums of the disme and quinzime yet running, whereunto the same towns or people of the same were assessed. So that always, the same disme and quinzime ended, all the same money, liveries, and prices, or the value of the same liveries, which (as afore is said) should be over and above received of them, and every of them, should be levied and gathered by them, whom the King will thereto assign, to the King's use, in alleviation, and supportation of the realm of England. And that they which for the same to serve, or the said sums so by them over and above received, and before assessed to pay, and their crafts and work to exercise do refuse, they shall be incontinently arrested by the taxers and collectors of the said disme and quinzime, or any of them, in every of the said towns deputed to execute the premisses, or by the bailiffs of the places, or constables of the towns, when they be thereof certified, and committed to the gaol, there to remain till they have found surety to serve, and shall pay that that they shall above receive, according to the same ordinances, or till the King shall some other thing thereof demand. And always it is the intent of the King and of his council, that according to the first ordinance it should be lawful, and shall be lawful to every man, to pursue against all exceeding the same, or not obeying to the same, and the thing recovered to be applied to his own use. And therefore our said sovereign lord the King hath commanded all archbishops, and bishops, that they do to be published the premises in all places of their dioceses, commanding the curates and other subdiocesans, that they compel their parochians to labour, according to the necessity of the time, and also their stipendiary priests of their said dioceses, which do now excessively take, and will not, as it is said, serve for a competent salary, as hath been accustomed, upon pain of suspension and interdiction. And that in no wise ye omit the same, as ye love us and the commonwealth of our realm. Dated the day and year aforesaid."

This Statute, it is seen, attempted not only to regulate the wages of labor, but the sale of "all manner of victual," and to compel its sale at "reasonable prices."

As to labor, however, it went beyond a mere attempt to fix prices. It also laid upon persons able to labor the legal obligation to work at those prices. Moreover, it gave to would-be employers a corresponding legal right to service. It thereupon proceeded to provide legal machinery, such as it was, for enforcing those rights and obligations.

This was logical and consistent. Evidently, statutes which fix the rates of wages to be paid by the employer ought also to provide proper legal process to enable him to procure employees at those rates. If the employer is not allowed to pay any higher rate than that fixed by the State, the State is surely bound to protect him by compelling the employee to accept service at the rates so fixed.

The legislators of that time duly accepted that obligation. They made the attempt, not only to fix the prices of labor, but also to compel the laborer to accept those prices. The same feature will be found to exist in other early English statutes, and in some early American statutes.

This feature of those early statutes will be found, in my opinion, to have a most important bearing on the general situation under the later English and American law.

Although this Statute of Labourers purported to regulate the prices of labor and of merchandise, it did not fix the rates of wages or the prices of merchandise in specific amounts of money, but merely enacted that the able-bodied persons named in the statute should " take only the wages, livery, meed, or salary, which were accustomed to be given in the places where he oweth to serve the XX. year of our reign of England, or five or six other common years next before ;" and that, as to prices of " victual," " all manner of victual" should be sold at " prices which were reasonable."

This left matters vague. Evidently, too, other practical difficulties intervened to prevent the statute from having the full degree of efficiency which had been anticipated. So we find very soon thereafter another Act, the 25 Edw. III., Stat. 1 (A.D. 1350), which begins with a recital showing the contempt with which the former act had been treated by all classes.

This later statute is as follows :

" A Statute of Labourers, made Anno 25 Edw. III. Stat. I. and A. D. 1350.

" Whereas late against the malice of servants, which were idle, and not willing to serve after the pestilence, without taking excessive wages, it was ordained by our lord the King, and by assent of the prelates, earls, barons, and other of his council, That such manner of servants, as well men as women, should be bound to serve, receiving salary and wages, accustomed in places where they ought to serve in the twentieth year of the reign of the King that now is, or five or six years before ; and that the same servants refusing to serve in such manner should be punished by imprisonment of their bodies, as in the said statute is more plainly contained; (2) whereupon *commissions were made to divers people in every county to enquire and punish all them which offend* against the same. (3) And now forasmuch as *it is given the King to understand in this present parliament, by the petition of the commonalty, that the said servants having no regard to the said ordinance, but to their ease and singular covetise, do withdraw themselves to serve great men and other, unless they have livery and wages to the double or treble of that they were wont to take the said twentieth year, and before*, to the great damage of the great men, and impoverishing of all the said commonalty, whereof the said commonalty prayeth remedy; (4) wherefore in the same parliament, by the assent of the said prelates, earls, barons, and other great men of the same commonalty there assembled, to *refrain the malice of the said servants*, be ordained and established the things underwritten.

"CAP. I.

" The *year and day's wages of servants and labourers in husbandry.*

" First, That carters, ploughmen, drivers of the plough, shepherds, swineherds, deies, and all other servants, shall take liveries and wages, accustomed the said twentieth year, or four years before, so that in the country, where wheat was wont to be given, they shall take for the bushel *ten pence*, or wheat at the will of the giver, till it be otherwise ordained. And that they be allowed to serve by a whole year, or by other usual terms, and not by the day. And that none pay in the time of sarcling or hay-making but *a penny the day.* And a mower of meadows for the acre *five pence*, or by the day *five pence*. And reapers of corn in the first week of August *two pence*, and the second *three pence*, and so till the end of August, and less in the country where less was wont to be given, *without meat or drink*, or other courtesy to be demanded, given, or taken. And that all workmen *bring openly in their hands to the merchant towns their instruments, and there shall be hired* in a common place and not privy.

" CAP. II.

" How much shall be given for threshing all sorts of corn by the quarter. *None shall depart from the town in summer where he dwelt in winter.*

" Item, That *none take for the threshing of a quarter of wheat or*

*rye over ii.d.ob. and the quarter of barley, beans, pease, and oats,
i.d.ob.* if so much were wont to be given, and in the country, where
it is used to reap by certain sheaves, and to thresh by certain
bushels, they shall take no more nor in other manner than was wont
the said xx. year and before. And that the same *servants be sworn
two times in the year before lords, stewards, bailiffs, and constables
of every town, to hold and do these ordinances.* And that *none of
them go out of the town, where he dwelleth in the winter, to serve the
summer,* if he may serve in the same town, taking as before is said.
Saving that the people of the counties of Stafford, Lancaster, and
Derby and people of Craven, and of the marches of Wales and Scotland, and other places, may come in time of August, and labour in
other counties, and safely return, as they were wont to do before
this time. And that those, which refuse to make such oath, or to
perform that that they be sworn to, or have taken upon them, shall
be put in the stocks by the said lords, stewards, bailiffs, and constables of the towns by three days or more, or sent to the next gaol,
there to remain, till they will justify themselves. And that stocks
be made in every town by such occasion betwixt this and the feast
of Pentecost.

"CAP. III.

" The wages of several sorts of artificers and labourers.

" ITEM, That carpenters, masons, and tilers, and other workmen
of houses, shall not take by the day for their work, but in manner
as they were wont, that is to say ; *A master carpenter, iii.d. and an
other ii.d. A master free mason iiii.d. and other masons iii.d. and
their servants i.d.ob. tylers iii.d. and their knaves i.d.ob. and other
coverers of fern and straw iii.d. and their knaves i.d.ob. plaisterers
and other workers of mudwalls, and their knaves, by the same manner,
without meat or drink.* s. from Easter to Saint Michael. And from
that time less, according to the rate and discretion of the justices,
which should be thereto assigned. And that they that make carriage by land or by water, shall take no more for such carriage to be
made, than they were wont the said xx. year, and iiii. years before.

"CAP. IV.

" Shoes, &c., shall be sold as in the 20th year of King EDWARD
the 3d. Artificers sworn to use their crafts as they did in the 20th
year of the same King.

"ITEM, That cordwainers and shoemakers, shall not sell boots nor shoes, nor none other thing touching their mystery, in any other manner than they were wont the said xx. year, and that goldsmiths, sadlers, horsesmiths, spurriers, tanners, curriers, tawers of leather, taylors, and *other workmen, artificers and labourers, and all other servants here not specified,* shall be *sworn before the justices, to do and use their crafts and offices in the manner as they were wont to do the said xx. year, and in the time before, without refusing the same because of this ordinance.* And if any of the said servants, labourers, workmen, or artificers, after such oath made, come against this ordinance, he shall be punished by *fine, and ransom, and imprisonment* after the discretion of the justices.

"CAP. V.

"The several punishments of persons offending against this statute.

" ITEM, That the said stewards, bailiffs, and constables of the said towns, be sworn before the same justices, to inquire diligently by all the good ways they may, of all them that come against this ordinance, and to certify the same justices of their names at all times, when they shall come into the country to make their sessions, so that the same justices in certification of the same stewards, bailiffs, and constables, of the names of the rebels, shall do them to be attached by their body, to be before the said justices, to answer of such contempts, so that they make fine and ransom to the King, in case they be attainted. And moreover to be commanded to prison, there to remain, till they have found surety, to serve, and take and do their work, and to sell things vendable in the manner aforesaid. And in case that any of them come against his oath, and be thereof attainted, he shall have imprisonment of forty days. And if he be another time convict, he shall have imprisonment of a quarter of a year, so that at every time that he offendeth and is convict, he shall have double pain. And that the same justices, at every time they come into the country, shall enquire of the said stewards, bailiffs, and constables, if they have made a good and lawful certificate, or any conceal for gift, procurement, or affinity, and punish them by fine and ransom, if they be found guilty. And that the same justices have power to enquire and make due punishment of the said ministers, labourers, workmen and other servants. And also of hostlers, herbergers, and of those that sell victual by retail, or other things here not specified, as well at the suit of the party, as by presentment, and to hear and determine, and put the things in execution by the exigend after the first capias, if need be, and to depute other under them, as many and such as they shall see best for the keeping of the same ordinance. And that they, which will sue against such servants, workmen, labourers, and artificers, for excess taken of them, and they be thereof attainted at their suit, they shall have again such excess. And in case that none will sue, to have again such excess, then it shall be levied of the said servants, labourers, workmen and artificers, and delivered to the collectors of the quinzime, in alleviation of the towns where such excesses were taken.

"CAP. VI.

"Sheriffs, constables, bailiffs, gaolers, nor other officers, shall exact any thing of the same servants. The forfeitures of servants shall be employed to the aid of dismes and quinzimes granted to the King by the commons.

"Item, That no sheriffs, constables, bailiffs, and gaolers, the clerks of the justices, or of the sheriffs, nor other ministers whatsoever they be, take any thing for the cause of their office of the same servants, for fees, suit of prison, nor in other manner, and if they have any thing taken in such manner, they shall deliver the same to the collectors of dismes and quinzimes, in aid of the commons, for the time that the dismes and quinzimes doth run, as well for the time past, as for the time to come. And that the said justices enquire in their sessions, if the said ministers have any thing received of the same servants, and that that they shall find by such inquests, that the said ministers have received the same justices shall levy of every of the said ministers, and deliver to the said collectors, together with the excess and fines and ransoms made, and also the amerciaments of all them which shall be amerced before the said justices, in alleviation of the said towns, as afore is said. And in case the excess found in one town doth exceed the quantity of the quinzime of the same town, the remnant of such excess shall be levied and paid by the said collectors to the next poor towns, in aid of their quinzime, by advice of the said justices. And that the fines and ransoms, excesses and amerciaments of the said servants, labourers and artificers, for the time to come running of the said quinzime, be delivered to the said collectors, in the form aforesaid, by indentures to be made betwixt them and the said justices, so that the same collectors may be charged upon their accompt by the same indentures, in case that the said fines, ransoms, amerciaments, and excesses be not paid in aid of the said quinzime. And sessing the said quinzime, it shall be levied to the King's use, and answered to him by the sheriffs of the counties.

"CAP. VII.

" The justices shall hold their sessions four times a year, and at all times needful. *Servants which flee from one country to another shall be committed to prison.*

" ITEM, That the said justices make their sessions in all the counties of England at the least four times a year, that is to say, at the feast of the Annunciation of our Lady Saint Margaret, Saint Michael, and Saint Nicholas. And also at all times that shall need, according to the discretion of the said justices. And that those that speak in the presence of the said justices, or other things do in their absence or presence, in encouraging or maintenance of the said servants, labourers or artificers against this ordinance, shall be grievously punished by the discretion of the same justices. And *if any of the said servants, labourers, or artificers do flee from one county to another*, because of this ordinance, that the *sheriffs* of the county where such fugitive persons shall be found, *shall do them to be taken*, at the commandment of the justices of the counties from whence they shall flee, *and bring them to the chief gaol of the same county*, there to abide till the next sessions of the same justices. And that the sheriffs return the same commandments before the same justices at their next sessions. And that this ordinance be holden and kept, as well in the city of London, as in other cities and boroughs, and other places throughout the land, as well within franchises as without."

Of like nature were the following series of enactments, intended to fix the prices of certain classes of merchandise, to prevent an increase in the prices thereof by wholesale dealers, termed " ingrossers," to prevent dealing by any single merchant in merchandise of more than one class, to prevent artisans from following more than one craft, to regulate the quality of goldsmiths' ware, and to regulate the diet and clothing, of servants, and of subjects of all classes.

Act 37 Edw. III., Cap. III., V., VI., VII., VIII., XV.

"CAP. III.

"The several prices of a hen, capon, pullet, and goose.

"Item, for the great dearth that is in many places of the realm of poultry ; it is ordained, That the price of a young capon shall not pass 3*d*. and of an old 4*d*. of an hen 2*d*. of a pullet 1*d*. of a goose 4*d*. and in places where the prices of such victuals be less, they shall hold, without being enhanced by this ordinance. And that in the towns and markets of up-land they shall be sold at a less price, according as may be agreed between the seller and the buyer. And justices shall be thereupon assigned by commission to put the thing duely in execution.

"CAP. V.

"Merchants *shall not ingross merchandises to inhance the prices* of them, nor use but one sort of merchandise.

"Item, for the *great mischiefs which have happened*, as well to the King, as to the great men and commons, of that that the merchants, called grocers, do ingross all manner of merchandise vendible : and suddenly do enhance the price of such merchandise within the realm, putting to sale by covin and ordinance made betwixt them, called the fraternity and gild of merchants, the merchandises, which be most dear, and keep in store the other, till the time that dearth or scarcity be of the same : hath ordained, That no English merchant shall use no ware nor merchandise, by him nor by other, nor by no manner of covin, one only one, which he shall choose betwixt this and the feast of Candlemas next coming. And such as have other wares or merchandises in their hands, than those that they have chosen, may set them to sale before the feast of the Nativity of Saint John next ensuing. And if any do to the contrary of this ordinance in any point, and be thereof attainted, in the manner as hereafter followeth, he shall forfeit against the King the merchandise, which he hath so used against this ordinance : and moreover, shall make a fine to the King, according to the quantity of the trespass. And how this ordinance shall be put in execution, it is ordained, That good people and lawful of every merchandise shall be chosen and sworn, to survey that this ordinance be holden and executed, that is to say, two merchants in every merchandise in every town and burgh, and two merchants of every county, and redress the defaults, and of that that they may not redress, they shall certify the chancellor, and the King's council. And commissions shall be made to certain people, to whom and when it shall please the King to assign, to enquire in cities, burghs, and counties, where need shall be, as well of trespasses in this behalf, as of surveyors, in case that they be negligent, or of covin with the trespassers, by the oath of six men sworn: and moreover, to make process for to hear and determine daily, and to punish the trespassers and surveyors, that is to say, the trespassers according as is above ordained, and the surveyors according to the discretion of the justices, and that by the jury of xii. in case they will put themselves upon the country of their accusement. And whosoever will sue for the King in such case, shall be thereto received, and shall have the fourth peny of the forfeiture of him that so shall be attainted at his suit.

"CAP. VI.

"*Handicraftsmen shall use but one mystery*, but workwomen may work as they did.

"ITEM, it is ordained, That artificers, handicraft people, hold them every one to one mystery, which he will choose betwixt this and the said feast of Candlemas. And two of every craft shall be chosen to survey, that none use other craft than the same which he hath chosen, and that justices be assigned to enquire by process, to hear and determine in this article, as is ordained in the article before said, saving that the trespassers in this article shall be punished by imprisonment of half a year, and moreover to make fine and ransom, according to the quantity of the trespass. And the surveyors by the discretion of the justices, as before. But the intent of the King and of his council is, that women, that is to say, brewers, bakers, carders, and spinners, and workers as well of wool, as of linen cloth and of silk, brawdefters, and breakers of wool, and all other that do use and work all handy works, may freely use and work as they have done before this time, without any impeachment, or being restrained by this ordinance.

"CAP. VII.

"Goldsmiths work shall be of good sterling, and marked with his own mark. None shall make white vessel and also gild.

"ITEM, it is ordained, That goldsmiths, as well in London as elsewhere within the realm, shall make all manner of vessel and other work of silver well and lawfully of the allay of good sterling. (2) And every master goldsmith shall have a mark by himself, and the same mark shall be known by them which shall be assigned by the King to survey their work and allay. (3) And that the said goldsmiths set not their mark upon their works till the said surveyors have made their essay, as shall be ordained by the King and his council; and after the essay made, the surveyors shall set the King's mark, and after the goldsmith his mark, for which he will answer. (4) And that no goldsmith take for vessel white and full for the weight of a pound, that is to say, of the price of two marks of Paris weight, but eighteen pence, as they do at Paris. (5) And that no goldsmith making white vessel shall meddle with gilding, nor they that do gild shall meddle to make white vessel. (6) And they which shall be so assigned in every town, shall make their searches as oftentimes shall be ordained. (7) And for that which shall be in the goldsmith's default, they shall incur the pain of forfeiture to the King the value of the metal which shall be found in default.

"CAP. VIII.

"The diet and apparel of servants.

"ITEM, for the outragious and excessive apparel of divers people against their estate and degree, to the great destruction and impoverishment of all the land: it is ordained, That grooms, as well servants of lords, as they of mysteries and artificers, shall be served to *eat and drink once a day of flesh or of fish,* and the remnant of other victuals, as of milk, butter, and cheese, and other such victuals, according to their estate. And that they have cloths for their vesture, or hosing, whereof the whole cloth shall not exceed two marks, and that they wear no cloth of higher price, of their buying, nor otherwise, nor nothing of gold nor of silver embroidered, aimeled, nor of silk, nor nothing pertaining to the said things. And their wives, daughters, and children of the same condition in their clothing and apparel, and they shall *wear no veils passing xii.d. a veil.*"

Subsequent chapters in the same statute regulated the

apparel of handicraftsmen and yeomen, of "gentlemen under the estate of knights," of "esquires of two hundred mark-land," of "merchants, citizens, burgesses, and handicraftsmen," of "knights which have lands within the yearly value of two hundred marks and of knights and ladies which have four hundred mark-land," of "several sorts of clerks," of "ploughmen and others of mean estate."

Another chapter regulating the making of cloths reads as follows:

"CAP. XV.

"Clothiers shall make cloths sufficient of the foresaid prices, so that this statute for default of such cloths be in no wise infringed.

"ITEM, to the intent that this ordinance, for the taking and wearing of cloths be maintained and kept in all points without blemish: it is ordained, that all the makers of cloths within the realm, as well men as women, shall confirm them to *make their cloths according to the price limited by this ordinance.* And that all the drapers shall *buy and purvey* their sorts *according to the same price.* So that so *great plenty of such cloths be made and set to sale in every city, borough, and merchant, town, and elsewhere within the realm,* that for default of such cloths the said ordinance be in no point broken. And to that shall the said *clothmakers and drapers be constrained by any manner way that best shall seem to the King and his council.* And this ordinance of new apparel shall begin at candlemas next coming."

In time these statutes, with others of like character, were found to be of no effect. The Statute 5 Elizabeth, c. 4, A.D. 1562, entitled "An Act containing divers orders for artificers, labourers, servants of husbandry and apprentices," was therefore passed. It repealed many of the former acts. It began with the following recital:

"CAP. IV.

"An act containing divers orders for artificers, labourers, servants of husbandry and apprentices.

"ALTHOUGH there remain and stand in force presently a *great number of acts and statutes* concerning the *retaining, departing, wages and orders* of apprentices, servants and labourers, as well in husbandry as in divers other arts, mysteries and occupations ; (2) yet partly for the imperfection and contrariety that is found, and doth appear in sundry of said laws, and for the *variety and number* of them, (3) and chiefly for that the *wages and allowances limited and rated in many of the said statutes, are in divers places too small and not answerable to this time, respecting the advancement of prices* of all things belonging to the said servants and labourers ; (4) the *said laws cannot conveniently, without the great grief and burden of the poor labourer and hired men, be put in good and due execution ;* (5) and as the said several acts and statutes were, at the time of the making of them, *thought to be very good and beneficial for the commonwealth of this realm* (as divers of them are), so if the substance of as many of the said laws as are meet to be continued, shall be digested and reduced into one sole law and statute, and in the same an uniform order prescribed and limited concerning the wages and other orders for apprentices, servants and labourers, there is *good hope* that it will come to pass, that the same law (being duly executed) should *banish idleness, advance husbandry, and yield unto the hired person, both in the time of scarcity, and in the time of plenty, a convenient proportion of wages.''*

The Act then proceeded to repeal, among others, all such statutes '' as touch or concern the hiring, keeping, departing, working, wages, or order of servants, workmen, artificers, apprentices and labourers, or any of them.''

The Act then proceeded to impose manifold restrictions on the freedom of contract between employers and employees, and to establish elaborate machinery for carrying out its provisions. It provided, among other things, that in a large number of handicrafts no person should hire another '' to work for any less time or term than for one whole year ;'' that every person having certain specified qualifications '' shall during the time that he or they shall be so unmarried, or under the said age of thirty years, *upon request* made by any person using the art or mystery wherein the said person so required hath been exercised (as is aforesaid) *be retained ;* and shall *not refuse to serve* according to the tenor of this statute, upon the pain and penalty hereafter mentioned." It provided, that no person should put away his servant, nor should any servant depart from his master, before the end of his term, "unless it be for some reasonable and sufficient cause or matter to be allowed before two justices of the peace" or other specified officials. It provided, also, "that none of the said retained persons in husbandry, or in any of the arts or sciences above remembered after the time of his retainer expired, shall *depart forth of one city, town or parish to another;* (2) nor out of the lath, rape, wapentake or hundred; . . . unless he have a testimonial under the seal of the said city or town corporate," or of certain specified officials in form prescribed by the statute. It contained also minute provisions as to the hours of labor, and the times to be allowed for breakfast, dinner, drinking, and for sleep.

It then abandoned the attempt to fix wages or prices at definite rates specified in the Act itself. But it provided, "That the justices of the peace of every shire . . . shall before the tenth day of June next coming, and afterward shall *yearly* . . . assemble themselves together (2) and they (so assembled) calling unto them such discreet and grave persons of the said country or of the said city or town corporate, as they shall think meet, and conferring together, respecting the plenty or scarcity of the time and other circumstances necessarily to be considered, shall have authority by virtue thereof, within the limits and precincts of their several commissions, to *limit, rate and appoint the wages*" of artificers, husbandmen, laborers, servants, and workmen. The statute further provided for the printing and proclamation of the rates so established. It also contained provisions for compelling "such artificers and persons as be meet to labor" to work at mowing, reaping and other farm labor "in the time of hay or corn harvest." Penalties were provided for violations of the provisions of the act.

The sections of this Act which have importance to this discussion are as follows :

"II. Be it therefore enacted by the authority of this present parliament, That as much of all the estatutes heretofore made, and every branch of them, as touch or concern the hiring, keeping, departing, working, wages, or order of servants, workmen, artificers, apprentices and labourers, or any of them, and the penalties and forfeitures concerning the same, shall be from and after the last day of September next ensuing, repealed and utterly void and of none effect ; (2) and that all the said statutes, and every branch thereof, or any matter contained in them, and not repealed by this statute, shall remain and be in full force and effect ; any thing in this statute to the contrary notwithstanding.

"III. And be it further enacted by the authority aforesaid, That no manner of person or persons, after the aforesaid last day of September now next ensuing, shall retain, hire or take into service, or cause to be retained, hired or taken into service, nor any person shall be retained, hired or taken into service, by any means or colour, to work for any less time or term than for one whole year, in any of the sciences, crafts, mysteries or arts of clothiers, woolen cloth weavers, tuckers, fullers, clothworkers, sheremen, dyers, hosiers, taylors, shoemakers, tanners, pewterers, bakers, brewers, glovers, cutlers, smiths, farriers, curriers, sadlers, spurriers, turners, cappers, hatmakers or feltmakers, bowyers, fletchers, arrowhead-makers, butchers, cooks or millers.

"IV. And be it further enacted, That every person being unmarried ; (2) and every other person being under the age of thirty years, that after the feast of Easter next shall marry ; (3) and having been brought up in any of the said arts, crafts or sciences ; (4) or that hath used or exercised any of them by the space of three years or more ; (5) and not having lands, tenements, rents or hereditaments, copyhold or freehold, of an estate of inheritance, or for term of any life or lives, of the clear yearly value of forty shillings ; (6) nor been worth of his own goods the clear value of ten pounds ; (7) and so allowed by two justices of the peace of the county where he hath most commonly inhabited by the space of one whole year, and under their hands and seals ; (8) or by the mayor or other head officer of the city, borough or town corporate where such person hath most commonly dwelt by the space of one whole year, and two aldermen, or two other discreet burgesses of the same city, borough or town corporate, if there be no aldermen, under their hands and seals ; (9) nor being retained with any person in husbandry, or in any of the aforesaid arts and sciences, according to this statute ; (10) nor lawfully retained in any other art or science ; (11) nor being lawfully retained in household, or in any office, with any nobleman, gentleman or others, according to the laws of this realm ; (12) nor having a convenient farm, or other holding in tillage, whereupon he may employ his labour ; (13) shall, during the time that he or they shall be so unmarried, or under the said age of thirty years, upon request made by any person using the art or mystery wherein the said person so required hath been exercised (as is aforesaid) be retained ; (14) and shall not refuse to serve according to the tenor of this statute, upon the pain and penalty hereafter mentioned.

" V. And be it further enacted, That no person which shall retain any servant shall put away his or her said servant ; (2) and that no person retained according to this statute, shall depart from his master, mistress or dame, before the end of his or her term ; (3) upon the pain hereafter mentioned ; (4) unless it be for some reasonable and sufficient cause or matter to be allowed before two justices of peace, or one at the least, within the said county, or before the mayor or other chief officer of the city, borough or town corporate wherein the said master, mistress or dame inhabiteth, to whom any of the parties grieved shall complain ; (5) which said justices or justice, mayor or chief officer, shall have and take upon them or him the hearing and ordering of the matter betwixt the said master or mistress, or dame and servant, according to the equity of the cause.

" VI. And that no such master, mistress or dame, shall put away any such servant at the end of his term, or that any such servant shall depart from his said master, mistress or dame at the end of his term, without one quarter's warning given before the end of the said term, either by the said master, mistress or dame, or servant, the one to the other, upon the pain hereafter ensuing.

" VII. And be it further enacted by the authority aforesaid, That every person between the age of twelve years and the age of sixty years, not being lawfully retained, nor apprentice with any fisherman or mariner haunting the seas ; (2) nor being in service with any kidder or carrier of any corn, grain or meal, for provision of the city of London ; (3) nor with any husbandman in husbandry ;

(4) nor in any city, town corporate or market-town, in any of the arts or sciences limited or appointed by this estatute to have or take apprentices ; (5) nor being retained by the year, or half the year at the least, for the digging, seeking, finding, getting, melting, fining, working, trying, making of any silver, tin, lead, iron, copper, stone, sea-coal, stone-coal, moor-coal or cherk-coal ; (6) nor being occupied in or about the making of any glass ; (7) nor being a gentleman born, nor being a student or scholar in any of the universities, or in any school ; (8) nor having lands, tenements, rents or hereditaments, for term of life, or of one estate of inheritance, of the clear yearly value of forty shillings ; (9) nor being worth in goods and chattels to the value of ten pounds ; (10) nor having a father or mother then living, or other ancestor whose heir apparent he is, then having lands, tenements or hereditaments, of the yearly value of ten pound or above, or goods or chattels of the value of forty pound ; (11) nor being a necessary or convenient officer or servant lawfully retained, as is aforesaid ; (12) nor having a convenient farm or holding, whereupon he may or shall imploy his labour ; (13) nor being otherwise lawfully retained, according to the true meaning of this estatute ; (14) *shall* after the aforesaid last day of September, now next ensuing, by virtue of this estatute, *be compelled to be retained to serve in husbandry by the year, with any person that* keepeth husbandry, and *will require* any such person so to serve, within the same shire where he shall be so required.

* * * * * * *

" XII. And be it further enacted by the authority aforesaid, That all artificers and labourers, being hired for wages by the day or week, shall betwixt the midst of the months of March and September be and continue at their work at or before five of the clock in the morning, and continue at work and not depart until betwixt seven and eight of the clock at night (except it be in the time of breakfast, dinner or drinking, the which times at the most shall not exceed above two hours and a half in a day, that is to say, at every drinking one half hour, for his dinner one hour, and for his sleep when he is allowed to sleep, the which is from the midst of May to the midst of August, half an hour at the most, and at every breakfast one half hour ; (2) and all the said artificers and labourers, between the midst of September and the midst of March, shall be and continue at their work from the spring of the day in the morning until the night of the same day, except it be in time afore appointed for breakfast and dinner; (3) upon pain to lose and forfeit one penny for every hour's absence, to be deducted and defaulked out of his wages that shall so offend.

"XIII. And be it also enacted by the authority aforesaid, That *every artificer and labourer* that shall be lawfully retained in and for the building or repairing of any church, house, ship, mill or every other piece of work taken in great, in task or in gross, or that shall hereafter take upon him to make or finish any such thing or work, *shall continue and not depart from the same*, unless it be for not paying of his wages or hire agreed on, or otherwise lawfully taken or appointed to serve the Queen's majesty, her heirs or successors, or for other lawful cause, or *without licence of the master or owner of the work*, or of him that hath the charge thereof, *before the finishing of the said work;* (2) upon pain of imprisonment by one month, without bail or mainprise; (3) and the forfeiture of the sum of five pounds to the party from whom he shall so depart; for the which the said party may have his action of debt against him that shall so depart, in any of the Queen's majesty's courts of record, over and besides such ordinary costs and damages as may or ought to be recovered by the common laws, for or concerning any such offence: in which action no protection, wager of law or essoin shall be admitted.

* * * * * * *

"XV. And for the *declaration and limitation what wages servants, labourers and artificers, either by the year or day or otherwise, shall have and receive,* Be it enacted by the authority of this present parliament, That the *justices of peace* of every shire, riding and liberty within the limits of their several commissions, or the more part of them, being then resiant within the same, and the *sheriff of that county* if he conveniently may, and every mayor, *bailiff or other head officer* within any city or town corporate wherein is any justice of peace, within the limits of the said city or town corporate, and of the said corporation, shall before the tenth day of June next coming, and afterward shall *yearly* at every general sessions first to be holden and kept after Easter or at some time convenient within six weeks next following every of the said feasts of Easter, assemble themselves together; (2) and they (so assembled) calling unto them such discreet and grave persons of the said county or of the said city or town corporate, as they shall think meet, and conferring together, *respecting the plenty or scarcity of the time and other circum-*

stances necessarily to be considered, shall have authority by virtue thereof, within the limits and precincts of their several commissions, *to limit, rate and appoint the wages,* as well of such and so many of the said *artificers, handicraftsmen, husbandmen or any other labourer, servant or workman,* whose wages in time past hath been by any law or statute rated and appointed ; (3) as also the wages of *all other labourers, artificers, workmen or apprentices of husbandry,* which have not been rated ; (4) as they the same justices, mayors or head officers within their several commissions or liberties shall think meet by their discretions to be rated, limited or appointed by the year or by the day, week, month or otherwise, with meat and drink or without meat and drink ; (5) and what wages every workman or labourer shall take by the great, for mowing, reaping or threshing of corn and grain, or for mowing or making of hay, or for ditching, paving, railing or hedging, by the rod, pearch, lugg, yard, pole, rope or foot, and for any other kind of reasonable labours or service ; (6) and shall yearly before the twelfth day of July next after the said assessments and rates so appointed and made, certify the same ingrossed in parchment, with the considerations and causes thereof, under their hands and seals, into the Queen's most honourable court of chancery ; (7) whereupon it shall be lawful to the lord chancellor of England, or lord keeper of the great seal for the time being, upon declaration thereof to the Queen's majesty, her heirs or successors, or to the lords and others of the privy council for the time being, attendant upon their persons, to cause to be printed and sent down before the first day of September next after the said certificate, into every county, to the sheriff and justices of peace there, and to the said mayor, bailiff and head officers, ten or twelve proclamations or more, containing in every of them the several rates appointed by the said justices and other head officers, as is aforesaid, with commandment by the said proclamations, to all persons, in the name of the Queen's majesty, her heirs or successors, straightly to observe the same, and to all justices, sheriffs and other officers, to see the same duly and severally observed, upon the danger of the punishment and forfeiture limited and appointed by this statute ; (8) upon receipt whereof the said sheriffs, justices of peace and the mayor and head officer in every city or town corporate, shall cause the same proclamations to be entered of record by the clerk of the peace or by the clerk of the city or town corporate ; (9) and the said sheriffs, justices, and other the said mayor and head officers, shall forthwith in open markets, upon the market-days before Michaelmas then ensuing, cause the same proclamation to be proclaimed in every city or market-town within the limits of their commission, and the same proclamation to be fixed in some convenient place of the said city and town, or in such of the most occupied market-towns, as to the said sheriffs, justices of peace and to the said mayor and head officers shall be thought meet.

* * * * * * *

"XVIII. And be it further enacted by the authority aforesaid, That if any person after the said proclamation shall be so sent down and published, shall by any secret ways or means, directly or indirectly retain or keep any servant, workman or labourer, or shall give any more or greater wages or other commodity, contrary to the true intent and purport of this estatute, or contrary to the rates or wages that shall be assessed or appointed in the said proclamations ; that then every person that shall so offend, and be thereof lawfully convicted before any the justices or other head officers above-remembred, or either of the said presidents and councils, shall suffer imprisonment by the space of ten days, without bail or mainprise, and shall lose and forfeit five pounds of lawful money of England.

"XIX. And that every person that shall be so retained and take wages contrary to this estatute or any branch thereof, or of the said proclamations, and shall be thereof convicted before the justices aforesaid, or any two of them, or before the mayor or other head officers aforesaid, shall suffer imprisonment by the space of one and twenty days, without bail or mainprise.

"XX. And that every retainer, promise, gift or payment of wages or other thing whatsoever contrary to the true meaning of this estatute, and every writing and bond to be made for that purpose, shall be utterly void and of none effect.

* * * * * * *

"XXII. Provided always, and be it enacted by the authority aforesaid, That *in the time of hay or corn harvest*, the *justices of peace* and every of them, and also the *constable or other head officer of every township* upon request, and for the avoiding of the loss of any corn, grain or hay, shall and may *cause all such artificers and persons as be meet to labour*, by the discretions of the said justices or constables, or other head officers, or by any of them, *to serve by the day for the mowing, reaping, shearing, setting or inning of corn, grain*

PRIVATE EMPLOYMENTS. 33

and hay, according to the skill and quality of the person ; (2) and that none of the *said persons shall refuse so to do, upon pain to suffer imprisonment in the stocks* by the space of two days and one night ; (3) and the constable of the town or other head officer of the same, where the said refusal shall be made, upon complaint to him made, shall have authority by virtue hereof to *set the said offender in the stocks* for the time aforesaid, and shall punish him accordingly, upon pain to lose and forfeit for not doing thereof the sum of forty shillings.

"XXIII. Provided also, That *all persons* of the counties where they have accustomed to go into other shires for harvest work, and *having at that time no harvest-work* sufficient in the same town or county where he or they dwelt in the winter then last past, bringing with him or them a testimonial under the hand and seal of one justice of the peace of the shire, or other head officer of the town or place that he or they come from, testifying the same, for the which he shall pay not above one penny (other than such persons as shall be retained in service, according to the form of this estatute) *may repair and resort in harvest of hay or corn, from the counties wherein their dwelling-places are, into any other place or county*, for the only mowing, reaping and getting of hay, corn or grain, and for the only working of harvest-works, as they might have done before the making of this estatute ; any thing herein contained to the contrary notwithstanding.

"XXIV. And be it further enacted by the authority aforesaid, That two justices of peace, the mayor or other head officer of any city, borough or town corporate, and two aldermen, or two other discreet burgesses of the same city, borough or town corporate, if there be no aldermen, shall and may, by virtue hereof, appoint any such woman as is of the age of twelve years, and under the age of forty years and unmarried, and forth of service, as they shall think meet to serve, to be retained or serve by the year, or by the week or day, for such wages, and in such reasonable sort and manner as they shall think meet ; (2) and if any such woman shall refuse so to serve, then it shall be lawful for the said justices of peace, mayor or head officers, to commit such woman to ward, until she shall be bounden to serve as is aforesaid.

"XXV. And for the better advancement of husbandry and tillage, and to the intent that such as are fit to be made apprentices to husbandry, may be bounden thereunto ; (2) be it enacted by the authority of this present parliament, That every person being an housholder, and having and using half a ploughland at the least in tillage, may have and receive as an apprentice any person above the age of ten years, and under the age of eighteen years, to serve in husbandry, until his age of one and twenty years at the least, or until the age of twenty-four years, as the parties can agree, and the said retainer and taking of an apprentice, to be made and done by indenture.

"XXVI. And be it further enacted, That every person being an housholder, and twenty-four years old at the least, dwelling or inhabiting, or which shall dwell and inhabit in any city or town corporate, and using and exercising any art, mystery or manual occupation there, shall and may, after the feast of Saint John Baptist next coming, during the time that he shall so dwell or inhabit in any such city or town corporate, and use and exercise any such mystery, art or manual occupation, have and retain the son of any freeman, not occupying husbandry, nor being a labourer, and inhabiting in the same, or in any other city or town that now is or hereafter shall be and continue incorporate, to serve and be bound as an apprentice after the custom and order of the city of London, for seven years at the least, so as the term and years of such apprentice do not expire or determine afore such apprentice shall be of the age of twenty-four years at the least.

"XXVII. Provided always and be it enacted, That it shall not be lawful to any person dwelling in any city or town corporate, using or exercising any of the mysteries or crafts of a merchant trafficking by traffick or trade into any the parts beyond the sea, mercer, draper, goldsmith, ironmonger, imbroiderer or clothier, that doth or shall put cloth to making and sale, to take any apprentice or servant to be instructed or taught in any of the arts, occupations, crafts or mysteries which they or any of them do use or exercise; except such servant or apprentice be his son; (2) or else that the father and mother of such apprentice or servant, shall have, at the time of taking such apprentice or servant, lands, tenements or other hereditaments, of the clear yearly value of forty shillings of one estate of inheritance or freehold at the least, to be certified under the hands and seals of three justices of the peace of the shire or shires where the said lands, tenements or other hereditaments, do or shall lie, to the mayor, bailiff or other head officers of such city or town corporate, and to be inrolled among the records there."

This Act (5 Eliz. c. 4) was explained and extended by the 1 Jac. I. c. 6, of which the third section read as follows:

"III. Be it enacted by authority of this present parliament, That the said statute, and the authority by the same statute given to any person or persons for assessing and rating of wages, and the authority to them in the said act committed, shall be expounded and construed, and shall by force of this act give authority to all persons having any such authority, to *rate wages of any labourers, weavers, spinsters, and workmen or workwomen whatsoever*, either working by the day, week, month, year, or taking any work at any person or persons' hand whatsoever, to be done in great or otherwise."

This last statute, which purported to re-enforce the statute 5 Eliz. c. 4, began with an admission of the inefficiency of that statute in the following words: "And whereas the *said act hath not, according to the true meaning thereof, been duly put in execution*, whereby the rates of wages for poor artificers, labourers and other persons whose wages was meant to be rated by the said act, *have not been rated and proportioned according to the plenty, scarcity, necessity, and respect of the time*, which was politickly intended by the said act."

The Act 5 Eliz. c. 4 was not repealed until the year 1875, by the Conspiracy and Protection of Property Act, 38 & 39 Vict. ch. 86, sect. 17.

Similar in purpose were the statutes of different kinds which were intended to regulate the manufacture of different kinds of goods in respect to measurements and quality.

One of these is The Statute 4 Edw. IV., Cap. I., entitled "The Length and Breadth of Cloths to be sold. No cloths wrought beyond Sea shall be brought into England." It begins with the recital "First, Whereas many years past, and now at this day, the workmanship of cloths, and things requisite to the same, is and hath been of such fraud, deceit, and falsity, that the said cloths in other lands and countries be had in small reputation, to the great shame of this land ; (2) and by reason thereof a great quantity of cloths of other strange lands be brought into this realm, and here sold at an high and excessive price, evidently showing the offence, default, and falshood of the making of woolen cloths of this land." The Statute then proceeds to prescribe the length and breadth of different kinds of cloths, and prohibits the use of certain materials in making them. It also enacts, that "every of the said cloths and half cloths shall perfectly and rightly pursue and follow one order of workmanship from one end to the other," and that a seal of lead shall be set on faulty cloths. It also provides that every clothmaker shall pay his carders, spinsters and other laborers in lawful money, and that every such laborer "shall duly perform his duty in his occupation."

Another Statute of the same character was the Statute 7 Edw. IV. Cap. I., "For making of worsteds." It begins by reciting "For that there be as well within the City of Norwich, as elsewhere within the County of Norfolk, divers persons which do make untrue wares of all manner of worsteds, not being of the assise in length nor in breadth, nor of good stuff and right making as they ought to be, and of old time were accustomed, and the sleyes and yarn pertaining to the same not well made and wrought, in great deceit as well of denizens as of strangers inhabiting or repairing to this realm, which have used and do use to buy such merchandises, trusting that they were within as they seemed without, where indeed it is contrary : (2) And for that the worsteds in times past were lawfully wrought, and merchandise well liked, and greatly desired and esteemed in the parts beyond the sea ; now because they be of no right making, nor good stuff, they be reported and esteemed deceitful and unlawful merchandise, and of little regard, to the great damage of our lord the King, and great prejudice of his loyal subjects." The Act then proceeds to empower the worsted weavers in the City of Norwich to choose four wardens, who "shall have full power for the year then next following to *survey the workmanship* of the said artificers, and that they *make and work rightfully and well*, and of *good stuff*, and to ordain such *rules and ordinances* within the said craft as often as it shall seem needful or necessary for the amendment of the said worsteds and craft." The Act then prescribes the length and breadth of Worsteds, and gives the wardens power to seize all defective cloths and stuff, giving them a power of search for the purposes of the execution of the Act.

These statutes are quoted at some length, for two purposes: the one is, to show how thorough and complete was the experience already had under the English law prior to our separation from the mother country, in attempts to control trade and commerce, and especially prices, by statute; the other is, to show the magnitude and intricacy of the undertaking which lies before legislators of the present day, if they enter on that line of legislation. Utterly hopeless, and utterly fruitless, in anything save annoyance, all such legislation always has been, and, so far as we can form a judgment in the light of history, always will be.

It will appear, too, that the latest attempts in this country to control the so-called "trusts" and "monopolies" of to-day are on the same line with these statutes here set forth.

In addition to all these statutes, intended to fix directly the prices, and quality, of labor and merchandise, by their operation on laborers and producers, we find another wholly different class of legislation, the purpose of which was to prevent any raising of the prices of merchandise, by wholesale dealers and middlemen. These wholesale dealers and middlemen were in the ancient statutes grouped together under the terms "forestallers," "regrators," and "engrossers."

Although the assertion has been often made that "forestalling," "regrating," and "engrossing" were criminal offenses at the common law, a careful examination shows, that these offenses were made crimes by statute from a very early period; and there is no authentic record, which my efforts have been able to discover, of the existence of either of these offenses prior to those statutes, which are cited by Coke, in the third volume of his Institutes. The earliest statute of this kind after the Norman conquest, which it is necessary to mention, is the Act 25 Edw. III. Stat. 4, A.D. 1350, which reads as follows:

"CAP. III.

"The penalty of him that doth *forestal wares, merchandise, or victual.*

"ITEM, it is accorded and established, That the forestallers of wines, and *all other victuals, wares, and merchandises that come to the good towns of England by land or by water,* in damage of our lord the King and of his people, if they be thereof attainted at the suit of the King, or of the party, before mayor, bailiff, or justices thereto assigned, or elsewhere in the King's court; and if they be attainted at the King's suit by indictment, or in other manner, the things forestalled shall be forfeited to the King, if the buyer thereof hath made gree to the seller; (2) and if he have not made gree of all, but by earnest, the buyer shall incur the forfeiture of as much as the forestalled goods forfeited do amount to, after the value as he bought them, if he have whereof; (3) and if he have not whereof, then he shall have two years' imprisonment, and more, at the King's will, without being let to mainprise, or delivered in other manner; (4) and if he be attainted at the suit of the party, the party shall have the one half of such things forestalled and forfeit, or the price, of the King's gift, and the King the other half."

Thereafter came the Act 3 & 4 Edw. VI., Cap. XXI., " An act for the buying and selling of butter and cheese," which provided, " Be it enacted by the authority of this present parliament, That no person or persons after the feast of the Annunciation of our Lady next coming, shall *buy to sell again* any butter or cheese, *unless he or they sell the same again by retail* in open shop, fair or market, and *not in gross:* (2) upon pain of forefeiture of the double value of the same butter and cheese so sold contrary to the tenor of this present act."

Thereafter came the Statute 5 & 6 Edward VI., Cap. XIV., entitled "An Act against Regrators, Forestallers, and Ingrossers," which gave a general definition of these offenses, and provided their punishments. Section I provided, "that whatsoever person or persons, that after the first day of May next coming shall *buy or cause to be bought*, any *merchandise, victual, or any other thing whatsoever, coming* by land or by water *toward any market or fair* to be sold in the same, or *coming toward any city, port, haven, creek or road of this realm or Wales*, from any parts beyond the sea to be sold, (3) or *make any bargain, contract or promise, for the having or buying*, of the same or any part thereof so coming as aforesaid, before the said merchandise, victuals or other things, shall be in the market, fair, city, port, haven, creek or road, ready to be sold ; (4) or shall make *any motion by word, letter, message or otherwise*, to any person or persons, *for the inhancing of the price or dearer selling of any thing or things above mentioned*, (5) or else dissuade, move or stir any person or persons coming to the market or the fair, to abstain or forbear to bring or convey any of the things, above rehearsed, to any market, fair, city, port, haven, creek or road to be sold, as is aforesaid, (6) shall be deemed, taken, and adjudged a *forestaller*."

Section II. provided, "That whatsoever person or persons, that after the said first day of May shall by any means *regrate, obtain, or get into his or their hands or possession*, in any fair or market, any corn, wine, fish, butter, cheese, candles, tallow, sheep, lambs, calves, swine, pigs, geese, capons, hens, chickens, pigeons, conies, or other dead victual whatsoever, that shall be brought to any fair or market within this realm or Wales to be sold, and do *sell the same again in any fair or market holden or kept in the same place, or in any other fair or market within four miles thereof*, shall be accepted, reputed and taken for a *regrator* or *regrators.*"

Section III. provided, "That whatsoever person or persons, that after the said first day of May shall *ingross* or *get into his or their hands by buying, contracting, or promise-taking*, other than by demise, grant, or lease of land or tithe, any corn growing in the fields, or any other corn or grain, butter, cheese, fish, or other dead victuals whatsoever, within the realm of England, *to the intent to sell the same again*, shall be accepted, reputed and taken an unlawful *ingrosser or ingrossers.*"

Section VII. contained certain specific exceptions to the sweeping general provisions of the act, such as the cases of innkeepers buying for the purpose of selling to their guests, fishmongers, butchers, and poulterers buying "such thing . . . as concern his or their own faculty, craft or mystery (otherwise than by forestalling), *which shall sell the same again upon reasonable prices by retail,*" with others which need not here be mentioned.

Section IX. prohibited the sale of cattle and sheep by any person within five weeks after his purchase thereof. Section XIII. allowed any person to "buy, engross and keep in his or their granaries or houses, such corn of the kinds aforesaid" as should be bought under prices specified in the act, "at all times hereafter, when wheat shall be commonly at the price of vi. s. viii. d. the quarter or under," and when other grains should be under certain other specified prices.

As to this act and other similar acts, it is to be noted, that no distinction is made between the acts of single individuals, and of combinations of individuals. The crime consisted in "buying to sell again," in "making *any motion* by word, letter, message, or otherwise . . . for the *inhancing of the price or dearer selling* of anything or things above mentioned," in "getting into his or their hands by buying, contracting, or promise-taking . . . to the *intent to sell again.*" It was the attempt to raise prices which constituted the crime. The crime was the same, whether committed by one person singly, or by several persons in combination. It is evident that these statutes, as to "regrating," "ingrossing," and "forestalling," were part of the comprehensive attempt to control prices by statute.

The Act 5 & 6 Edward VI., Cap. XV., entitled "An Act against Regrators and Ingrossers of Tanned Leather," provided "That from and after the first day of May next coming, no person or persons, of what estate, degree or condition soever he or they be, shall *buy or engross*, or cause to be bought or engrossed, any kind of tanned leather, *to the intent to sell the same again*." Other sections allowed saddlers, cordwainers and other artificers to buy such quantities of leather as should be necessary for the carrying on of their trades. Section V. prohibited altogether the shipping of boots, shoes and similar articles "to the intent to carry, transport or convey over the seas as merchandise to be sold or exchanged there." Section VII. provided "That no sadler, girdler, cordwainer, nor other artificer, dwelling within the City of London and the suburbs of the same, which shall cut the same tanned leather as is aforesaid, to the intent to make wares thereof, shall curry or dress any of the aforesaid tanned leather in his or their own house or houses, or by his or their servant or servants."

It is seen, that these and other similar statutes, if enforced, would have compelled producers to be their own salesmen, would have abolished the occupation of the middleman or merchant, and made utterly impossible the trade and commerce which experience has shown to be necessary for the life of all large communities. Buying and selling at wholesale is always conducted with the purpose of "inhancing prices." It is a commercial process which is absolutely necessary, in order to ensure the presence in the market of merchandise in quantities sufficiently large, to supply the needs of large communities. Such statutes could be passed only in a rudimentary stage of society, when its needs are imperfectly comprehended, and when the actual practical results of such legislation have not been ascertained by experience.

So far the protection of the law had been in the main given to buyers. But every member of the community is a seller as well as a buyer. He is a seller of his own labor, or of its products. He is a buyer of the labor of others, or of its products. In the one capacity, he is no more entitled to artificial and arbitrary aid from the law, than he is in the other. But if this were not so, if the entire community were, in fact, divided into two distinct classes, of buyers and sellers, if the law undertakes to keep prices down for the benefit of buyers, it is also under the obligation to keep prices up for the benefit of sellers.

This obligation the lawgivers of the time recognized and accepted.

Accordingly we find statutes passed with the intent of keeping prices up. Of such we find an example in the Acts 14 Rich. II., Cap. IV. and VI., which are as follows:

14 RICHARD II., A.D. 1390.

"CAP. IV.

"Of whom denizens may buy wools, and where; but they shall not regrate them.

"ITEM, to *keep the price of wools the better*, That no denizen of England, shall *buy* no wools *but of the owners* of the sheep and of the tithes, except in the staple: and that no denizen regrate wools nor other merchandises of the staple privily nor apertly, upon pain to forfeit the value of the thing regrated: and that the justices of peace in the country have power to enquire, and shall enquire from time to time of such English regrators and of the weights of the staple, and punish them by the pain aforesaid. And that *no Englishman buy any wool of any person, but for himself or for his own use*, as to sell at the staple, and for *to make cloth.*"

"CAP. VI.

"English merchants shall freight only in English ships.

"ITEM, That all merchants of the realm of England shall freight in the said realm the ships of the said realm, and not strange ships ; so that the *owners* of the said ships *take reasonable gains* for the freight of the same."

In the same line of legislation, for like purposes, were the class of statutes which were absolutely prohibitory of trade and commerce of certain classes. Such was the Act 14 Rich. II., Cap. V., which is as follows :

"CAP. V.

"No denizen shall transport any merchandise of the staple forth of the realm.

"ITEM, That no denizen carry wools, leather, woolfels, nor lead out of the realm of England, to the parties beyond the sea, upon pain of forfeiture of the same, but only strangers."

So, too, we find specimens of limited prohibition for the purpose of the special protection of a particular locality, of which the 14 Rich. II., Cap. VII., is an example.

"CAP. VII.

"Tin shall pass forth of the realm only at Dartmouth.
"ITEM, that the passage of tin out of the realm shall be at the port of Dartmouth, and in no place else."

The statutes against forestalling, regrating, and engrossing, as we have seen, were directed against all attempts to raise prices, whether on the part of single individuals, or of individuals in combination. At an early period, however, statutes were passed giving a criminal character to attempts of the same kind by individuals in combination. It was made a crime, to combine or confederate to raise prices. Combinations to raise prices of labor were placed on the same legal footing with combinations to raise prices of merchandise.

The earliest statute of this nature, which has come under my observation, is the Statute 2 & 3 Edw. VI.,

c. 15, entitled "The bill of conspiracies of victuallers and craftsmen."

Prior to this statute the crime of conspiracy was virtually limited to illegal combinations having some connection with the administration of justice. The crime was defined by the Statute 33 Edw. I., quoted by Hawkins in his "Pleas of the Crown." In his definition of the crime of conspiracy Hawkins begins by stating

"As to the First Point, viz., *Who may be said to be guilty of Conspiracy*, Sect. 1. There can be *no better rule than the statute* of 33 or rather 21 Edw. I., *the intent whereof was to make a final definition of* CONSPIRATORS, to which purpose it declared "that conspirators be they that do confeder or bind themselves by oath, covenant, or other alliance, that every of them shall aid and bear the other falsly and maliciously to indict, or cause to indict, or falsly to move and maintain pleas ; and also such as cause children within age to appeal men of felony, whereby they are imprisoned and sore grieved ; and such as retain men in the country with liveries or fees for to maintain their malicious enterprizes ; and this extendeth as well to the takers as to the givers ; and to stewards and bailiffs of great lords, who by their seigniory, office, or power, undertake to bear or maintain quarrels, pleas, or debates that concern other parties than such as touch the estate of their lords or themselves."

No doubt in time other conspiracies came to be recognized in addition to those there described. But so far as appears by any record which has come under my observation, a mere combination to raise prices was not punishable as a conspiracy prior to the passage of that Act, 2 & 3 Edw. VI., c. 15.

The Act was as follows :

"Forasmuch as of late divers sellers of victuals, not contented with moderate and reasonable gain, but minding to have and to take for their victuals so much as list them, have conspired and covenanted together to sell their victuals at *unreasonable prices ;* (2) and likewise artificers, handicraftsmen and labourers have made confederacies and promises, and have sworn mutual oaths not only that they should not meddle one with another's work, and perform and finish that another hath begun, but also to constitute and appoint how much work they shall do in a day, and what hours and times they shall work, *contrary to* the laws and *statutes* of this realm, and to the great hurt and impoverishment of the King's majesty's subjects ; (3) for reformation thereof it is ordained and enacted by the King our sovereign lord, the lords and commons in this present parliament assembled, and by the authority of the same, That if any butchers, brewers, bakers, poulterers, cooks, costermongers or fruiterers, shall at any time from and after the first day of March next coming, conspire, covenant, promise or make any oaths, *that they shall not sell their victuals but at certain prices ;* (4) or if any artificers, workmen, or labourers do conspire, covenant or promise together, or make any oaths, *that they shall not make or do their works but at a certain price or rate,* or shall not enterprize or take upon them to finish that another hath begun, *or shall do but a certain work in a day, or shall not work but at certain hours and times,* (5) that then every person so conspiring, covenanting, swearing or offending, being lawfully convict thereof by witness, confession or otherwise, shall forfeit for the first offence ten pounds to the King's highness" with provisions for higher penalties for later offences.

" II. And if it fortune any such conspiracy, covenant or promise to be had and made by any society, brotherhood or company of any craft, mystery or occupation of the victuallers above mentioned, with the presence or consent of the more part of them, that then immediately upon such act of conspiracy, covenant or promise had or made, over and besides the particular punishment before in this act appointed for the offender, their corporation shall be dissolved to all intents, constructions and purposes."(*a*)

This statute, it is apparent, was one step in the general system of legislation, of which the purpose was to regulate prices by statute. Under this statute, too, it is apparent, that any combination to raise prices was a crime, even if strictly limited in its intended effect to the prices of the labor or merchandise of the combining parties, and involving no interference with the legal rights of others.

Especially is it to be noted, that this crime of conspir-

(*a*) Repealed with a long list of other statutes, 5 Geo. IV., c. 95.

acy, as defined by the statute itself, consisted in a combination to raise prices and fix hours of work " contrary to the laws and statutes of this realm." The mere combination constituted no crime provided there were to be no ultimate act which was unlawful. It was necessary that the act, which was the object of the combination, should be in itself a violation of law or statute. And that has always been the well-established doctrine of the English law, as well as of the American law, until the recent decisions before alluded to.

So far as concerned combinations to raise the prices of merchandise, this Act seems to have been a dead letter from the very time of its passage. It was apparently ignored by common consent. Hardly a pretence was ever made of enforcing it. Even as to combinations to raise prices of labor, it practically never formed part of the living body of the English law. Only one conviction, so far as my reading has been able to discover, was ever had under it on a mere combination to raise the price of the labor of the combining parties, when such combination was unaccompanied by an unlawful interference with the legal rights of others. That was the case of *Rex* v. *Journeymen Taylors of Cambridge*, 8 Modern, 11. There have, no doubt, been many cases of indictments for combinations by workmen, when those combinations have been accompanied by unlawful interference with the legal rights of others. But the case just mentioned is the only reported case, which I have been able to find, of a conviction, or even of a trial, for a mere combination to raise the prices of the labor of the combining parties. As to prices of merchandise, however, I have been unable to discover a single reported case of a prosecution for a combination to raise or maintain such prices.(*a*) Black-

---

(*a*) *Rex* v. *Norris*, 2 Ld. Kenyon, 300,can be hardly called a prosecution, being according to the report only an *ex parte* application for leave to file an information, accompanied by some language from Lord Mansfield.

If, however, that case be deemed " a prosecution," it was a case arising

stone, in that part of his Commentaries which treats of the crime of conspiracy, makes no mention of a combination to raise or maintain prices, whether of merchandise or labor. (*a*) He treats the crime of conspiracy almost entirely as an offense connected with the administration of justice. What he says of it is comprised in his Chapter X. of Book IV., which is entitled "Of Offenses against Public Justice." Serjeant Hawkins, in his "Pleas of the Crown," follows the same course, and treats the offense of conspiracy almost wholly as one connected with the administration of justice. Neither does he make any mention of a conspiracy to raise or maintain prices, of either labor or merchandise.

But as to mere combinations to raise or maintain the prices of merchandise, I have failed to find any evidence that such a combination was ever practically treated as a criminal offense, save that it was nominally made such by the language of the statute above quoted. That statute was repealed, as a matter of form, by the Statute 5, George IV., chap. 95. But, as a matter of fact, and substance, it had been ignored by the entire community from the time of its passage. At the time of the writing of Blackstone's Commentaries it had become an obsolete antiquity.

As to the prices of labor, the various later amending statutes as to combinations or conspiracies of workmen all recognized the right of workmen to make combinations merely to raise the prices of their own labor, so long as they refrained from violence, intimidation, or other unlawful interference with the rights of others. So, too, did the opinions of the courts. Other than the case of *Rex* v. *Journeymen Taylors of Cambridge*, I find no case in the English reports where workmen were convicted for a mere peaceable and orderly combination to raise their own wages.

---

under the statute before quoted, which, according to the authorities, never formed part of our American law.

(*a*) 4 Blackstone Com. 136.

By the Act 12 Geo. III., chap. 71, A.D. 1772, the statutes as to forestalling, regrating, and engrossing were repealed. The intention evidently was both to repeal them, and to abolish the offenses.

The reason given for the repeal in the preamble of the Act is as follows: "Whereas it hath been *found by experience*, that the *restraints laid by several statutes* upon the dealing in corn, meal, flour, cattle, and sundry other sorts of victuals, by *preventing a free trade* in the said commodities, have a *tendency to discourage the growth*, and to *inhance the price* of the same; which statutes, if put in execution, would *bring great distress upon the inhabitants of many parts of this Kingdom*, and in particular upon those of the cities of London and Westminster."

Although it was evidently the intention of the legislature, by this statute not merely to repeal the former statutes as to forestalling, regrating, and engrossing, but also to abolish the offenses, Lord Kenyon nevertheless held in *Rex* v. *Waddington*, 1 East, 167, that those offenses had been offenses at common law; and consequently that the offenses had not been abolished by the mere repeal of the statutes. To meet this situation, a later statute was passed, 7 & 8 Victoria, Cap. XXIV., A.D. 1844, which in express terms abolished the offenses. No authority exists, so far as I have been able to find, for this decision of Lord Kenyon. It is somewhat singular, too, that the original statutes creating those offenses should have been passed, if the offenses existed already. It is also very clear, that the lawyers who drafted the repealing act would have abolished the offenses, if they had supposed that the offenses still continued to exist at common law.

In *Rex* v. *Waddington* there was a remarkable array of counsel, including Erskine, for the prosecution; and the indications are very strong, that the prosecution was merely the work of business rivals. The prosecution was not for conspiracy, but for the mere offense of engrossing, by a single individual. Lord Kenyon, in his opinion, dilated on the dreadful dangers from such practices on the part of single individuals. With the exception of this *Waddington* case, my examinations have failed to find any cases of trials for either of those antiquated offenses. It is, therefore, an accurate statement, that the statutes creating these offenses by individuals were virtually ignored, almost from the time of their passage. That fact admits of only one explanation, which is, that no practical injury ever resulted from the business of buying and selling at wholesale, which is invariably conducted with the intent of selling at an advanced price.

The same thing can be said as to combinations to put up the prices of merchandise on the part of several individuals in combination. Without doubt there were numberless instances of such combinations. Such combinations, too, under the statutes above mentioned were criminal offenses. But we find no records in the reports, of prosecutions for such offenses, unless *Rex* v. *Norris*, before cited, be such a case.(*a*) The evident reason is that such combinations did no harm.

With these repealing and abolishing statutes, the law in England was finally established, permitting any and all efforts to merely raise prices, whether of labor or merchandise, whether on the part of single individuals or individuals in combination, provided those efforts were limited to the prices of the labor and merchandise of the parties making the attempts, and provided also that the efforts were accompanied by no legal injury to others. Contracts of combination, to raise or maintain prices, or to prevent competition, were not enforced by the courts. But they were never held to be criminal. Nor were they held to be violations of the legal rights of other individuals.

As to such combinations, the most important and instructive case in the English reports, so far as my read-

---

(*a*) *Rex* v. *Norris*, 2 Ld. Kenyon, 300.

ing goes, is the case of *Mogul Steamship Company* v. *McGregor*,(a) wherein the law as to contracts in restraint of trade had a more thorough discussion than in any other which has come within my knowledge.

The action was brought against the combining parties as defendants, by the Mogul Steamship Company, the owner of a line of steamships which had been driven out of a contested field by the combination, to enjoin the further operation of the combination to the injury of the plaintiff. The cause came on for hearing in the first instance before Lord Chief Justice Coleridge, on a motion for an injunction. The injunction was refused, after elaborate argument by the leaders of the English bar, the present Lord Chief Justice Russell being leading counsel for the defense, Sir Henry James being the leading counsel for the complainant. Lord Coleridge's judgment was affirmed in the Court of Appeal, and afterward in the House of Lords. In the Court of Appeal the case was heard before Lord Esher, Master of the Rolls, with Judges Bowen and Fry, each of whom delivered an opinion. In the House of Lords opinions were delivered by Lord Halsbury, Lord Watson, Lord Bramwell, Lord Morris, Lord Field, and Lord Hannen; and there was a memorandum of concurrence by Lord Macnaghten. The Master of the Rolls alone dissented.

In all there were ten opinions, by the first jurists in England. It is seldom that any case has received a consideration so exhaustive. The principles and authorities of the English law bearing on the case were thoroughly examined, and carefully stated.

The point decided was the legality, under the English law, of a combination of shipowners, formed for the avowed purpose of controlling prices, and preventing competition—of preventing all competition between the parties combining, and destroying all competition by outsiders. It was, too, the case of a combination of com-

---

(a) Law Rep. 21 Q. B. Div. 544, 23 Q. B. Div. 598, App. Cas. 1892, 25.

mon carriers, for the avowed purpose of absorbing, and controlling, the entire transportation of tea from Canton, and all the ports on the Hankow River, in China. The means to be used to accomplish that purpose included the fixing of rates by one common authority for all the combining owners, the boycotting of all outside competitors, the refusal to do business with parties who did business with any outside competitors, and the putting down of freights to any figure that might be necessary to drive away those competitors, with the intent to subsequently restore rates to a profitable figure after the suppression of the outside competition.

A few extracts from the opinions are here selected, in order to give an authoritative statement of the facts and the decision of the court.

The opinion of Lord Coleridge, C. J., was in part:

"The plaintiffs are a company of shipowners trading, or desirous of trading, between Australia and this country, taking China by the way; and desirous in particular of sharing in the transport of what has been called the 'tea harvest,' the time of which is in the late spring and early summer months, and the places for loading which, as far as this case is concerned, are Shanghai at the mouth of the Yangtze-kiang and Hankow, a place about 600 miles up the stream of that great river. The defendants are a number of great shipowners, companies, and private partnerships, trading for the most part from this country to China and from China to this country direct, and who, being desirous to keep this very valuable trade in their own hands, and to prevent, if they can, the lowering of freights (the ruinous lowering as they contend), which must follow, as they say, from absolutely unrestricted competition, entered into what they call a conference for the purpose of working the homeward trade, by offering a rebate of 5 per cent. upon all freights paid by the shippers to the conference vessels, such rebate not to be paid to any shipper who shipped any tea at Shanghai or Hankow (the rebate was not confined to these ports, but I think that an immaterial circumstance) in any vessels but those belonging to the conference.

* * * * * * *

"The complaint, then, is this, that the defendants unlawfully combined or conspired to prevent the plaintiffs from carrying on their trade, that they did prevent them by the use of unlawful means in furtherance of such unlawful combination or conspiracy, and that from such unlawful combination or conspiracy therefore damage has resulted to the plaintiffs.

"The defendants answer that neither was their combination unlawful in itself, nor were any unlawful means used in furtherance of it; but that the damage, if any, to the plaintiffs was the necessary and inevitable result of the defendants carrying on their lawful trade in a lawful manner.

"These are the contentions on the two sides. Is there anything in the law applicable to this subject in which they are agreed? In the statement of the law, as might be expected from the counsel who argued the case, there was often a close apparent agreement; but when it came to the application of it, the same words were evidently not always used on both sides in the same sense. I have carefully read over again and considered the arguments, and it seems to me it will be better that I should endeavour to state what I conceive to be the law upon the matter in dispute, and then apply it to the facts before me, which, as most of them depended upon written documents, can hardly be said to have been much disputed.

"It cannot be, nor indeed was it, denied that in order to found this action there must be an element of *unlawfulness* in the combination on which it is founded, and that this *element of unlawfulness must exist* alike *whether the combination is the subject of an indictment or the subject of an action.* But in an indictment it suffices if the combination exists, *and is unlawful,* because it is the combination itself which is mischievous, and which gives the public an interest to interfere by indictment. Nothing need be actually done in furtherance of it. In the Bridgewater Case(1), referred to at the bar, and in which I was counsel, nothing was done in fact; yet a gentleman was convicted because he had entered into an unlawful combination from which almost on the spot he withdrew, and withdrew altogether. No one was harmed, but the public offence was complete. This is in accordance with the express words of Bayley, J., in *Rex* v. *De Berenger.*(2) It is otherwise in a civil action: it is the damage which results from the unlawful combination itself with which the civil action is concerned. It is not every combination which is unlawful, and if the combination is lawful, that is to

---

(1) Unreported.   (2) 3 M. & S. 67, at p. 76.

say, is for a lawful end pursued by lawful means, or being unlawful there is no damage from it to the plaintiff, the action will not lie. In these last sentences damage means legal injury ; mere loss or disadvantage will not sustain the action.

" Once more, to state the proposition somewhat differently with a view to some of the arguments addressed to me, the law may be put thus. *If the combination is unlawful, then the parties to it commit a misdemeanour, and are offenders against the State; and if, as the result of such unlawful combination and misdemeanour, a private person receives a private injury, that gives such person a right of private action.*

" It is, therefore, no doubt necessary to consider the object of the combination as well as the means employed to effect the object, in order to determine the legality or illegality of the combination. And in this case it is clear that if the *object* were *unlawful*, or if the object were lawful, but the *means* employed to effect it were *unlawful*, and if there were a *combination either* to *effect the unlawful object* or to *use the unlawful means,* then the *combination was unlawful, then those who formed it were misdemeanants,* and a person injured by their misdemeanour has an action in respect of his injury.

* * * * * * *

" It will appear from the statement which I have given of what I believe to be the law, that I cannot assent without some qualification to the propositions which were pressed upon me by the learned counsel for the contending parties in this case. For the same reason I do not propose to enter into a detailed examination of the many cases which were cited in argument. I believe that, fairly considered and rightly looked at, every case, including the much canvassed one of *Rex* v. *Turner,* (1) will be found to be consistent with the principles I have stated, although there are isolated *dicta* of very great judges, probably in their actual terms—if the terms are rightly reported—going beyond the law, certainly quite at variance with each other. On one side are extreme cases, such as *Keble* v. *Hickringill*(2), in which at first Lord Holt doubted, but finally gave judgment for the plaintiff, and *Reg* v. *Druitt*(3), in which, unless he is misreported, Bramwell, B., said he thought a combination to treat a man with ' black looks ' was an indictable misdemeanour

---

(1) 13 East, 228.   (2) 11 Mod. 74, 131.   (3) 10 Cox, C. C. 592.

(a decision, if it be one, which might assuredly land us in unexpected and singular results) ; and the very broad dictum of Pratt, C. J., in *Rex* v. *Journeyman Tailors of Cambridge*(1), that ' a conspiracy of any kind is illegal, though the matter they conspired about might have been quite lawful for them to do.' These are perhaps as extreme as can be found on one side ; on the other is the questioned and possibly overruled case of *Rex* v. *Turner*(2), decided by Lord Ellenborough, C. J., and Grose, Le Blanc and Bayley, JJ. The view which Lord Ellenborough took of the facts of that case appears rather from his interlocutory observation at p. 230 than from his judgment on the page following. It is difficult not to acquiesce in the good sense of Lord Ellenborough's observations, and speaking, as I wish, and, indeed, ought to speak, with grateful respect of Lord Campbell, I do not feel so sure that Lord Ellenborough was wrong simply because Lord Campbell in *Reg* v. *Rowlands*(3) says he has no doubt he was so. Be that as it may, and if Lord Ellenborough and the Court did wrongly apply the principles of law in *Rex* v. *Turner*(2), the principles are clearly and forcibly stated in accordance with what I have endeavoured to express by Lord Ellenborough himself. The case of *Rex* v. *Eccles*(4), before Lord Mansfield, C. J., Willes and Buller, JJ., turned upon pleading ; the motion was in arrest of judgment ; the decision was that after verdict the indictment was good ; and the case itself is expressly commented on, explained and distinguished by Lord Ellenborough in *Rex* v. *Turner*.(2)

"There were a number of cases, of which *Winsmore* v. *Greenbank*(5), *Lumley* v. *Gye*(6), and *Bowen* v. *Hall*(7), were examples, in which the question of conspiracy did not arise ; but they were cited to shew what cases of interference with what sort of contracts had been held actionable by the courts at the suit of one individual against another. Now all these cases bind me sitting here, and I neither question nor desire to evade their authority. But they do not help me much. I do not doubt the acts done by the defendants here, if done *wrongfully* and maliciously, or if done in furtherance of a *wrongful* and malicious combination, would be

(1) 8 Mod. 11.
(2) 13 East, 228.
(3) 17 Q. B. 671, at p. 686.
(4) 1 Leach, C. C. 274.
(5) Willes, 577.
(6) 2 E. & B. 216.
(7) 6 Q. B. D. 333.

ground for an action on the case at the suit of one who suffered injury from them. The question comes at last to this, what was the character of these acts, and what was the motive of the defendants in doing them? The defendants are traders with enormous sums of money embarked in their adventures, and naturally and allowably desirous to reap a profit from their trade. They have a right to push their *lawful* trade by all *lawful* means. They have a right to endeavour by lawful means to keep their trade in their own hands and by the same means to exclude others from its benefits, if they can. Amongst lawful means is certainly included the inducing by profitable offers customers to deal with them rather than with their rivals. It follows that they may, if they think fit, endeavour to induce customers to deal with them exclusively by giving notice that only to exclusive customers will they give the advantage of their profitable offers. I do not think it matters that the withdrawal of the advantages is out of all proportion to the injury inflicted on those who withdraw them by the customers, who decline to deal exclusively with them, dealing with other traders. It is a bargain which persons in the position of the defendants here had a right to make, and those who are parties to the bargain must take it or leave it as a whole. Of coercion, of bribing, I see no evidence; of inducing, in the sense in which that word is used in the class of cases to which *Lumley* v. *Gye*(1) belongs, I see none either.

"One word in passing only on the contention that this combination of the defendants was *unlawful* because it was in *restraint of trade*. It seems to me it was no more in restraint of trade, as that phrase is used for the purpose of avoiding contracts, than if two tailors in a village agreed to give their customers five per cent. off their bills at Christmas on condition of their customers dealing with them and with them only. *Restraint of trade*, with deference, *has in its legal sense nothing to do with this question.*

"But it is said that the motive of these acts was to ruin the plaintiffs, and that such a motive, it has been held, will render the combination itself wrongful and malicious, and that if damage has resulted to the plaintiffs an action will lie. I concede that if the premises are established the conclusion follows. It is too late to dispute, if I desired it, as I do not, that a *wrongful* and malicious combination to ruin a man in his trade may be ground for such an

(1) 2 E. & B. 216.

action as this. Was then this combination such? The answer to this question has given me much trouble, and I confess to the weakness of having long doubted and hesitated before I could make up my mind. There can be no doubt that the defendants were determined, if they could, to exclude the plaintiffs from this trade. Strong expressions were drawn from some of them in cross-examination, and the telegrams and letters shewed the importance they attached to the matter, their resolute purpose to exclude the plaintiffs if they could, and to do so without any consideration for the results to the plaintiffs, if they were successfully excluded. This, I think, is made out, and I think no more is made out than this. Is this enough? It must be remembered that all trade is and must be in a sense selfish; trade not being infinite, nay, the trade of a particular place or district being possibly very limited, what one man gains another loses. In the hand-to-hand war of commerce, as in the conflicts of public life, whether at the bar, in Parliament, in medicine, in engineering (I give examples only), men fight on without much thought of others, except a desire to excel or to defeat them. Very lofty minds, like Sir Philip Sidney with his cup of water, will not stoop to take an advantage, if they think another wants it more. Our age, in spite of high authority to the contrary, is not without its Sir Philip Sidneys; but these are counsels of perfection which it would be silly indeed to make the measure of the rough business of the world as pursued by ordinary men of business. The line is in words difficult to draw, but I cannot see that these defendants have in fact passed the line which separates the reasonable and legitimate selfishness of traders from wrong and malice. In 1884 they admitted the plaintiffs to their conference; in 1885 they excluded them, and they were determined no doubt, if they could, to make the exclusion complete and effective, not from any personal malice or ill will to the plaintiffs as individuals, but because they were determined, if they could, to keep the trade to themselves; and if they permitted persons in the position of the plaintiffs to come in and share it they thought, and honestly and, as it turns out, correctly thought, that for a time at least there would be an end of their gains.

"The plaintiffs' conduct cannot affect their right of action, if they have it; but it is impossible not to observe that they were as reckless of consequences in regard to the defendants as they accuse the defendants of being in regard to themselves; they were as determined to break in as the defendants were determined to shut out ; and they made their threats of smashing freights and injuring the defendants a mode of rather forcible suasion to the defendants to let them into the conference. If they have their right of action, why they have it ; if they have it not, their own conduct disentitles them to much sympathy.

" On the whole I come to the conclusion that the combination was *not wrongful* and malicious, and that the defendants were *not guilty of a misdemeanour*. I think that the acts done in pursuance of the combination were *not unlawful, not wrongful*, not malicious ; and that therefore the defendants are entitled to my judgment."

Opinion of Lord Bowen, Law Rep. 23 Q. B. Div. 613 :

" The English law, which in its earlier stages began with but an imperfect line of demarcation between torts and breaches of contract, presents us with no scientific analysis of the degree to which the intent to harm, or, in the language of the civil law, the animus vicino nocendi, may enter into or affect the conception of a personal wrong ; see *Chasemore* v. *Richards*.(1) *All personal wrong means the infringement of some personal right*. ' It is essential to an action in tort,' say the Privy Council in *Rogers* v. *Rajendro Dutt*,(2) ' that the act complained of should under the circumstances be legally wrongful as regards the party complaining ; that is, it must prejudicially affect him in some legal right ; merely that it will, however directly, do a man harm in his interests, is not enough.' What, then, were the rights of the plaintiffs as traders as against the defendants ? The plaintiffs had a right to be protected against certain kind of conduct ; and we have to consider what conduct would pass this legal line or boundary. Now, intentionally to do that which is calculated in the ordinary course of events to damage, and which does, in fact, damage another in that other person's property or trade, is actionable if done without just cause or excuse. Such intentional action when done without just cause or excuse is what the law calls a malicious wrong (see *Bromage* v. *Prosser* ;[3] *Capital and Counties Bank* v. *Henty*, per Lord Blackburn[4]). The acts of the defendants which are complained of here were intentional, and were also calculated, no doubt, to do the plaintiffs damage in their

---

(1) 7 H. L. C. 349, at p. 388. (3) 4 B. & C. 247.
(2) 13 Moore, P. C. 209. (4) 7 App Cas. 741, at p. 772.

trade. But in order to see whether they were wrongful we have still to discuss the question whether they were done without any just cause or excuse. Such just cause or excuse the defendants on their side assert to be found in their own positive right (subject to certain limitations) to carry on their own trade freely in the mode and manner that best suits them, and which they think best calculated to secure their own advantage.

"What, then, are the limitations which the law imposes on a trader in the conduct of his business as between himself and other traders? There seem to be no burdens or restrictions in law upon a trader which arise merely from the fact that he is a trader, and which are not equally laid on all other subjects of the Crown. His right to trade freely is a right which the law recognises and encourages, but it is one which places him at no special disadvantage as compared with others. No man, whether trader or not, can, however, justify damaging another in his commercial business by *fraud* or *misrepresentation*. *Intimidation*, *obstruction*, and *molestation* are forbidden; so is the *intentional procurement of a violation of individual rights, contractual or other*, assuming always that there is no just cause for it. The intentional driving away of customers by show of violence: *Tarleton* v. *M'Gawley* ;(1) the obstruction of actors on the stage by preconcerted hissing: *Clifford* v. *Brandon* ;(2) *Gregory* v. *Brunswick* ;(3) the disturbance of wild fowl in decoys by the firing of guns: *Carrington* v. *Taylor*,(4) and *Keeble* v. *Hickeringill* ;(5) the impending or threatening servants or workmen: *Garret* v. *Taylor* ;(6) the inducing persons under personal contracts to break their contracts: *Bowen* v. *Hall* ;(7) *Lumley* v. *Gye* ;(8) all are instances of such forbidden acts. But the defendants have been guilty of none of these acts. They have done nothing more against the plaintiffs than pursue to the bitter end a war of competition waged in the interest of their own trade. To the argument that a competition so pursued ceases to have a just cause or excuse when there is ill will or a personal intention to harm, it is sufficient to reply (as I have already pointed out) that there was here no personal intention to do any other or greater harm to the plaintiffs than

---

(1) Peak, N. P. C. 270.
(2) 2 Camp. 358.
(3) 6 Man. & G. 205.
(4) 11 East, 571.
(5) 11 East, 574, n.
(6) Cro. Jac. 567.
(7) 6 Q. B. D. 333.
(8) 2 E. & B. 216.

such as was necessarily involved in the desire to attract to the defendants' ships the entire tea freights of the ports, a portion of which would otherwise have fallen to the plaintiffs' share. I can find no authority for the doctrine that such a commercial motive deprives of 'just cause or excuse' acts done in the course of trade which would but for such a motive be justifiable. So to hold would be to convert into an illegal motive the instinct of self-advancement and self-protection, which is the very incentive to all trade. *To say that a man is to trade freely, but that he is to stop short at any act which is calculated to harm other tradesmen, and which is designed to attract business to his own shop, would be a strange and impossible counsel of perfection.*

* * * * * * *

" It is urged, however, on the part of the plaintiffs, that even *if the acts complained of would not be wrongful had they been committed by a single individual, they become actionable when they are the result of concerted action among several.* In other words, the plaintiffs, it is contended, have been injured by an *illegal* conspiracy. Of the general proposition, that certain kinds of conduct not criminal in any one individual *may* become criminal if done by combination among several, there can be no doubt. The distinction is based on sound reason, for a combination may make oppressive or dangerous that which if it proceeded only from a single person would be otherwise, and the very fact of the combination may shew that the object is simply to do harm, and not to exercise one's own just rights. In the application of this undoubted principle it is necessary to be very careful not to press the doctrine of illegal conspiracy beyond that which is necessary for the protection of individuals or of the public ; and it may be observed in passing that as a rule it is the damage wrongfully done, and not the conspiracy, that is the gist of actions on the case for conspiracy : see *Skinner* v. *Gunton ;*(1) *Hutchins* v. *Hutchins.*(2) But what is the definition of an illegal combination ? It is an agreement by one or more to do an *unlawful act,* or to do a lawful act by *unlawful means: O'Connell* v. *The Queen ;*(3) *Reg* v. *Parnell ;*(4) and the question to be solved is whether there has been

---

(1) 1 Wms. Saund. 229.
(2) 7 Hill's New York Cases, 104 ; Bigelow's Leading Cases on Torts, 207.
(3) 11 Cl. & F. 155.
(4) 14 Cox, Criminal Cases, 508.

any such agreement here. Have the defendants combined to do an *unlawful act?* Have they combined to do a lawful act by *unlawful means?* A moment's consideration will be sufficient to shew that this new inquiry only drives us back to the circle of definitions and legal propositions which I have already traversed in the previous part of this judgment. The unlawful act agreed to, if any, between the defendants must have been the intentional doing of some act to the detriment of the plaintiffs' business without just cause or excuse. Whether there was any such justification or excuse for the defendants is the old question over again, which, so far as regards an individual trader, has been already solved. The only differentia that can exist must arise, if at all, out of the fact that the acts done are the joint acts of several capitalists, and not of one capitalist only. The next point is whether the means adopted were unlawful. The means adopted were competition carried to a bitter end. Whether such means were unlawful is in like manner nothing but the old discussion which I have gone through, and which is now revived under a second head of inquiry, except so far as a combination of capitalists differentiates the case of acts jointly done by them from similar acts done by a single man of capital. But *I find it impossible myself to acquiesce in the view that the English law places any such restriction on the combination of capital as would be involved in the recognition of such a distinction. If so, one rich capitalist may innocently carry competition to a length which would become unlawful in the case of a syndicate with a joint capital no larger than his own, and one individual merchant may lawfully do that which a firm or a partnership may not.* What limits, on such a theory, would be imposed by law on the competitive action of a joint-stock company limited, is a problem which might well puzzle a casuist. The truth is, that the *combination of capital for purposes of trade and competition is a very different thing from such a combination of several persons against one, with a view to harm him, as falls under the head of an indictable conspiracy.* There is no just cause or excuse in the latter class of cases. There is such a just cause or excuse in the former. There are cases in which the very fact of a combination is evidence of a design to do that which is hurtful without just cause —is evidence—to use a technical expression—of malice. But it is *perfectly legitimate, as it seems to me, to combine capital for all the mere purposes of trade for which capital may, apart from combination, be legitimately used in trade.* To limit *combinations of capital, when used for purposes of competition, in the manner proposed by the argument of the plaintiffs, would, in the present day, be impossible— would be only another method of attempting to set boundaries to the tides.* Legal puzzles which might well distract a theorist may easily be conceived of imaginary conflicts between the selfishness of a group of individuals and the obvious wellbeing of other members of the community. Would it be an indictable conspiracy to agree to drink up all the water from a common spring in a time of drought; to buy up by preconcerted action all the provisions in a market or district in times of scarcity: see *Rex* v. *Waddington*;(1) to combine to purchase all the shares of a company against a coming settling-day; or to agree to give away articles of trade gratis in order to withdraw custom from a trader? May two itinerant match-vendors combine to sell matches below their value in order by competition to drive a third match-vendor from the street? In cases like these, *where the elements of intimidation, molestation, or the other kinds of illegality to which I have alluded are not present,* the question must be decided by the application of the test I have indicated. Assume that what is done is intentional, and that it is calculated to do harm to others. Then comes the question, Was it done with or without 'just cause or excuse'? If it was bona fide *done in the use of a man's own property, in the exercise of a man's own trade,* such legal justification would, I think, exist not the less because what was done might seem to others to be selfish or unreasonable; see the summing-up of Erle, J., and the judgment of the Queen's Bench in *Reg.* v. *Rowlands.*(2) But such legal justification would not exist when the act was merely done with the intention of causing temporal harm, without reference to one's own lawful gain, or the lawful enjoyment of one's own rights. The good sense of the tribunal which had to decide would have to analyze the circumstances and to discover on which side of the line each case fell. But if the real object were to *enjoy what was one's own, or to acquire for one's self some advantage in one's property or trade, and what was done was done honestly, peaceably, and without any of the illegal acts above referred to*, it could not, in my opinion, properly be said that it was done without just cause or excuse. One may with advantage borrow for the *benefit of traders* what was said by Erle, J., in *Reg.* v. *Rowlands,*(3), of *workmen and of masters:* 'The intention

---

(1) 1 East, 143.   (2) 17 Q. B. 671.   (3) 17 Q. B. 671, at p. 687, n.

of the law is at present to allow either of them to *follow the dictates of their own will, with respect to their own actions, and their own property ;* and either, I believe, has a right to *study to promote his own advantage*, or to *combine with others to promote their mutual advantage.*'

"Lastly, we are asked to hold the defendants' conference or association illegal, as being in restraint of trade. The term 'illegal' here is a misleading one. *Contracts*, as they are called, *in restraint of trade*, are *not*, in my opinion, *illegal in any sense, except that the law will not enforce them.* It *does not prohibit* the making of such contracts ; it merely *declines*, after they have been made, to *recognise their validity.* The law considers the disadvantage so imposed upon the contract a sufficient shelter to the public. The language of Crompton, J., in *Hilton* v. *Eckersley*(1), is, I think, *not to be supported. No action at common law will lie or ever has lain against any individual or individuals for entering into a contract* merely because it is in *restraint of trade.* Lord Eldon's equity decision in *Cousins* v. *Smith*(2) is not very intelligible, even if it be not open to the somewhat personal criticism passed on it by Lord Campbell in his 'Lives of the Chancellors.' If indeed it could be plainly proved that the mere formation of 'conferences,' 'trusts,' or 'associations' such as these were always necessarily injurious to the public—a view which involves, perhaps, the disputable assumption that, in a country of free trade, and one which is not under the iron régime of statutory monopolies, such confederations can ever be really successful—and if the evil of them were not sufficiently dealt with by the common law rule, which held such agreements to be void as *distinct from holding them to be criminal*, there might be some reason for thinking that the common law ought to discover within its arsenal of sound common-sense principles some further remedy commensurate with the mischief. Neither of these assumptions are, to my mind, at all evident, *nor is it the province of judges to mould and stretch the law of conspiracy in order to keep pace with the calculations of political economy. If peaceable and honest combinations of capital for purposes of trade competition are to be struck at, it must, I think, be by legislation, for I do not see that they are under the ban of the common law.*

"In the result, I agree with Lord Coleridge, C. J., and differ,

---

(1) 6 E. & B. 47.   (2) 13 Ves. 542.

with regret, from the Master of the Rolls. The substance of my view is this, that *competition*, however severe and egotistical, if *unattended by circumstances of dishonesty, intimidation, molestation*, or *such illegalities* as I have above referred to, gives rise to *no cause of action at common law*. I myself should deem it to be a misfortune if we were to attempt to prescribe to the business world how honest and peaceable trade was to be carried on in a case where no such illegal elements as I have mentioned exist, or were to adopt some standard of judicial ' reasonableness,' or of ' normal ' prices, or ' fair freights,' to which commercial adventurers, otherwise innocent, were bound to conform."

Opinion of Lord Fry, Law Rep., 23 Q. B. Div. 624.

" The plaintiffs allege that the conference was an unlawful conspiracy ; that the agreement then entered into was carried into execution by the sending up of the three ships expressly to compete with the plaintiffs' vessels, by the circular and by the reduction of freights ; that these acts were wrongful, and have caused damage to them, and consequently were actionable.

" I cannot doubt that whenever persons enter into an agreement which constitutes at law an indictable conspiracy, and that agreement is carried into execution by the conspirators by means of an unlawful act or acts which produce private injury to some person, that person has a cause of action against the conspirators. Was the agreement in the present case an unlawful conspiracy ?

" ' The crime of conspiracy,' said Tindal, C. J., speaking for the judges attending the House of Lords in *O'Connell's case*,(1) ' is complete if two, or more than two, should agree to do an illegal thing ; that is, to effect something in itself unlawful, or to effect, by unlawful means, something which in itself may be indifferent or even lawful.' ' A conspiracy,' said Willes, J., ' consists in the agreement of two or more to do an unlawful act, or to do a lawful act by unlawful means.'(2) In *all cases*, therefore, a *conspiracy is an agreement to do an unlawful act*. It is immaterial whether that act be (a) the principal object and end of the agreement, as an agreement to kill, or (b) a subordinate act toward the principal object, as in an agreement to support a true title by forged deeds or suborned wit-

---

(1) 11 Cl. & F. 155, at p. 233.
(2) *Mulcahy* v. *Reg.*, Law Rep. 3 H. L. 306, at p. 317.

nesses. Again, the act may be unlawful (a) because it would be unlawful in each of the agreeing parties, even if he did it alone, or (b) because though lawful in one it is unlawful in two or more.

"The first inquiry, then, which arises, is this : Was the principal object and end of the agreement illegal ? I answer that that object and end was the acquisition of gain by the defendants. That is lawful, and, I suppose, even commendable, according to the law of this country, provided the means used be lawful. What, then, were the means intended to be used ? They were, as I have already said, the exclusion of competition in the remoter future by severe competition in the near future. Was that lawful or unlawful ?

"It is not necessary to consider whether competition directed by one man or by a combination of men against another man, if instigated and put in motion from mere malice and ill will towards him, as a means of doing him ill service, and for no benefit to the doer, would or would not be unlawful or actionable. There is in the present case no evidence of express malice or of any activity of the defendants against the plaintiffs, except as rival and competing shipowners. The defendants did not aim at any general injury of the plaintiffs' trade, or any reduction of them to poverty or insolvency ; they only desired to *drive them away from particular ports, where the defendants conceived that the plaintiffs' presence interfered with their own gain.* The damage to be inflicted on the plaintiffs was to be strictly limited by the gain which the defendants desired to win for themselves. In the observations I am about to make I shall, therefore, lay out of consideration this case of competition used as a mere engine of malice, even where I do not in terms repeat the exception. I will only add on this part of the case that the charge of Erle, J., in the case of *Reg.* v. *Rowlands,*(1) draws the same distinction which I have taken between combinations to promote the interests of those who combine, and combinations of which the hurt of another is the immediate purpose.

"We have then to inquire whether mere competition, directed by one man against another, is ever unlawful. It was argued that the plaintiffs have a legal right to carry on their trade, and that to deprive them of that right by any means is a wrong. But the right of the plaintiffs to trade is not an absolute, but a qualified right—a right conditioned by the like right in the defendants and all Her

(1) 17 Q. B. 671.

Majesty's subjects, and a right therefore to trade subject to competition. Now, I know no limits to the right of competition in the defendants—I mean, no limits in law. I am not speaking of morals or good manners. To draw a line between fair and unfair competition, between what is reasonable and unreasonable, passes the power of the courts. Competition exists when two or more persons seek to possess or to enjoy the same thing : it follows that the success of one must be the failure of another, and no principle of law enables us to interfere with or to moderate that success or that failure so long as it is due to mere competition. I say mere competition, for I do not doubt that it is unlawful and actionable for one man to interfere with another's trade by fraud or misrepresentation, or by molesting his customers, or those who would be his customers, whether by physical obstruction or moral intimidation. The cases of *Garret* v. *Taylor* ;(1) *Tarleton* v. *McGawley* ;(2) *Keeble* v. *Hickeringill* ;(3) *Carrington* v. *Taylor*,(4) are all cases of interferences by physical acts, driving away either the birds or the customers from the plaintiffs' places of business. Other cases were cited in which one man has persuaded another who is under some contract of service to a third to break that contract to the damage of such third person, and the persuasion has been held actionable. But no case has been or, I believe, can be cited where the only means used by the defendant to injure the plaintiff has been competition pure and simple. I think that if we were now to hold interference by mere competition unlawful, we should be laying down law both novel and at variance with that which modern legislation has shewn to be the present policy of the State.

" But if one man may by competition strive to drive his rival out of the field, is it lawful or unlawful for *several persons to combine together* to drive from the field their competitor in trade ? It is said that such an agreement is in restraint of trade, and therefore illegal. Be it so. But in what sense is the word ' illegal ' used in such a proposition ? In my opinion, it means that the agreement is one upon which *no action can be sustained, and no relief obtained at law or in equity ;* but it *does not mean that the entering into the agreement is either indictable or actionable.* The authorities on this point are, I think, with a single exception, uniform. In *Mitchel* v. *Reynolds*,(5)

---

(1) Cro. Jac. 567.   (3) 11 East, 574, n.
(2) Peake, N. P. 270.   (4) 11 East, 571.
    (5) 1 P. Wms. 181 ; 1 Sm. L. C. 430, 9th ed.

Parker, C. J., in discussing contracts in restraint of trade, says: 'It is not a reason against them that they are against law, I mean, in a proper sense, for in an improper sense they are.' In *Price* v. *Green*,(1) Patteson, J., in delivering the judgment of the Exchequer Chamber upon a covenant held void as in restraint of trade, said expressly that it was 'void only, not illegal.' In *Hilton* v. *Eckersley*,(2) the bond was addressed, not as in *Mitchel* v. *Reynolds*,(3) only to negative acts, such as not trading, but to positive acts, such as carrying on works under particular directions, and closing the works at the dictation of a majority of the combining owners. In this case all the judges, both in the courts of Queen's Bench and in the Exchequer Chamber, held that the bond could not be enforced; but Crompton, J., alone thought that it created an indictable offence, Lord Campbell, C. J., and Erle, J., expressing an opposite opinion, and the Court of Exchequer Chamber carefully abstaining from expressing any opinion on the point. The language of all the judges in the cases of *Hornby* v. *Close*(4) and *Farrer* v. *Close*(5) is consonant with that of Lord Campbell and Erle, J., in *Hilton* v. *Eckersley*,(2) and *Crompton, J., is, I believe, the only judge who has ever hitherto held such contracts illegal as well as void.*

"If every agreement in restraint of trade were not only void, but unlawful in the stricter sense of the word, it would follow that, as every agreement must be between at least two persons, every such agreement would constitute an indictable offence, and yet *not a single case has been cited of a conspiracy constituted by a mere agreement between two persons in undue restraint of the trade of one of the contractors.* This silence of the books is very significant.

"It was forcibly urged upon us that combinations like the present are in their nature calculated to interfere with the course of trade, and that they are, therefore, so directly opposed to the interest which the State has in freedom of trade, and in that competition which is said to be the life of trade, that they must be indictable. It is plain that the intention and object of the combination before us is to check competition; but the means it uses is competition, and it is difficult, if not impossible, to weigh against one another the

---

(1) 16 M. & W. 346.
(2) 6 E. & B. 47.
(3) 1 P. Wms. 181; 1 Sm. L. C. 430, 9th ed.
(4) Law Rep. 2 Q. B. 153.
(5) Law Rep. 4 Q. B. 602.

probabilities of the employment of competition on the one hand and its suppression on the other ; nor is it easy to say how far the success of the combination would arouse in others the desire to share in its benefits, and by competition to force a way into the magic circle. In *Wickens* v. *Evans*(1) it was suggested that the brewers or distillers of London might enter into an agreement to divide the metropolis into districts, the effect of which might be to supply the public with an inferior commodity at a higher price. This argument was met by Hullock, B., by this observation : ' If the brewers or distillers of London were to come to the agreement suggested, many other persons would soon be found to prevent the result anticipated ; and the consequences would, perhaps, be, that the public would obtain the articles they deal in at a cheaper rate.' A similar observation may be made in the present instance, and corroborated by what has actually happened. For the case before us strikingly illustrates the difficulty of foretelling the probable results of such a combination on the public interest ; *in fact, the competition between the plaintiffs and defendants in May and June,* 1885, *brought down the freights from Hankow, to the benefit, it must be supposed, of the consumer in England. The conference came to an end in August,* 1885, *and in the summer of* 1886 *the rate of freight from Hankow was determined by free competition in an open market in which the defendants were competing with one another.*

" But I do not rest my conclusion on any speculations as to the probable effect of such agreements as the one before us, but on this : that the combination, if in restraint of trade, is, prima facie, *void only and not illegal;* that *no statute in force makes such competition criminal;* and that the *policy of our law, as at present declared by the legislature, is against all fetters on combination and competition unaccompanied by violence or fraud, or other like injurious acts.*

" The ancient common law of this country, and the statutes with reference to the acts known as badgering, forestalling, regrating, and engrossing, indicated the mind of the legislature and of the judges that certain large operations in goods which interfered with the more ordinary course of trade were injurious to the public ; they were held criminal accordingly. But early in the reign of George III. the mind of the legislature shewed symptoms of change in this matter, and the penal statutes were repealed (12 Geo. III., c. 71), and

(1) 3 Y. & J. 318.

the common law was left to its unaided operation. This repealing statute contains in the preamble the statement that it had been found by experience that the restraint laid by several statutes upon the dealing in corn, meal, flour, cattle, and sundry other sorts of victuals, by preventing a free trade in the said commodities, had a tendency to discourage the growth and to enhance the price of the same. This statement is very noteworthy. It contains a confession of failure in the past; the indication of a new policy for the future.

"This new policy has been more clearly declared and acted upon in the present reign; for the legislature has by 7 & 8 Vict. c. 24, altered the common law by utterly abolishing the several offences of badgering, engrossing, forestalling and regrating. At the same time this repeal was accompanied by a proviso that nothing in the act contained should apply to the offence of knowingly and fraudulently spreading or conspiring to spread any false rumour with intent to enhance or decry the price of any goods or merchandise, or to the offence of preventing or endeavouring to prevent by force or threats any goods, wares, or merchandise being brought to any fair or market, but that every such offence might be punished as if this act had not been made. The comparison of the operative part of the statute with this proviso goes far to draw the line between lawful and unlawful interference with the ordinary course of trade or of the market. A consideration of the statutes relative to trade unions leads me to a similar conclusion. It is not necessary to consider in detail the provisions of the statutes of 1871 and 1875 (34 & 35 Vict. c. 31, and 39 & 40 Vict. c. 22); but one of their principal results was to enlarge the power of combination between workmen and workmen, and between masters and masters, for the purpose of maintaining and enforcing their respective interests, and to remove the objection of being in restraint of trade, to which some of such combinations had been obnoxious. But whilst the legislature thus set masters and men respectively free to combine, they reasserted the illegality of using violence, threats, molestation, obstruction, or coercion; and here again the contrast between the two pieces of legislation which stand side by side in the statute-book, the one declaring mere combinations lawful, and the other declaring violence and other like acts unlawful, helps to draw the line in the same direction as does the legislation in respect of trade combination. (See the statutes 34 & 35 Vict. c. 31, and c. 32.)

"Thus the stream of modern legislation runs strongly in favour of allowing great combinations of persons interested in trade, and intended to govern or regulate the proceedings of large bodies of men, and thus, necessarily, to interfere with what would have been the course of trade if unaffected by such combinations. I, therefore, conclude that the combination in the present case cannot be held illegal, as opposed to the policy of the law.

" It remains to inquire whether the authorities assist in the decision of the question before us. As regards an individual, I have already pointed out that for one man to interfere with the lawful trade or business of another by *molestation or any physical interference, or by fraud or misrepresentation*, may be an actionable wrong. But no authority appears to shew that for one man to injure the business of another by mere competition, even though it may be successfully directed to driving the rival out of the town where he dwells or out of the business which he carries on, is actionable. And the silence of the books is strong evidence that such acts are not actionable.

" With regard to like acts done by a *combination of persons*, the authorities are not very numerous. There are certain general statements in text-books, of which the passage in Hawkins' ' Pleas of the Crown,' vol. i., p. 446, may be taken as a fair specimen. ' There can be no doubt,' he says, ' but that all confederacies whatsoever, wrongfully, to prejudice a third person are highly criminal at common law, as where divers persons confederate together by indirect means to impoverish a third person.' For this proposition Hawkins cites authorities relative to two cases : first, *Rex* v. *Kimberty*,(1) which was a conspiracy to indict the prosecutor for having begotten a bastard child on the body of one of the conspirators ; a case, therefore, which has nothing to do with the question now in hand ; secondly, *Rex* v. *Sterling*,(2) in which the indictment charged certain brewers of London with a conspiracy to refuse to sell small-beer, with a view to impoverish the excisemen, and with intent to move the common people to pull down the excise house, and to bring the excisemen into hatred of the people, and to impoverish and disable them from paying their rent to the King ; the defendants were found guilty of counselling and assembling to impoverish the excisemen, and not guilty of the residue ; and thereupon ultimately judgment

---

(1) 1 Levinz, 62.
(2) 1 Levinz, 126 ; 1 Siderfin, 174 ; and 1 Keble, 650, 655.

went for the Crown. The real ground of the decision was, as stated by Holt, C. J., in *Reg.* v. *Daniell*, (1) that the offence of the defendants was of a public nature and levelled at the Government, and it is therefore no authority in respect of a combination which has no such object or effect. But one argument, as it appears in Siderfin is important. It was urged for the defendants that it was no offence punishable by our law for one man to depauperate another with a view to enrich himself, or by selling commodities at cheaper rates. The court did not deny this proposition, but drew a distinction based upon the allegations of the information, which were supported by the verdict, that the excise was parcel of the revenue of the King, and that to impoverish the excisemen was to render them incapable of paying these revenues to the King. So far, therefore, as the case goes it is an authority rather for the defendants than for the plaintiffs in this case.

"The next case that seems relevant is *Rex* v. *Eccles*, (2) before Lord Mansfield and the Court of King's Bench. The defendant and six other persons had been convicted on two counts, charging that the defendants and others, devising unlawfully and by indirect means to impoverish one Booth, and to hinder him from exercising the trade of a tailor, conspired by wrongful and indirect means to impoverish him and to hinder him from exercising his said business, and that the defendants, according to their said conspiracy, did so hinder him. It was moved in arrest of judgment that the means by which the mischief was to be effected ought to have been set out, but the indictment was held sufficient. The nature of the acts done by the defendants does not appear, nor is it easy to learn precisely on what principle the court proceeded. Lord Ellenborough, in *Rex* v. *Turner*, (3) said that the case seemed to have been determined on the ground of restraint of trade, in which case it would probably be no authority since the legislation of this reign with reference to trade unions. If regarded as an authority merely on the sufficiency of the indictments, it appears open to some question. In any event, it throws no clear light on the matter now for decision.

"The case of *Cousins* v. *Smith*(4) is probably not applicable, since it proceeded on the view of a Court of Equity of forestalling and regrating, and those practices are not now unlawful. The

---

(1) 6 Mod. 99.
(2) 1 Lea. C. C. 274.
(3) 13 East, 228.
(4) 13 Ves. 542.

equitable shadow of these crimes must, I think, have disappeared with the crimes themselves.

" These are, so far as I am aware, all the relevant authorities, and none of them appears to me to support the proposition that mere competition of one set of men against another man carried on for the purpose of gain and not out of actual malice is actionable, even though intended to drive the rival in trade away from his place of business, and though that intention be actually carried into effect.

" For these reasons, I hold that the judgment of the Lord Chief Justice was right, and that the appeal should be dismissed with costs."

In the House of Lords(a) opinions were delivered by Lord Halsbury, Lord Watson, Lord Bramwell, Lord Morris, Lord Field, and Lord Hannen.

Opinion of Lord Halsbury, L. C., p. 35.

" My Lords, notwithstanding the elaborate examination which this case has undergone, both as to fact and law, I believe the facts may be very summarily stated, and when so stated the law seems to me not open to doubt.

" An associated body of traders endeavour to get the whole of a limited trade into their own hands by offering exceptional and very favourable terms to customers who will deal exclusively with them ; so favourable that but for the object of keeping the trade to themselves they would not give such terms ; and if their trading were confined to one particular period they would be trading at a loss, but in the belief that by such competition they will prevent rival traders competing with them, and so receive the whole profits of the trade to themselves.

" I do not think that I have omitted a single fact upon which the appellants rely to show that this course of dealing is unlawful and constitutes an indictable conspiracy.

" Now it is not denied and cannot be even argued that prima facie a trader in a free country in all matters ' not contrary to law may regulate his own mode of carrying on his trade according to his own discretion and choice.' This is the language of Baron Alderson in delivering the judgment of the Exchequer Chamber,(1) and no author-

---

(a) Law Rep. App. Cas. 1892, pp. 35 et seq.
(1) Hilton v. Eckersley, 6 E. & B., at pp. 74, 75.

ity, indeed no argument, has been directed to qualify that leading proposition. It is necessary, therefore, for the appellants here to show that what I have described as the course pursued by the associated traders is a 'matter contrary to law.'

"Now, after a most careful study of the evidence in this case, I have been unable to discover anything done by the members of the associated body of traders other than an offer of reduced freights to persons who would deal exclusively with them ; and if this is unlawful it seems to me that the greater part of commercial dealings, where there is rivalry in trade, must be equally unlawful.

* * * * * * *

"I entirely adopt and make my own what was said by Lord Justice Bowen in the court below : 'All commercial men with capital are acquainted with the ordinary expedient of sowing one year a crop of apparently unfruitful prices, in order by driving competition away to reap a fuller harvest of profit in the future ; and until the present argument at the Bar it may be doubted whether shipowners or merchants were ever deemed to be bound by law to conform to some imaginary 'normal' standard of freights or prices, or that law courts had a right to say to them in respect of their competitive tariffs, "Thus far shalt thou go, and no further."'

"Excluding all I have excluded upon my view of the facts, it is very difficult indeed to formulate the proposition. What is the *wrong done?* What *legal right* is *interfered with?* What *coercion of the mind, or will, or of the person* is effected ? *All are free to trade* upon what terms they will, and nothing has been done except in rival trading which can be supposed to interfere with the appellants' interests.

"I think this question is the first to be determined. What injury, if any, has been done ? What *legal right* has been *interfered with?* Because *if no legal right has been interfered with, and no legal injury inflicted, it is vain to say that the thing might have been done by an individual, but cannot be done by a combination of persons.* My Lords, I do not deny that there are many things which might be perfectly lawfully done by an individual, which, when done by a number of persons, become unlawful. I am unable to concur with the Lord Chief Justice's criticism(1) (if its meaning was rightly interpreted, which I very much doubt) on the observations made by my noble

---

(1) 21 Q. B. D. 551.

and learned friend Lord Bramwell in *Reg.* v. *Druitt,*(1) if that was intended to treat as doubtful the proposition that a combination to insult and annoy a person would be an indictable conspiracy. I should have thought it as beyond doubt or question that such a combination would be an indictable misdemeanour, and I cannot think the Chief Justice meant to throw any doubt upon such a proposition.

"But in this case the thing done, *the trading by a number of persons together, effects no more and is no more, so to speak, a combined operation than that of a single person.* If the thing done is rendered unlawful by combination, the course of trade by a person who singly trades for his own benefit and apart from partnership or sharing profits with others, but nevertheless avails himself of combined action, would be open to the same objections. The merchant who buys for him, the agent who procures orders for him, the captain who sails his ship, and even the sailors (if they might be supposed to have knowledge of the transaction) would be acting in combination for the general result, and would, whether for the benefit of the individual, or for an associated body of traders, make it not the less combined action than if the combination were to share profits with independent traders ; and if a combination to effect that object would be unlawful, the sharers in the combined action could, in a charge of criminal conspiracy, make no defence that they were captain, agent, or sailors, respectively, if they were knowingly rendering their aid to what, by the hypothesis, would be unlawful if done in combination.

"A totally separate head of unlawfulness has, however, been introduced by the suggestion that the thing is unlawful because in *restraint of trade.* There are two senses in which the word 'unlawful' is not uncommonly, though, I think, somewhat inaccurately used. There are some contracts to which the law will not give effect ; and therefore, although the parties may enter into what, but for the element which the law condemns, would be perfect contracts, the law would not allow them to operate as contracts, notwithstanding that, in point of form, the parties have agreed. Some such contracts may be void on the ground of immorality ; some on the ground that they are contrary to public policy ; as, for example, in restraint of trade : and contracts so tainted the law will not lend its aid to enforce. It treats them as if they had not been made at all. But the more accurate use of the word 'unlawful,' which would bring the contract

(1) 10 Cox, C. C. 592.

within the qualification which I have quoted from the judgment of the Exchequer Chamber, namely, as contrary to law, is not applicable to such contracts.

"It has *never been held that a contract in restraint of trade is contrary to law in the sense that I have indicated.* A judge in very early times expressed great indignation at such a contract ; and *Mr. Justice Crompton undoubtedly did say (in a case where such an observation was wholly unnecessary to the decision, and therefore manifestly obiter) that the parties to a contract in restraint of trade would be indictable. I am unable to assent to that dictum. It is opposed to the whole current of authority ;* it was dissented from by Lord Campbell and Chief Justice Erle, and found no support when the case in which it was said came to the Exchequer Chamber, and it seems to me *contrary to principle.*"

* * * * * * *

Opinion of Lord Watson, p. 42.

"There is nothing in the evidence to suggest that the parties to the agreement had any other object in view than that of defending their carrying-trade during the season against the encroachments of the appellants and other competitors, and of attracting to themselves custom which might otherwise have been carried off by these competitors. That is an object which is strenuously pursued by merchants great and small in every branch of commerce ; and it is, in the eye of the law, perfectly legitimate. If the respondents' combination had been formed, not with a single view to the extension of their business and the increase of its profits, but with the main or ulterior design of effecting an unlawful object, a very different question would have arisen for the consideration of your Lordships. But no such case is presented by the facts disclosed in this appeal.

"The object of the combination being legal, was any illegal act committed by the respondents in giving effect to it? The appellants invited your Lordships to answer that question in the affirmative, on the ground that the respondents' competition was unfair, by which they no doubt meant that it was tainted by illegality. The facts which they mainly relied on were these : that the respondents allowed a discount of 5 per cent. upon their freight accounts for the year to all customers who shipped no tea to Europe except by their vessels ; that, whenever the appellants sent a ship to load tea at Hankow, the respondents sent one or more of their ocean steamers to underbid her, so that neither vessel could obtain cargo on remunerative terms ; and lastly, that the respondents took away the agency of their vessels from persons who also acted as shipping agents for the appellants and other trade competitors outside the combination.

" I cannot for a moment suppose that it is the proper function of English courts of law to *fix the lowest prices* at which traders can sell or hire, for the purpose of protecting or extending their business, without committing a legal wrong which will subject them in damages. *Until that becomes the law of the land, it is, in my opinion, idle to suggest that the legality or mercantile competition ought to be gauged by the amount of the consideration for which a competing trader thinks fit to part with his goods or to accept employment.* The withdrawal of agency at first appeared to me to be a matter attended with difficulty ; but on consideration, I am satisfied that it *cannot be regarded as an illegal act*. In the first place, it was impossible that any honest man could impartially discharge his duty of finding freights to parties who occupied the hostile position of the appellants and respondents ; and, in the second place, the respondents gave the agents the option of continuing to act for one or other of them in circumstances which placed the appellants at no disadvantage.

" My Lords, in this case it has not been proved, and it has not been suggested, that the respondents used either *misrepresentation or compulsion* for the purpose of attaining the object of their combination. The only means by which they endeavoured to obtain shipments for their vessels, to the exclusion of others, was the inducement of cheaper rates of freight than the appellants were willing to accept. I entertain no doubt that the judgment appealed from ought to be affirmed. I am quite satisfied with the reasons assigned for it by Bowen and Fry, L. JJ.; and the observations which I have made were not meant to add to these reasons, but to make it clear that in my opinion the appellants have presented for decision no question of fact or law attended with either doubt or difficulty."

* * * * * * *

Opinion of Lord Bramwell, p. 45.

" The first position of the plaintiffs is that the agreement among the defendants is illegal as being in restraint of trade, and therefore against public policy, and so illegal. 'Public policy,' said Burrough, J. (I believe, quoting Hobart, C. J.), ' is an unruly horse, and dangerous to ride.'(1) I quote also another distinguished judge more modern, Cave, J.: ' Certain kinds of contracts have been held void at common law on the ground of public policy ; a branch of the law, however, which certainly should not be extended, as judges are more to be trusted as interpreters of the law than as expounders of what is called public policy.'(2) I think the present case is an illustration of the wisdom of these remarks. I venture to make another. No evidence is given in these public policy cases. The tribunal is to say, as matter of law, that the thing is against public policy, and void. How can the judge do that without any evidence as to its effect and consequences ? If the shipping in this case was sufficient for the trade, a further supply would have been a waste. There are some people who think that the public is not concerned with this—people who would make a second railway by the side of one existing, saying ' only the two companies will suffer,' as though the wealth of the community was not made up of the wealth of the individuals who compose it. I am by no means sure that the conference did not prevent a waste, and was not good for the public. Lord Coleridge thought it was—see his judgment.

" As to the suggestion that the Chinese profited by the lowering of freights, I cannot say it was not so. There may have been a monopoly or other cause to give them a benefit ; but, as a rule, it is clear that the expense of transit, and all other expenses, borne by an exported article that has a market price, are borne by the importer, therefore, ultimately, by the consumer. So that low freights benefit him. To go on with the case, take it that the defendants had bound themselves to each other ; I think they had, though they might withdraw. Let it be that each member had tied his hands ; let it be that that was in restraint of trade ; I think upon the authority of *Hilton* v. *Eckersley*,(3) and other cases, we should hold that the agreement was illegal, that is, *not enforceable by law*. I will assume, then, that it was, though I am not quite sure. But that is not enough for the plaintiffs. To maintain their action on this ground they must make out that it was an *offence*, a *crime*, a *misdemeanour*. I am *clearly of opinion it was not*. Save the opinion of Crompton, J. (entitled to the greatest respect, but not assented to by Lord Camp-

---

(1) *Richardson* v. *Mellish*, 2 Bing. at p. 252.
(2) *In Re Mirams*, L. R., 1 Q. B. [1891] 595.
(3) 6 E. & B. 47.

bell or the Exchequer Chamber), there is *no authority for it in the English law.*

" It is quite certain that an agreement may be void, yet the parties to it not punishable. Take the case I put during the argument : a man and woman agree to live together as man and wife, without marrying. The agreement is illegal, and could not be enforced, but clearly the parties to it would not be indictable. It ought to be enough to say that the fact that there is *no case where there has been a conviction for such an offence as is alleged against the defendants is conclusive.*

" It is to be remembered that it is for the plaintiffs to make out the case that the defendants have committed an indictable offence, not for the defendants to disprove it. There needs no argument to prove the negative. There are some observations to be made. It is admitted that there may be fair competition in trade, that *two may offer to join and compete against a third.* If so, what is the definition of ' fair competition ' ? *What is unfair that is neither forcible nor fraudulent ?* It does seem strange that to enforce freedom of trade, of action, the law should punish those who make a perfectly honest agreement with a belief that it is fairly required for their protection.

" There is one thing that is to me decisive. I have always said that *a combination of workmen, an agreement among them to cease work except for higher wages, and a strike in consequence, was lawful at common law ;* perhaps *not enforceable* inter se, but *not indictable.* The legislature has now so declared. The enactment is express, that agreements among workmen shall be binding, whether they would or would not, but for the acts, have been deemed unlawful, as in restraint of trade. *Is it supposable that it would have done so in the way it has, had the workmen's combination been a punishable misdemeanour ?* Impossible. This seems to me conclusive, that though agreements which fetter the freedom of action in the parties to it may not be enforceable, they are not indictable. See also the judgment of Fry, L. J., on this point. Where is such a contention to stop ? Suppose the case put in the argument : In a small town there are two shops, sufficient for the wants of the neighbourhood, making only a reasonable profit. They are threatened with a third. The two shopkeepers agree to warn the intending shopkeeper that if he comes they will lower prices, and can afford it longer than he. Have they committed an indictable offence ? Remember the *conspiracy is the offence, and they have conspired.* If he, being warned, does not set up his shop, *has he a cause of action?* He might prove damages. He might shew that from his skill he would have beaten one or both of the others. See in this case the judgment of Lord Esher, that the plaintiffs might recover for 'damages at large for future years.' Would a shipowner who had intended to send his ship to Shanghai, but desisted owing to the defendants' agreement, and on being told by them they would deal with him as they had with the plaintiffs, *be entitled to maintain an action against the defendants?* Why not? *If yes, why not every shipowner who could say he had a ship fit for the trade, but was deterred from using it?*

"The Master of the Rolls cites Sir William Erle, that 'a combination to violate a private right in which the public has a sufficient interest is a crime, such violation being an actionable wrong.' True. Sir William Erle means that *where the violation of a private right is an actionable wrong, a combination to violate it, if the public has a sufficient interest, is a crime.* But, in this case, I hold that there is *no private right violated.* His Lordship further says : ' If one goes beyond the exercise of the course of trade, and does an act beyond what is the course of trade, in order—that is to say, with intent—to molest the other's free course of trade, he is not exercising his own freedom of a course of trade, he is not acting in but beyond the course of trade, and then it follows that his act is an unlawful obstruction of the other's right to a free course of trade, and if such obstruction causes damage to the other he is entitled to maintain an action for the wrong' (1) I may be permitted to say that this is not very plain. I think it means that it is not in the course of trade for one trader to do acts the motive of which is to damage the trade of another. Whether I should agree depends on the meaning to be put on ' course of trade ' and ' molest.' But it is clear that the Master of the Rolls means conduct which would give a cause of action against an individual. He cites Sir William Erle in support of his proposition, who *clearly is speaking of acts which would be actionable in an individual,* and there is *no such act here.* The Master of the Rolls says the lowering of the freight far beyond a lowering for any purpose of trade was not an act done in the exercise of their own free right of trade, but for the purpose of interfering with the plaintiffs' right to a free course of trade ; therefore a wrongful act as against the plaintiffs' right ; and as injury to the plaintiffs followed,

---

(1) 23 Q. B. D. 607.

they had a right of action. I cannot agree. If there were two shopkeepers in a village and one sold an article at cost price, not for profit therefor, but to attract customers or cause his rival to leave off selling the article only, it could not be said he was liable to an action. I cannot think that the defendants did more than they had a legal right to do. I adopt the vigorous language and opinion of Fry, L. J.: 'To draw a line between fair and unfair competition, between what is reasonable and unreasonable, passes the power of the courts.'(1) It is a strong thing for the plaintiffs to complain of the very practices they wish to share in, and once did.

"I am of opinion that the judgment should be affirmed."

* * * * * * *

Opinion of Lord Morris, p. 49.

"The object was a lawful one. It is *not illegal* for a trader to aim at *driving a competitor out of trade, provided* the *motive be his own gain* by appropriation of the trade, and the *means* he uses be *lawful* weapons. Of the first four of the means used by the defendants, the rebate to customers and the lowering of the freights are the same in principle, being a bonus by the defendants to customers to come and deal exclusively with them. The sending of ships to compete, and the indemnifying other ships, was 'the competition' entered on by the defendants with the plaintiffs. The fifth means used, viz., the dismissal of agents, might be questionable according to the circumstances; but in the present case, the agents filled an irreconcilable position in being agents for the two rivals, the plaintiffs and the defendants. Dismissal under such circumstances became, perhaps, a necessary incident of the warfare in trade.

"All the acts done, and the means used, by the defendants were acts of competition for the trade. There was nothing in the defendants' acts to disturb any existing contract of the plaintiffs, or to induce any one to break such. Their action was aimed at making it unlikely that any one would enter into contracts with the plaintiffs, the defendants offering such competitive inducements as would probably prevent them. The use of rhetorical phrases in the correspondence cannot affect the real substance and meaning of it.

"Again, *what one trader may do in respect of competition, a body or set of traders can lawfully do; otherwise a large capitalist could do*

(1) 23 Q. B. D. 625, 626.

what a number of small capitalists, combining together, could not do, and thus a blow would be struck at the very principle of co-operation and joint-stock enterprise. I entertain no doubt that a *body of traders,* whose motive object is to promote their own trade, *can combine* to acquire, and thereby in so far to injure the trade of competitors, provided they do no more than is incident to such motive object, and *use no unlawful means.* And the defendants' case clearly comes within the principle I have stated.

* * * * * * *

" But *suppose the combination* in this case was such as might be held to be in *restraint of trade, what follows? It could not be enforced.* None of the parties to it could sue each other. It might be held void, because its tendency might be held to be against the public interests. *Does that make, per se, the combination illegal? What a fallacy would it be that what is void and not enforceable becomes a crime ;* and *cases abound of agreements which the law would not enforce, but which are not illegal;* which you *may enter* into, if you like, but which you *will not get any assistance to enforce.*

" My Lords, I have merely summarised my views, because I adopt entirely the principles laid down by Lord Justice Bowen in his judgment with such felicitous illustrations, and I concur in the opinion already announced by your Lordships, that the judgment of the Court of Appeals should be affirmed."

* * * * * * *

Opinion of Lord Hannen, p. 58.

" It was contended that the agreement between the defendants to act in combination which was proved to exist, was illegal as being in *restraint of trade.* I think that *it was so, in the sense that it was void,* and *could not have been enforced* against any of the defendants who might have violated it : *Hilton v. Eckersley.*(1) But it does not follow that the entering into such an agreement would, as contended, subject the persons doing so to an indictment for conspiracy, and I think that the *opinion to that effect expressed by Crompton, J., in Hilton v. Eckersley*(1) *is erroneous.*

" The question, however, raised for our consideration in this case is whether a person who has suffered loss in his business by the

---

(1) 6 E. & B. 47.

joint action of those who have entered into such an agreement, can recover damages from them for the injury so sustained. In considering this question it is necessary to determine upon the evidence what was the object of the agreement between the defendants and what were the means by which they sought to attain that object. It appears to me that their *object* was to secure to themselves the benefit of the carrying trade from certain ports. It *cannot, I think, be reasonably suggested that this is unlawful* in any sense of the word. The object of every trader is to procure for himself as large a share of the trade he is engaged in as he can. If then the object of the defendants was legitimate, were the *means* adopted by them *open to objections? I cannot see that they were.* They sought to induce shippers to employ them rather than the plaintiffs by offering to such shippers as should during a fixed period deal exclusively with them the advantage of a rebate upon the freights they had paid. This is, in effect, nothing more than the ordinary form of competition between traders by offering goods or services at a cheaper rate than their rivals.

*   *   *   *   *   *   *

"It only remains for me to refer to the argument that an act which might be *lawful for one* to do, becomes *criminal*, or the *subject of civil action* by any one injured by it, *if done by several combining together.* On this point I think the law is accurately stated by Sir William Erle in his treatise on the law relating to trades unions. The principle he lays down is equally applicable to combinations other than those of trades unions. He says (p. 23) : ' As to combination, *each person has a right to choose whether he will labour or not,* and also to choose *the terms on which he will consent to labour,* if labour be his choice. The *power of choice* in respect of labour and terms which *one person may exercise and declare singly,* many, *after consultation,* may *exercise jointly,* and they may make a *simultaneous declaration* of their choice, and may *lawfully act thereon for the immediate purpose of obtaining the required terms,* but they cannot create any mutual obligation having the legal effect of binding each other not to work or not to employ unless upon terms allowed by the combination.'

"In considering the question, however, of what was the motive of the combination, whether it was for the purpose of injuring others, or merely in order to benefit those combining, the fact of several agreeing to a common course of action may be important. There are some forms of injury which can only be effected by the combination of many. Thus, if several persons agree not to deal at all with a particular individual, as this could not, under ordinary circumstances, benefit the persons so agreeing, it might well lead to the conclusion that their real object was to injure the individual. But it appears to me that, in the present case, there is nothing indicating an intention to injure the plaintiffs, except in so far as such injury would be the result of the defendants obtaining for themselves the benefits of the carrying trade, by giving better terms to customers than their rivals, the plaintiffs, were willing to offer.

"For these reasons I think that the judgment of the Court of Appeals should be affirmed."

This case definitely established the position, that, under the common law of England, a combination for the express purpose of preventing competition between the parties combining, and of destroying competition from all outside parties, even in the case of common carriers, was lawful; not only that it did not constitute a crime, but that it did no individual a civil legal injury. If such a combination had ever been a crime under the English common law, it still remained so, notwithstanding all repealing statutes. The case, therefore, is an authority in the most conclusive form, that such a combination, in England, though the law might not enforce it, never was illegal, in the absence of a statute making it so, either civilly or criminally, notwithstanding all the *dicta* in the opinions of different judges, and the remarks of writers of legal treatises.

A review of the course of development of the English law on the matters here under consideration leads us then to these conclusions:

I. The English law as to combinations in restraint of trade, on its criminal side, was only one feature of the attempts, in the early rudimentary stages of the growth of that law, to control and regulate trade and commerce by statute, as to times and manner of labor, prices of labor, quality of merchandise, and prices of merchandise. Those attempts to control trade and commerce went hand in hand with attempts to regulate apparel, and the ways of living, by statute.

II. Combinations to raise the prices of merchandise, from the earliest times, were on the same legal footing with combinations to raise the prices of labor.

III. Attempts to raise prices by single individuals were on the same legal footing, as to their criminality, with like attempts by individuals in combination.

IV. The right to sell his own property at his own price, whether that property be labor or merchandise, and whether that price be fixed by single individuals separately, or by individuals in combination, has at last been fully recognized by the English law.

V. There is no authentic record of any authoritative decision of any English Court, which holds that a combination merely to raise prices, of the labor or merchandise of the parties combining, ever constituted a crime independently of statute.

VI. The case *Mogul Steamship Company* v. *McGregor* necessarily *holds* that such a contract of combination, independently of any statute, though the courts might not enforce it, never constituted a crime, or a legal wrong.

CHAPTER II.

THE COURSE OF THE ENGLISH LAW AS TO PUBLIC EMPLOYMENTS.

In the earlier stages of the growth of the English law no distinction was drawn, as to the right of the State to control the prices of merchandise and the manner of carrying on trades and professions, between employments that were private and employments that were public.

That distinction is a product of a later date. Its chief development, due to questions of our constitutional law, has been in this country.

That distinction is, however, now well established. It is also now well established as the fundamental law in this country, where legislatures are the creatures of constitutions, and where their powers have legal limitations, that the State has the lawful power to control prices, and methods, in employments and properties that are public, while it has no such power as to employments and properties that are private. As Chief Justice Waite declared in *Munn* v. *People of Illinois*, 4 Otto, 113, "Undoubtedly, in mere *private contracts*, relating to matters in which the public has no interest, what is reasonable must be ascertained judicially. But this is because the *legislature has no control over such a contract*. So, too, in matters which do *affect the public interest*, and as to which *legislative control may be exercised*, if there are no statutory regulations upon the subject, the court must determine what is reasonable. The *controlling fact is the power to regulate at all. If that exists, the right to establish the maximum of charge, as one of the means of regulation*, is implied. In fact, the *common law rule*, which requires the charge to be *reasonable*, is itself a *regulation as to price*. Without it the *owner could make his rates at will*, and *compel the public to yield to his terms, or forego the use.*"

In early times the number and importance of these public employments were comparatively small. Innkeepers, common carriers, millers, wharfingers, and the owners of ferries, were nearly the only private persons who followed public employments. Among these, it is to be noted that common carriers, wharfingers, and the owners of ferries, constituted part of the existing system of public transportation—were, in a sense, a part of the existing system of public highways. Indeed, innkeepers almost fell within the same classification, and therefore fell within its reason. The inns were the stopping-places for all the king's subjects, in their ordinary use of the king's highways.

The right of state control of innkeepers was asserted in England from a very early date, in statutes which regulated both prices and labor, in employments and trades which it would now be conceded are private. The law, from a very early time, took from innkeepers the ordinary contractual freedom which the subject naturally enjoyed in matters of private trade and commerce. The innkeeper was required to admit to his inn all persons who applied peaceably to be admitted as guests. In case of refusal he was liable to indictment.(a) He was held liable as an insurer, for the goods of his guest. In modern times the right of state control of inns has continually been asserted, and is never questioned.

So, too, the right of the state to control common carriers, as to their charges, and the manner of performance of their duties, has for a long time been unquestioned under the English law. Common carriers, too, from a very early period were deprived of the ordinary contractual freedom of the subject. From an early time

---

(a) *Rex* v. *Ivens*, 7 C. & P. 213.

public control of common carriers was exercised by statute. The Act 3 William and Mary, Cap. XII., sect. 24, provided: "That the justices of the peace of every county and other place . . . shall have power or authority, and are hereby enjoined and required at their next respective quarter or general sessions after Easter Day, yearly, to assess and rate the prices of all land carriage of goods whatsoever, to be brought into any place or places within their respective limits and jurisdictions, by any common waggoner or carrier, and the rates and assessments so made to certify to the several mayors and other chief officers of each respective market town within the limits and jurisdictions of such justices of the peace, to be hung up in some publick place in every such market town, to which all persons may resort for their information; and that no such common waggoner or carrier shall take for carriage of such goods and merchandises above the rates and prices so set, upon pain to forfeit for every such offense the sum of five pounds, to be levied by distress and sale of his and their goods, by warrant of any two justices of the peace, where such waggoner or carrier shall reside, in manner aforesaid, to the use of the party grieved." The Act 2 & 3 Will. IV., c. 120, regulated duties, licenses, number of passengers, luggage, etc., as regarded stage carriage. By the Act 2 & 3 Victoria, chap. 66, sect. 1, those duties were changed. The Railway and Canal Traffic Act, 1854, 17 & 18 Vict., c. 31, provided that "every railway company, canal company and railway and canal company shall, according to their respective powers, afford all reasonable facilities for the receiving and forwarding and delivering of traffic upon and from the several railways and canals belonging to or worked by such companies respectively, and for the return of carriages, trucks, boats and other vehicles; and no such company shall make or give any undue or unreasonable preference or advantage to or in favor of any particular person or company, or any particular description of traffic, in any respect whatsoever, nor shall any such company subject any particular person or company, or any particular description of traffic, to any undue or unreasonable prejudice or disadvantage in any respect whatsoever ; and every railway company and canal company and railway and canal company having or working railways or canals, which form part of a continuous line of railway or canal or railway and canal communication, or which have the terminus, station or wharf of the one near the terminus, station or wharf of the other, shall afford all due and reasonable facilities for receiving and forwarding all the traffic arriving by one of such railways or canals by the other, without any unreasonable delay, and without any such preference or advantage, or prejudice or disadvantage as aforesaid, and so that no obstruction may be offered to the public desirous of using such railways or canals or railways and canals as a continuous line of communication, and so that all reasonable accommodation may, by means of the railways and canals of the several companies, be at all times afforded to the public in that behalf."

Section third provided, that any company or person complaining against any such companies or company of anything done, or of any omission made, in violation or contravention of the act, could apply in a summary way by motion or summons to the Court of Common Pleas, or to a judge thereof ; that the Attorney-General could also apply to the court or a judge thereof, to hear and determine the matter of such complaint, and in the discretion of the court could direct and prosecute by engineers, barristers or other persons, all such inquiries as might be deemed necessary to enable the court or judge to form a just judgment on the matter of such complaint ; and if it appeared to the court or judge on such hearing, and on the report of such persons, that anything had been done or omission made in violation or contravention of the act, a writ of injunction could be issued restraining the company or companies from further continuing such violation or contravention, and enjoining obedience thereto. The section also provided for the issuing of a writ of attachment against any one or more of the directors of the company, or against any owner, lessee, director or other person failing to obey the writ, and for an order directing the payment by any of such companies of any such sum of money as the court or any judge might determine, not exceeding 200 pounds for every day of a failure to obey the injunction.

By the Act 36 & 37 Victoria, Chap. 48, the Regulation of Railways Act, 1873, three railway commissioners were appointed, to whom was transferred the jurisdiction exercised by the Court of Common Pleas under the Railway and Canal Act, 1854.

It would not be within the purview of this present examination to go into any detailed statement of the cases which have arisen, or of the decisions that have been made, under those acts. It is sufficient to say, that the practice is eminently simple, as is usually the case in all modern English provisions for the administration of justice, and the act has been found, so far as my information goes, amply sufficient to redress any substantial injuries done by common carriers to the public.

It is evident, from this short statement, that the course of the English law as to common carriers has been directly the reverse of its course as to private employments. In the early stages of the English law, the attempts by the state to regulate private employments and private trade were manifold. On the other hand, the regulation and control of common carriers was comparatively imperfect. As to private employments, the growth of the law has been continuous to its present condition of virtually complete non-interference. As to common carriers, on the other hand, the state control is now practically unrestricted, and is ample for the protection of all rights of the citizen. The growth in the one branch of the law has been from a condition of minute and annoying restriction to one of complete freedom. In the other, it has been from a condition of comparative freedom to one of complete and adequate supervision and control.

CHAPTER III.

THE COURSE OF THE AMERICAN LAW AS TO PRIVATE EMPLOYMENTS UNTIL CERTAIN RECENT DECISIONS.

RECENT criminal prosecutions in this country for mere combinations to raise or maintain the prices of merchandise of the parties combining, or to prevent competition in the sale of merchandise between the parties combining, though arising under special statutes, have almost invariably been classified, in the decisions of the courts under those statutes, as "Conspiracies to commit acts injurious to trade or commerce."

Before considering those decisions, it is necessary to ascertain exactly the course of the law down to the time when the statutes in question were passed. We shall also thereafter trace the course of judicial interpretation of those statutes down to the time of the making of those decisions.

In the first place, we have the position, that under the English common law, independently of any statute, combinations of this character were not unlawful, either civilly or criminally. They violated no legal right, of any individual, or of the public. The *Mogul Steamship* case conclusively establishes that. Such combinations are no novelty. They have long been known to the English law, and have been made the subject of adjudication in the English Courts. It had long been the established law in England, that combinations of that character would not always be enforced by the Courts. But that was all. They were lawful.

In the next place, it is evident, as already stated, that in England the criminal law as to combinations to raise prices of merchandise, and as to combinations to raise prices of labor, rested on the same footing ; that both became crimes only by statute ; that the statutes as to both formed part of the ancient general scheme of legislation for state control of prices ; and that those statutes had become virtually obsolete in England long before the American colonies separated from the mother country.

That this was the situation in England will be made still more clear from the treatment of the law of conspiracy by Sir William Blackstone. The entire text of Blackstone on the crime of "conspiracy" is to be found in his chapter " Of offences against *public justice*." The fifteenth of those offences is mentioned as follows :

" A conspiracy also to indict an innocent man of felony falsely and maliciously, who is accordingly indicted and acquitted, is a farther abuse and perversion of public justice ; for which the party injured may either have a civil action by writ of conspiracy, (of which we spoke in the preceding book,) or the conspirators, for there must be at least two to form a conspiracy, may be indicted at the suit of the king, and were by the ancient common law to receive what is called the villenous judgment, viz., to lose their *liberam legem*, whereby they are discredited and disabled as jurors or witnesses ; to forfeit their goods and chattels, and lands for life ; to have those lands wasted, their houses razed, their trees rooted up, and their own bodies committed to prison. . . . To this head may be referred the offence of sending letters threatening to accuse any person of a crime punishable with death, transportation, pillory, or other infamous punishment, with a view to extort from him any money or other valuable chattels. This is punishable by statute 30 Geo. II., c. 24, at the discretion of the court with fine, imprisonment, pillory, whipping, or transportation for seven years."

But there is no mention, in that connection, of conspiracies in restraint of trade, or of conspiracies to raise or maintain prices.

It is not to be maintained, of course, that, because Blackstone omits to mention any other conspiracies, no others existed. But this fact, taken in connection with the *Mogul Steamship* case, and with the other facts hereinbefore stated, makes it quite evident that a mere combination to raise wages or prices, or to prevent competition between the parties combining, was not an indictable conspiracy independently of statute.

Having gone so far, let us next see what was the English criminal law as to acts "injurious to trade and commerce" irrespective of the element of conspiracy.

Here we find that there was a well-recognized class of such crimes. They were enumerated by Blackstone in his Chapter XII. of Book IV., entitled "Of Offences against Public Trade."

Under that classification he enumerates the following:

1. "Owling, so called from its being usually carried on in the night, which is the offence of carrying wool or sheep out of this kingdom, to the detriment of its staple manufacture."

2. Smuggling.

3. Fraudulent bankruptcies.

4. Usury.

5. Cheating.

Thereafter he gives forestalling, regrating, engrossing, and other offences enumerated in the following extract, which it will be well to quote *verbatim*(a).

"6. The offence of forestalling the market is also an offence against public trade. This, which (as well as the two following) is also an offence at common law, was described by statute 5 & 6 Edw. VI. c. 14 to be the buying or contracting for any merchandise or victual coming in the way to market; or dissuading persons from bringing their goods or provisions there; or persuading them to *enhance the price*, when there: any of which practices make the market dearer to the fair trader.

"7. Regrating was described by the same statute to be the buying of corn, or other dead victual, in any market, and selling it again in the same market, or within four miles of the place. For this also *enhances the price* of the provisions, as every successive seller must have a successive profit.

(a) 4 Blackstone, Com., 158–160.

" 8. Engrossing was also described to be the getting into one's possession, or buying up, large quantities of corn, or other dead victuals, with *intent to sell them again.* This *must of course be injurious to the public*, by putting it in the power of one or two rich men to raise the price of provisions at their own discretion. And so the total *engrossing of any other commodity*, with an *intent to sell it at an unreasonable price*, is an offence indictable and fineable at the common law. And the general penalty for these three offences by the common law (for *all the statutes concerning them were repealed by* 12 *Geo. III. c.* 71) (*a*) is, as in other minute misdemeanors, discretionary fine and imprisonment. Among the Romans these offences and other mal-practices to raise the price of provisions, were punished by a pecuniary mulct. 'Poena viginti aureorum statuitur adversus eum, qui contra annonam fecerit, societatemve coierit quo annona carior fiat.'

" 9. Monopolies are much the same offence in other branches of trade, that engrossing is in provisions : being a licence or privilege allowed by the king for the sole buying and selling, making, working, or using of anything whatsoever ; whereby the subject in general is restrained from that liberty of manufacturing or tracing which he had before. These had been carried to an enormous height during the reign of queen Elizabeth ; and were heavily complained of by sir Edward Coke, in the beginning of the reign of king James the First : but were in great measure remedied by statute 21 Jac. I. c. 3, which declares such monopolies to be contrary to law and void (except as to patents, not exceeding the grant of fourteen years, to the authors of new inventions ; and except also patents concerning printing, saltpetre, gunpowder, great ordnance, and shot) ; and monopolists are punished with the forfeiture of treble damages and double costs, to those whom they attempt to disturb ; and if they procure any action, brought against them for these damages, to be stayed by an extra-judicial order, other than of the court wherein it is brought, they incur the penalties of praemunire. *Combinations* also among victuallers or artificers, to *raise the price* of provisions, or *any commodities*, or the rate of labour, are in many cases severely *punished by particular statutes;* and in general by statute 2 & 3 Edw. VI. c. 15 with the forfeiture of 10*l.* or twenty days' imprisonment, with an allowance of only bread and water for the first offence ;

(*a*) This was A.D. 1772.

20*l.* or the pillory, for the second ; and 40*l.* for the third, or else the pillory, loss of one ear, and perpetual infamy. In the same manner, by a constitution of the emperor Zeno, all monopolies and combinations to keep up the price of merchandise, provisions, or workmanship, were prohibited upon pain of forfeiture of goods and perpetual banishment.

" 10. To exercise a trade in any town, without having previously served as an apprentice for seven years, is looked upon to be detrimental to public trade, upon the supposed want of sufficient skill in the trader : and therefore is punished by statute 5 Eliz. c. 4 with the forfeiture of forty shillings by the month.

" 11. Lastly, to prevent the destruction of our home manufactures by transporting and seducing our artists to settle abroad, it is provided by statute 5 Geo. I. c. 27 that such as so entice or seduce them shall be fined 100*l.* and be imprisoned three months : and for the second offence shall be fined at discretion, and be imprisoned a year : and the artificers, so going into foreign countries, and not returning within six months after warning given them by the British ambassador where they reside, shall be deemed aliens, and forfeit all their land and goods, and shall be incapable of any legacy or gift. By statute 23 Geo. II. c. 13 the seducers incur, for the first offence, a forfeiture of 500*l.* for each artificer contracted with to be sent abroad, and imprisonment for twelve months ; and for the second, 1000*l.* and are liable to two years' imprisonment ; and by the same statute, connected with 14 Geo. III. c. 71 if any person exports any tools or utensils used in the silk, linen, cotton, or woollen manufactures (excepting woolcards to North America), he forfeits the same and 200*l.*, and the captain of the ship (having knowledge thereof) 100*l.* ; and if any captain of a king's ship, or officer of the customs, knowingly suffers such exportation, he forfeits 100*l.* and his employment ; and is forever made incapable of bearing any public office : and every person collecting such tools or utensils, in order to export the same, shall, on conviction at the assises, forfeit such tools and also 200*l.*"

Here we get additional light. The view of the law taken by Blackstone was this :

1. Forestalling, regrating, engrossing, and monopolies, so far as concerns the matter here under consideration, were the only "acts injurious to trade and commerce" which then constituted crimes.

2. The legal injury involved in those crimes, whether to any other individual, or to the community, consisted in "enhancing prices."

3. The offence of "enhancing prices" was the same, whether committed by an individual or a combination.

4. Mere "combinations" to raise prices were criminal only under "particular statutes."

Under those statutes, then, the only "offences against public trade," which concern us, were the four above named, "forestalling," "regrating," "engrossing," and "monopolies."

Let us see where we find ourselves at our next step.

One of these offences, that termed a "monopoly," is easily eliminated, that is, if legal terms are to be used with any degree of accuracy. It is here especially to be noted, that combinations to raise prices are by Blackstone classified under the heading of "monopolies." Moreover, it is from that point of view that such combinations have been considered in recent opinions of our own courts; and it is their tendency to create "monopolies," that these courts have considered to be the chief danger of these combinations.

But if legal terms are to be used with any accuracy, it must be said, with all possible deference to Sir William Blackstone, that combinations which have for their purpose only the raising of the prices of the property of the parties combining, or the preventing of competition among the parties combining, have no connection whatever with "monopolies," or the law relating thereto. A "monopoly" under the English law, according to Blackstone's own definition just quoted, which is in accordance with the authorities, was "a licence or privilege allowed *by the king* for the *sole buying* and *selling, making*, working, or *using* of anything whatsoever; whereby the *subject in general is restrained from that liberty of manufacturing or trading* which he had before."

As to "monopolies," therefore, these points are plain:

1. They were grants "by the king"—that is, by due authority of law.

2. They were exclusive; and barred all other subjects than their grantee from the right of selling or manufacturing.

3. They never became unlawful, in any sense, till the statute 21 Jac. I. c. 3, which provided simply that *some* monopolies, under grant of the sovereign alone, were "unlawful and void;" and which, so far as I am aware, for the first time visited their holders with a penalty, and then only in case of any attempt by those holders to disturb others in the exercise of their lawful rights.

It is easily apparent, from the foregoing statement, that a mere combination to raise prices of the property of the parties combining lacks all the essential features of a "monopoly." Those parties have no exclusive "license or privilege." They have no license or privilege of any kind. All other citizens retain the same right, and the same power, of manufacturing, buying, and selling, with the parties combining. A "monopoly," too, was lawful. Unless it was lawful, it had no existence. The stigmatizing such combinations as "monopolies," therefore, involves extreme looseness of thought and language.

The position, then, which we have now reached is this:

1. Under the English law there was a well-defined class of "Offences against Public Trade."

2. Those offences, so far as they concern us here, were forestalling, regrating, engrossing, and, to use the term in a loose, popular sense, "monopolies."

3. Combinations to raise prices, though mentioned by Blackstone under the heading of "monopolies," had nothing of the "monopoly" in their real legal nature.

4. All four of these offences were statutory.

We come next to a question which lies at the bottom of the entire situation. It is this: Did the English statutes which created these "Offences against Public Trade," ever become part of the body of our American law?

The weight of authority in this country is overwhelming, that the ancient English statutes which established prices, and which made crimes of mere efforts to enhance prices, never formed part of our law. As to this point let me first give an extract from the opinion of Chief Justice Shaw in *Commonwealth* v. *Hunt*(a). It reads:

"We have no doubt, that by the operation of the constitution of this Commonwealth, the *general rules of the common law*, making conspiracy an indictable offence, *are in force here*, and that this is included in the description of laws which had, before the adoption of the constitution, been used and approved in the Province, Colony, or State of Massachusetts Bay, and usually practised in the courts of law. Const. of Mass. c. VI. § 6. It was so held in *Commonwealth* v. *Boynton*, and *Commonwealth* v. *Pierpont*, cases decided before reports of cases were regularly published,* and in many cases since. *Commonwealth* v. *Ward*, 1 Mass. 473; *Commonwealth* v. *Judd*, and *Commonwealth* v. *Tibbetts*, 2 Mass. 329, 536; *Commonwealth* v. *Warren*, 6 Mass. 74. Still, it is proper in this connexion to remark, that although the *common law* in regard to conspiracy in this Commonwealth *is in force*, yet it will not necessarily follow that every indictment at common law for this offence is a precedent for a similar indictment in this state. The general rule of the common law is, that it is a criminal and indictable offence, for two or more to confederate and combine together, by concerted means, to do that which is unlawful or criminal, to the injury of the public, or portions or classes of the community, or even to the rights of an individual. This rule of law may be equally in force as a rule of the common law, in England and in this Commonwealth; and yet it must depend upon the local laws of each country to determine, whether the purpose to be accomplished by the combination, or the concerted means of accomplishing it, be unlawful or criminal in the respective countries. *All those laws of the parent country*, whether *rules of the common law, or early English statutes*, which were made for the purpose of *regulating the wages of laborers*, the *settlement of paupers*, and making it penal for any one to use a trade or handicraft to which he had not served a full apprenticeship—*not being adapted to the circumstances of our colonial condition*—were not adopt-

---

(a) *Commonwealth* v. *Hunt*, 4 Metcalf, 111, p. 121.
* See a statement of these cases in 3 Law Reporter, 295, 296.

ed, *used or approved*, and therefore do *not come within the description of the laws adopted and confirmed by the provision of the constitution already cited*. This consideration will do something towards reconciling the English and American cases, and may indicate how far the principles of the English cases will apply in this Commonwealth, and show why a conviction in England, in many cases, would not be a precedent for a like conviction here. *The King* v. *Journeymen Tailors of Cambridge*, 8 Mod. 10, for instance, is commonly cited as an authority for an indictment at common law, and a conviction of journeymen mechanics of a conspiracy to raise their wages. It was there held, that the indictment need not conclude *contra formam statuti*, because the gist of the offence was the conspiracy, which was an offence at common law. At the same time *it was conceded, that the unlawful object to be accomplished was the raising of wages above the rate fixed by a general act of parliament*. It was therefore a *conspiracy to violate a general statute law*, made for the regulation of a large branch of trade, affecting the comfort and interest of the public; and thus the *object to be accomplished by the conspiracy* was *unlawful, if not criminal.*"

Judge Gibson, of Pennsylvania, in *Commonwealth* v. *Carlisle*(*a*), uses this language:

" There are, indeed, a variety of British precedents of indictments against journeymen for combining to raise their wages, and precedents rank next to decisions as evidence of the law; but it has been thought sound policy in England to put this class of the community under restrictions so severe, by *statutes that never were extended to this country*, that we ought to pause before we adopt their law of conspiracy, as respects artisans, which may be said to have, in some measure, indirectly *received its form from the pressure of positive enactment*, and which, therefore, may be entirely unfitted to the condition and habits of the same class here."

Mr. Bishop says(*b*):

" Whatever the language of some of the old cases, no lawyer of the present day would hold it indictable for men simply to associate to *promote their own interests* or specifically to *raise their wages*. . . . Or if employers should combine *simply to reduce wages, not proposing*

(*a*) Brightly, 36. (*b*) 2 Bishop Crim. Law, § 233.

any unlawful means, perhaps we might not so much commend them, yet still they would stand under *no disfavor from the law*. The result of which is that a *conspiracy to enhance or reduce wages is not indictable per se*, while yet it may be so by reason of proposed *unlawful means*."

While some parts of the English criminal law beyond doubt formed part of the criminal law of the English colonies, yet the repeal of the statutes as to forestalling, regrating, and engrossing, took place before the separation of the colonies from the mother country; and there is no indication, so far as I am aware, that the crimes of forestalling, engrossing, and regrating ever existed on this side of the water, except under certain special statutes, which are next to be mentioned.

For we have had our own separate experience in attempts to regulate prices by statute, of the same nature, and with the same results, as in England, although the results with us were reached much more quickly, and were followed more quickly by the repeal of the obnoxious and pernicious legislation.

Our attempts of this character were made during the Revolutionary War, at the time when great financial distress had ensued from the issue of large quantities of paper currency. Naturally there was a great rise in prices, of both labor and merchandise. At once, by concerted action, attempts were made, especially in the New England States and in New York, to control prices by statute. The Journals of Congress, under the date of November 22d, 1777, contain the following resolution:

" To maintain our fleets and armies, large sums have been emitted in bills of credit, and the same method has been embraced by the respective states to answer their internal wants. By these expedients, our paper currency, notwithstanding the solid basis on which it is founded, is multiplied beyond the rules of good policy. No truth being more evident, than that where the quantity of money of any denomination exceeds what is useful as a medium of commerce, its comparative value must be proportionably reduced. To this cause, conspiring with the arts of our open and secret enemies, the shameful avidity of too many of our professed friends and the scarcity of foreign commodities are we to ascribe the depreciation of our currency : the consequences to be apprehended are equally obvious and alarming. They tend to the depravity of morals, the decay of public virtue, a precarious supply for the war, debasement of the public faith, injustice to individuals, and the destruction of the honour, safety and independence of the United States. Loudly, therefore, are we called on to provide a reasonable and effectual remedy.''

The resolutions thereupon proceeded to recommend to the different States :
1. The raising of five million dollars by taxes.
2. The refraining from the emission of further bills of credit, and the withdrawal of part of those already emitted.
3. Effectual provisions for the administration of justice.
4. The raising of money by loan.
5. The appointment of commissioners from the different States to convene " in order to regulate and ascertain the *price of labour, manufactures, internal produce, and commodities imported from foreign parts*, military stores excepted, and also to *regulate the charges of inn-holders :* and that on the report of the commissioners, each of the respective legislatures enact suitable laws, as well for enforcing the observance of such of the regulations as they shall ratify, and enabling such inn-holders to obtain the necessary supplies, as to authorise the purchasing commissaries for the army or any other person whom the legislatures may think proper, to take from any *engrossers, forestallers* or other person *possessed of a larger quantity of any such commodities or provisions than shall be competent for the private annual consumption of their families*, and who shall *refuse to sell the surplus* at the *prices to be ascertained* as aforesaid, paying only such price for the same.

" 6. And in order to introduce immediate economy in the public expense, the spirit of sharping and extortion, and the rapid and excessive rise of every commodity being confined within no bounds ; and considering how much time must unavoidably elapse before the plan directed by the foregoing resolution can be carried into effect,

"*Resolved*, That it be earnestly recommended to the respective legislatures of the United States, without delay, by their separate authority, to adopt and effectually enforce a temporary regulation of the prices of provisions and other commodities for the supply of the army, in such manner as they shall judge reasonable ; and to continue in force until the general regulation before proposed shall be adopted."

Pursuant to these resolutions we find an act passed by the legislature of the State of New York on April 3d, 1778, Chap. 34, entitled "An Act to regulate the *wages* of *mechanicks* and *labourers*, the *prices* of *goods and commodities* and the *charges* of *inn-holders* within this State, and for other purposes therein mentioned."

That act recited the Resolutions of Congress of November 22d, 1777, and proceeded to fix the wages of farmers, mechanics and teamsters, the prices of American manufactures, of hemp and wool, of European goods, woolen cloths, rum, sugar, and other commodities. It also purported to fix *profits*, of traders, retailers, and vendors, and of transactions in many classes of merchandise.

Its last section read : "And be it further enacted . . . That this law, unless sooner repealed by the legislature of this State, shall be and continue in full force and effect *during the present war* between the United States of America and Great Britain *and no longer.*"

This New York statute was repealed in the same year with its passage.

A similar experience was had in the New England States, which had united for common action almost a year earlier, of their own motion. On December 25th, 1776, a meeting was held at Providence, R. I., of a committee composed of delegates from New Hampshire, Massachusetts, Rhode Island, and Connecticut, for the purpose of securing common concerted action in relation to the currency, and the high prices for labor and merchandise. The deliberations of this meeting resulted in the passage on December 31st, 1776, of certain recommendations as to prices. These recommendations began with the following recital :

"This Committee taking into consideration the unbounded Avarice of many Persons, by daily adding to the now most intolerable exorbitant Price of every necessary and Convenient Article of Life, and also the most extravagant Prices of Labour in General, which at this time of Distress, unless a speedy and effectual stop be put thereto will be attended with the most Fatal and Pernicious Consequences. As it not only Disheartens and Disaffects the Soldiers who have nobly entered into Service, for the Best of causes, by obliging them to give such unreasonable Prices for those Things that are absolutely needful for their very existence, that their pay is not sufficient to subsist them ; but is also very Detrimental to the Country in General.

"Wherefore it is recommended by this Committee that the Rates and Prices hereafter enumerated be affixed and settled within the Respective States in New England, to wit, . . ."

Then follows a long schedule of prices, both of labor and merchandise.

The committee also recommended the passage of Acts containing many other provisions, which need not here be enumerated, inasmuch as the more important of them may be ascertained from the statement hereafter given of the legislation actually had, upon the committee's recommendation, in the State of Massachusetts.

In Massachusetts, on January 25th, 1777, there was passed a statute, Chap. 14, entitled "An Act to prevent Monopoly and Oppression." It began with the following recital :

"Whereas the avaritious conduct of many persons, by daily adding to the now exorbitant price of every necessary and convenient article of life and encreasing the price of labour in general, unless a speedy and effectual stop be put thereto, will be attended with the most fatal and pernicious consequences, as it not only disheartens and disaffects the soldiers who have nobly entered into the service of their country for the support of the best of causes, and distresses the poorer part of the community by obliging them to give unreasonable prices for those things that are absolutely necessary to their very existence, but will be also very injurious to the state in general; and whereas the Committee lately empowered by this state to proceed to Providence in Rhode Island, and in behalf of this state there to meet with committees from the other New England States, and among other things to confer upon measures necessary to *prevent monopoly*, and the high price of goods and the necessaries of life, and for regulation of vendues, have, in conjunction with the said committees, recommended that rates and prices be settled and affixed by an act of this state to the articles hereinafter enumerated."

It then proceeded:

" Be it therefore enacted by the Council and House of Representatives in General Court assembled, and by the authority of the same,

" (Sect. 1.) That from and after the twenty-eighth day of January, one thousand seven hundred and seventy-seven, the price of farming labour, in the summer season, shall not exceed three shillings by the day, and found, as usual, and so in usual proportion at other seasons in the year ; and the labour of mechanics and tradesmen, and other labour beside what is herein hereafter especially enumerated, in proportion thereunto, according to the usages and customs which have heretofore been adopted and practiced in this state, when compared with farming labour.

" And be it further enacted by the authority aforesaid,

" (Sect. 2.) That the following articles shall not be sold for a higher price than is herein hereafter settled and affixed to them respectively ; viz., good merchantable wheat, at seven shillings and six pence per bushel ; good merchantable rye or rye-meal, at five shillings a bushel ;" proceeding thereafter to fix in the same manner the prices of other grains, salt, West India rum, New England rum, sugar, molasses, shoes, beef, cotton, tow-cloth, flannel, wood, leather, cloth, flour, horse keeping, teaming work, and many other articles of merchandise.

Section 3 provided

" That the *prices* of all the articles produced in America *hereinbe-*

fore enumerated, excepting those to which the prices of transportation are affixed, *shall be taken and deemed to be the prices of such goods and articles in the town of Boston;* and that the *selectmen and the committees of the several towns* in this state shall be and hereby are *impowered to affix and settle in their respective towns what such articles and goods shall be sold for in their towns,* respectively, according to the *proportion the price such goods have borne in such towns with the price they have been at in the town of Boston,* according to the ancient usage and custom of such towns."

"(Sect. 4.) And the said selectmen and committees are in like manner impowered and directed to set and establish the prices of goods herein not enumerated, according to the proportion the price of them have usually borne in their respective towns to those herein enumerated. And the said selectmen and committees are also required to make out a fair list of all the articles to which they shall affix prices, and to post the same, with the prices by them so affixed, up, in some public place or places, in the town where they live, and also to return a list of such prices to the clerk of such town, there to remain upon record; and such prices by them affixed, pursuant to the duty herein enjoined and power hereby given them, shall be taken and deemed to be the price set and affixed by this Act in such town."

Section 6 then provided that the price of all goods and merchandise imported into the State should

"Not exceed the following rates; woolen goods, coarse linens, duck, cordage . . . shall not be sold, by wholesale, at a higher rate than in the proportion of two hundred and seventy-five pounds sterling for what usually cost one hundred pounds sterling in that part of Europe from whence they are imported (with similar provisions for other classes of merchandise), . . . and the seller by wholesale shall make out a bill of parcels at the sterling cost of the articles sold, with his advance thereupon, and deliver the same to the bearer, under penalty of the sum at which such articles are so sold by him; and the retailers of such goods, wares and merchandise shall not sell them at a higher advance than twenty per cent. upon the wholesale price, and shall, if requested by the buyer, give a bill of parcels, with the sterling cost and the advance."

Section 7 provided that persons having necessaries for

the army or navy, and refusing to sell them, thereby subjected their stores to be opened by warrant.

Section 9 prescribed penalties for selling at prices higher than those fixed by the act.

Section 12 provided

" That if any person shall *engross*, or have in his possession, by purchase or otherwise, *more of any article* in this act enumerated (or any other necessary of life) *than is necessary for the consumption of his own family and immediate dependants*, and which he holds with *an apparent design*, in the judgment of the major part of the selectmen of the town where he lives or where such article shall be, *to sell, trade upon, and not for his own consumption as aforesaid*, and shall *refuse to sell and dispose of the same* for the common currency of this state or the United States of America, and *at the prices affixed and settled by this act or by the selectmen and committee in pursuance of it*, and complaint being thereof made to the major part of said selectmen by or in the *behalf of any person who is in want of such article or articles for his own immediate support, the support of his family or immediate dependants*, and the said selectmen or the major part of them believing the same to be true, shall demand of such person so refusing to sell such article or articles for such price as is affixed by this act, or by the selectmen or committee in pursuance of it, and if such person shall refuse to comply therewith, or cannot be found to have such demand made of him, the major part of said selectmen shall apply to some justice of the peace within the same county, for a *warrant to open any store, warehouse or granary in which such article* or articles may be, or otherwise *to take possession of the same.*"

Section 13 prescribes the form of the warrant to be issued, which authorized the sheriff " to take possession of the articles in question and deliver them to the selectmen to the intent that the said selectmen may sell and deliver to the said N. O. the aforesaid (articles) or so much of that article as the said N. O. has absolute necessity for."

Section 14 provided "And the said selectmen, or the major part of them, having possession of such article or articles in manner aforesaid, shall *sell and deliver to such necessitous person* so named in such warrant, *so much of the article therein mentioned as he stands in need of for the support of his family and immediate dependants, at the price affixed as aforesaid.*"

This Act was logical, and consistent. Evidently, if there is any legal obligation resting on the owner of merchandise to sell at any other price than his own, there is a corresponding legal right on the part of some other person or persons to buy at that price. So this Massachusetts legislature considered. Therefore they enacted, that not only should the owners of merchandise be bound to sell at legislative prices, but the community, or any of its members in need, should have the right to buy at those prices. And they provided the machinery for enforcing this right.

This measure, however, was soon found to be ineffectual, as similar ones had been found in England. The consequence was the passage of a later Act (Province Laws, 1776-77, Chap. 46), entitled "An Act in addition to, and for amending and more effectually carrying into execution, an Act intitled ' An Act to prevent Monopoly and Oppression ' made in the present year."

" Whereas it appears that the prices at which sundry articles are fixed in the act to prevent monopoly and oppression *are not adequate to the expence which will hereafter probably be incurred in procuring such articles,* —

" Be it therefore enacted by the Council and House of Representatives in General Court assembled, and by the authority of the same,

" (Sect. 1.) That the *selectmen and committees of correspondence &c.* of the several towns in this state, be, and they are hereby, impowered to *settle* and *affix*, in their respective towns, *once in two months*, during the continuance of this act, the *price of farming and other labour*, the *price* at which *poultry, flour, and iron*, either imported by land or water into such town, or manufactured therein, may be *sold for*, having respect to the quality of such flour and iron ; and that said selectmen and committees cause the prices by them affixed and settled for said articles, to be posted up in some public place or places in their respective towns, and six days at least before such prices are to take effect ; and that the price of the several kinds of smith's work be set by the selectmen and committees of the several towns in this state, as the price affixed by them to iron may, in their opinion, make it necessary ; and also the prices beyond which innholders may not exceed, in disposing of mixed liquors to travellers and others in their respective towns.

" And be it further enacted,

" (Sect. 2.) That the following articles be hereafter sold at the prices following, or not exceeding such prices ; viz.

" Fleece wool, at two shillings and two pence per pound," followed by an enumeration of other articles with their prices, among which were rye, pork, cocoa, coffee, cotton, cotton and linen cloth, rum, molasses, and sugar.

Section 3 then provided

" That when any store, warehouse, or other building shall be opened by warrant from a justice of the peace, in the manner prescribed in the act to which this act is made in addition, or dwelling-house, or other building and apartment, which they are hereby, in like manner, impowered to enter, *the selectmen may not only sell and dispose to the necessitous person applying therefor, but to all others who shall appear to purchase,* by retail in small quantities ; and also, to innholders, rum, by the barrel, and to bakers, flour, by the barrel, upon the day of executing the said warrant," with sundry provisions then following for the protection of distillers and " retailers of rum and molasses."

The legislature did, however, recognize that legislation of this kind was to be used only under the stress of exceptional circumstances. This appears from the language used by them in Section 4 of this act, which read as follows :

" That the powers and authorities by the last preceding paragraph granted to selectmen and committees, *can only be justified in cases wherein the very existence of the community is depending ;* and must, whenever adopted, be, in its nature, short and temporary, and *cannot, with any propriety consistent with the preservation of the common rights of men, be adopted but only in cases wherein the avarice and wickedness of a few endanger the ruin and destruction of the state ;* and therefore that *this instance shall not, at any time hereafter, be drawn, into precedent, excepting in cases of like necessity.*"

In other words, *Inter arma silent leges.*

By this time the difficulty of enforcing any laws of this character had evidently begun to produce some effect on the minds of the legislators, for they proceeded to provide a body of special officials who were to attend to the *enforcement* of the act. By section 8 it was provided,

" That there shall be elected, some time on or before the last day of June next, in each town and plantation within this State, three, five, or seven persons, who shall be *under oath to prosecute all breaches of this act,* and of the ' Act for preventing monopoly and oppression,' which shall come to their knowledge, or of which they shall receive information . . . and any person chosen into said office, and refusing to serve therein . . . shall forfeit and pay the sum of Five pounds . . . and when any person chosen to said office shall refuse to serve therein, the town to which he belongs, shall choose some other person in his place, and so as often as the case may require."

The difficulties of enforcing any such act, even as they had already become apparent to the members of that legislature, were so great as to lead them to go even further, and provide (Sect. 11)

" That no execution shall, after the fifteenth day of June next, be issued from the office of any clerk of any inferior court of common pleas, or of the superior court of judicature &c., for any sum whatever, unless the plaintiff or plaintiffs suing in his or their own right, and dwelling within this state, shall first take the following oath ; viz., You A. B. do, in presence of God, solemnly declare, that you have not, since the fifteenth day of June, 1777, wittingly and willingly, directly or indirectly, either by yourself, or any by, for, or under you, been concerned in selling any article enumerated in the ' Act to prevent monopoly and oppression ' at a higher price than is by the said acts limited for such article, or by the selectmen or committees in pursuance thereof. So help you God."

This Act was passed May 10th, 1777.

A very short experience under these two acts brought the legislature to a full comprehension of the situation, and on October 13th of the same year both acts were repealed, by a very short statute of which the terms are very instructive. It was Chap. 6 of Province Laws 1777-78, entitled

"An Act for the repealing two acts of the General Court made the present year to *prevent monopoly and oppression.*"

"Whereas the several acts to prevent monopoly and oppression made the present year *have been very far from answering the salutary purposes for which they were intended,*—

"Be it therefore enacted by the Council and House of Representatives in General Court assembled, and by the authority of the same,

"That the aforesaid acts ... be, and they are hereby, repealed, and every part and paragraph of each of the acts aforesaid declared null and void."

The futility of acts of this nature is made further apparent by a letter from Governor Cooke of Rhode Island of May 14th, 1777, part of which is as follows: "Sir: The Consequences arising from the *not carrying into Execution* the late Acts passed by the several Legislative Bodies of the New England States affixing Prices of Labor and Goods enumerated, are *too obvious to need commenting upon.*

"This little State hath exerted itself in some measure by prosecuting Persons who have transgressed that Law: but in vain can she alone, put in Execution a matter upon which so much depends. The *Consequence hath been an almost intire stop of vending the necessary Articles of Life.*"

Thereafter, among the Massachusetts statutes, we find "An Act against *monopoly* and *forestalling,*" Chap. 31, Province Laws 1778-79, which provided in effect that no person should have in his possession grain more than sufficient for the use of his family and immediate dependents until the next harvest time. This act was passed February 8th, 1779, and by its terms was limited to be in force only until the next twentieth day of October. Thereafter it was renewed for two periods of about one year each, when it expired.

The lawyers who drafted those statutes were evidently cognizant of the class of "Offences against Public Trade" mentioned by Blackstone, that is, "engrossing," "forestalling," and "monopolies." Those were the technical offences which, in the minds of the lawyers of that time, constituted the wrongs done to the community by persons engaged in raising prices.

This review of these old statutes brings us forward one more step. Whereas the old English statutes as to sundry "Offences against Public Trade" did not form part of our American law, on the other hand, there were, as we have seen, in several of the States a number of early statutes, creating those same old offences, under the same old names, "engrossing," "forestalling," and "monopolies;" and those early statutes were either repealed, or thereafter became obsolete. I have been able to find no reported case in the reports of any State of a conviction for either of those "Offences against Public Trade," all of which consisted, in some form, in an attempt to "enhance prices."

This was the situation when the New York statute defining the offence of conspiracy was passed. In other States the situation was much the same when similar statutes were enacted. So, too, it was with what may be termed the common law of the United States. It will be sufficient for our purpose, if we follow, with a slight degree of detail, the situation as it developed in New York.

The Revised Statutes of the State of New York, which went into effect in 1830, contained the following definition of the offence of conspiracy :(a)

" § 8. If two or more persons shall conspire, either,

" 1. To commit any offence ; or,

" 2. Falsely and maliciously to indict another for any offence, or to procure another to be charged or arrested for any such offence ; or,

---

(a) 2 N. Y. Rev. Stat. 691.

"3. Falsely to move or maintain any suit ; or,

"4. To cheat and defraud any person of any property by any means which are in themselves criminal ; or,

"5. To cheat and defraud any person of any property by any means which, if executed, would amount to a cheat, or to obtaining money or property by false pretences ; or,

"6. To commit any act *injurious* to the public health, to public morals or to *trade or commerce ;* or for the perversion or obstruction of justice or the due administration of the laws ;

"They shall be deemed guilty of a misdemeanor.

"§ 9. No conspiracies, other than such as are enumerated, are punishable criminally."

As to this statute, the following points are to be noted :

1. The offences defined, as had been the case under the common law, were to a large degree connected with the administration of justice.

2. Those offences were largely combinations to commit acts which would be crimes, if committed by a single individual.

The first reported case of any importance which arose under this act was *People* v. *Fisher*.(a) That case may be said to have been the primal source in the State of New York of most of the heresies as to combinations to raise prices, of either labor or merchandise.

It is well, therefore, to see precisely what this case *People* v. *Fisher* really did decide.

Its syllabus reads thus :

"A conspiracy of journeymen workmen of any trade or handicraft *to raise their wages, by entering into combinations to coerce* journeymen and master workmen employed in the same trade or business, to conform to rules established by such combination for the purpose of regulating the price of labor and carrying such rules into effect by overt acts, is indictable as a misdemeanor ; and it was accordingly *held*, where journeymen shoemakers conspired together and fixed the price of making coarse boots, and entered into a combination that if a journeyman shoemaker should make such boots for a compensation below the rate established, he should pay a penalty of ten dollars ;

(a) 14 Wendell, 9, A.D. 1835.

and if any master shoemaker employed a journeyman who had violated their rules, that they would refuse to work for him, and would quit his employment, and carried such combination into effect by leaving the employment of a master workman in whose service was a journeyman who had violated their rules, and thus *compelled the master shoemaker to discharge such journeyman from his employ*—that the parties thus conspiring were guilty of a misdemeanor and punishable accordingly."

The first count of the indictment charged that the defendants conspired

" to *prevent any journeyman boot and shoemaker in the village of Geneva from working in his trade and occupation below certain rates and prices* prescribed by the defendants and their confederates to the great injury of the trade of the State of New York."

The second count, after stating the conspiracy, charged that the defendants

" in pursuance thereof did promise and agree to and among themselves, and to and with their confederates, that *neither of them would be employed for any master shoemaker who should thereafter employ Thomas J. Pennock*, a journeyman boot and shoemaker, although Pennock was a good and free citizen of the State, and a good and faithful workman ;" that Pennock's employer was thereby " *compelled to dismiss and did dismiss Pennock* from his employment and service, and ever since declined and refused to employ him in his trade and occupation of a journeyman shoemaker, to the great prejudice of Pennock and of Quin, to the *obstruction of free and voluntary labor* in the business of boot and shoemaking to the injury of trade."

The opinion states the question to be decided thus : " The question therefore is, is a conspiracy to raise the wages of journeymen shoemakers an act injurious to trade and commerce ?" This question is answered in the affirmative. But other passages in the opinion make it clear that this affirmative answer must be taken with limitations made necessary by the special facts of the case. Those limitations are apparent from the following extract :

"The man who owns an article of trade or commerce is *not obliged to sell it for any particular price, nor is the mechanic obliged by law to labor for any particular price.* He may say that he will not make coarse boots for less than one dollar per pair, but he has *no right to say that no other mechanic shall make them for less.* The cloth merchant may say that he will not sell his goods for less than so much per yard, but *has no right to say that any other merchant shall not sell for a less price. If one individual does not possess such a right over the conduct of another, no number of individuals can possess such a right.* All combinations, therefore, to effect *such an object are injurious,* not only to the *individual particularly oppressed,* but *to the public at large.* In the present case an industrious man was *driven out of employment by the unlawful measures pursued by the defendants,* and an injury done to the community by diminishing the quantity of productive labor, and of internal trade. In so far as the *individual suffers an injury,* the remedy by indictment is taken away by our revised statutes and the *sufferer is left to his action on the case;* but in so far as the public are concerned, in the embarrassment to trade by the discouragement of industry, the defendants are liable to punishment by indictment. . . . Competition is the life of trade. If the defendants cannot make coarse boots for less than one dollar per pair, *let them refuse to do so;* but *let them not* directly or indirectly *undertake to say that others shall not do the work for a less price.* It may be that Pennock, from greater industry or greater skill, made more profit by making boots at seventy-five cents per pair than the defendants at a dollar. *He had a right to work for what he pleased.* His employer had *a right to employ him for such price as they could agree upon.* The *interference of the defendants was unlawful;* its tendency is not only to individual oppression, but to public inconvenience and embarassment.*"

The opinion, of course, must be taken as a whole. Its point is not to be taken from a single detached sentence. As to the point actually decided, this case is good law. The *obiter dicta,* however, are not to be accepted as law. The case must not be interpreted as an authority to the broad proposition that a combination merely " to raise wages" is a crime, provided that combination involves no interference with the rights of others. If " Pennock had a right to work for what he pleased," as the court say he had, and if he had a right to agree as to his own rate of wages with his employer, he had also the right to agree as to his own rate of wages with his fellow-employee. If Pennock had that right, other workmen had the same right. Certainly the question, whether or not an agreement fixing the rate of wages is or is not unlawful, cannot depend on the mere fact of who is the other contracting party. If one may make an agreement with an employer to work at a specific rate, he may surely make the same agreement with a fellow-employee. But when any one "interferes" with that same right of other men, then he commits a wrong on those other men, for which the law gives a remedy by civil action ; and in the case of a combination, or conspiracy, to so "interfere," the law gives a remedy by indictment.

The subject had a further review in one of the ablest opinions in the State of New York on this branch of the law, in *The Master Stevedores' Association* v. *Walsh*.(a) In that case, after a careful examination of the authorities, Mr. Justice Daly reviewed the *Fisher* case in the following terms : " The feature which distinguishes this case from the one under consideration is, that *coercive measures* were there resorted to to *compel a compliance*, not only on the part of master shoemakers, but *of journeymen not members of the association*, with the regulations the combination had established. *This was undertaking to interfere with the rights of others*, and it has frequently been held that *combinations to prevent* any journeyman *from working* below certain rates, or to prevent master workmen *from employing* one except at certain rates, are *unlawful*, and that the parties engaging in such combination may be indicted for a conspiracy."

In the case of *People* v. *Fisher*, therefore, although one of its sentences, taken separately, is to the effect that a mere "combination to raise wages" is indictable, yet the case was not such a combination as matter of fact, nor

---

(a) 2 Daly, 1, in the year 1867.

did the court so consider it. The court considered the case, as it was pleaded in the indictment, and proved by the evidence, as a combination to interfere unlawfully with the lawful rights of others. The entire opinion must be read in that light, and single detached phrases must be disregarded.

Thereafter came the statute of 1870(*a*) entitled "An act in relation to employers and persons employed, and to amend subdivision six of section eight, chapter one, part four of the Revised Statutes," which is as follows:

"Sec. 1. The provisions of subdivision six of section one, chapter one, title six, part four of the Revised Statutes, shall not be construed in any court of this State to restrict or prohibit the orderly and peaceable assembling or co-operation of persons employed in any profession, trade or handicraft, for the purpose of securing an advance in the rate of wages or compensation or for the maintenance of such rate."

Under this statute was decided the case of *Johnston Harvester Co.* v. *Meinhardt*,(*b*) which was an action to enjoin unlawful interference by strikers with the business of the plaintiff. The court denied the application for an injunction on the ground that there was no unlawful interference with the plaintiff's legal rights. In a very able opinion the statute of 1870 was considered, and the well-established distinction, between combinations which did, and did not, interfere with the legal rights of others, was fully recognized. The language of the opinion on that point is as follows:

"This statute does not, however, permit an association or trades union, so called, or any body of men in the aggregate, to do *any act* which *each one* of such persons *in his individual capacity*, and *acting independently*, had not *a right to do before the act was passed*. This act does not shield a person from liability for his action in intimidating or coercing a fellow-laborer so that he shall leave his employer's

---

(*a*) Laws 1870, chap. 19.
(*b*) 9 Abbott's New Cases, 395, A.D. 1880.

service. Such conduct is, in its nature, a *trespass upon the rights of business of the employer*. If he compels, by assault or violence, by threats, by acts of coercion, a fellow craftsman to leave the employ of another, he commits an *offence against the rights of such person*, which is hardly distinguishable from an act which should itself *injure or destroy the product of that man's labor*. It is a direct *injury to property rights*, and may be regarded as the sole proximate cause of such injury, for the laborer, in such cases, has not *freedom of action*, and cannot himself be deemed to take any voluntary part in the transaction."

The act of 1870, as so often happens, had really made no modification in the common law.

There the law rested in the State of New York until the year 1893, when a decision was made, which will be considered later. But until that later decision, it may be stated with accuracy, that any mere contract, which looked only to the raising or maintaining of the prices of the property of the contracting parties, or which looked to the regulation only of the action of the contracting parties, or to the prevention of competition between the contracting parties, and went no further, was neither criminal nor unlawful. In the State of New York, in that respect, we were governed by the English common law. It need not be said, that in the period between the enactment of our Revised Statutes and the year 1893 there were undoubtedly many such contracts. A considerable number of them came before the courts. Some of them, as will be hereafter noted, were not only held to be lawful, but they were specifically enforced in equity. No doubt, it is possible to find in the numerous New York cases *obiter dicta*, to the effect that such contracts were "unlawful." But down to the case above alluded to, there was in the State of New York, so far as I am aware, no authority holding that doctrine. On this point, the courts of New York were thoroughly in accord with the English courts, and with the other courts of greatest weight in this country.

In short, independently of statutes, and under the New

York Revised Statutes, and similar statutes in other States, mere contracts of combination, in private employments, whether between employers or employees, and whether they concerned labor or merchandise, had been emancipated from the unreasonable and impracticable fetters of antiquated mediæval legislation.

CHAPTER IV.

THE COURSE OF THE AMERICAN LAW AS TO PUBLIC EMPLOYMENTS.

THE course of the American law as to public employments has been the same as that of the English law ; that is, there has been a remarkable increase in the degree of state control exercised over such employments.

The reason of that fact is to be found in the great increase in the number of such employments, and in the closeness of their relations with the ordinary life of the community. In the early history of this country, as in that of England, such employments were comparatively few in number, and of comparatively slight importance. The state control exercised over them, though well established in law, was very slight, as matter of fact.

With the construction of railroads, followed by the invention of the telegraph, and the introduction of water companies, gas companies, lighting companies, and others of the same character, the necessity of state supervision and control over the use of the properties involved in such enterprises, though the properties were in law private properties, became very manifest.

The necessity of such control was recognized at an early period. In the case of railroads, inasmuch as their property was largely acquired by the exercise of the right of eminent domain, it was natural, that at the outset there should be regulations by statute as to the use of that property.

We find, therefore, a large number of statutes, in the different States, which regulate the use of railroad properties, and the performance of the duties of railroad companies to the public.

We find also a considerable number of cases, where the courts have intervened by the writ of mandamus, to compel the performance by those companies of those duties to the public.

It is foreign to the purpose of this treatise to go into a detailed examination of the many cases in which this state control is exercised over public employments. Our purpose here is simply to show the difference between the tendencies and growth of the law in the two classes of employments, public and private.

It is sufficient, therefore, as to railroad companies, to quote from a very exhaustive and able opinion of Mr. Justice Davis(a) which gives a statement of the legal ground on which this right of state control rests, together with an enumeration of cases in which the law courts have compelled by mandamus the performance by railroad companies of their public duties.

"The question presented by the motion is one of signal importance. It is whether the people of the State can invoke the power of the courts to compel the exercise by railroad corporations of the most useful public functions with which they are clothed. If the people have that right, there can be no doubt that their attorney-general is the proper officer to set it in effective operation on their behalf. (1 R. S., 179, § 1 ; Code of Civ. Proc., § 1993 ; *People v. Halsey*, 37 N. Y., 344 ; *People v. Collins*, 19 Wend. 56.)

"The question involves a consideration of the nature of this class of corporations, the objects for which they are created, the powers conferred and the duties imposed upon them by the laws of their creation, and of the State. As bodies corporate, their ownership may be and usually is altogether private, belonging wholly to the holders of their capital stock ; and their management may be vested in such officers or agents as the stockholders and directors under the provisions of law, may appoint. In this sense they are to be regarded as trading or private corporations, having in view the profit or advantages of the corporators. But these conditions are in no just sense in conflict with their obligations and duties to the public. The objects of their creation are from their very nature, largely different

---

(a) *People* v. *New York Central, etc., R. R. Co.*, 28 Hun, 543.

from those of ordinary private and trading corporations. Railroads are, in every essential quality, public highways, created for public use, but permitted to be owned, controlled and managed by private persons. But for this quality the railroads of the respondents could not lawfully exist. Their construction depended upon the exercise of the right of eminent domain, which belongs to the State in its corporate capacity alone, and cannot be conferred, except upon a 'public use.' The State has no power to grant the right of eminent domain to any corporation or person for other than a public use. Every attempt to go beyond that is void by the constitution; and although the legislature may determine what is a necessary public use, it cannot by any sort of enactment divest of that character any portion of the right of eminent domain which it may confer. This characteristic of public use is in no sense lost or diminished by the fact that the use of the railroad by the corporation which constructs or owns it, must, from its nature, be exclusive. That incident grows out of the method of use which does not admit of any enjoyment in common by the public. The general and popular use of a railroad as a highway is therefore handed over exclusively to corporate management and control because that is for the best and manifest advantage of the public. The progress of science and skill has shown that highways may be created for public use, of such form and kind that the best and most advantageous enjoyment by the people can only be secured through the ownership, management and control of corporate bodies created for that purpose, and the people of the State are not restricted from availing themselves of the best modes for the carriage of their persons and property. There is nothing in the Constitution hostile to the adoption and use by the State of any and every newly developed form or kind of travel and traffic, which have a public use for their end and aim, and giving to them vital activity by the use of the power of eminent domain.

"When the earliest Constitution of our State was adopted, railroads were unknown. The public highways of the State were its turnpikes, ordinary roads and navigable waters. The exercise of eminent domain in respect of them, was permitted by the Constitution for the same reasons that adapt it now to the greatly improved methods of travel and transportation; and in making this adaptation, there is no enlarged sense given to the language of the Constitution, so long as its inherent purpose—the creation only of public use—be faithfully observed.

"These principles are abundantly sustained by authority. In *Bloodgood* v. *The Mohawk and Hudson River Railroad Company* (18 Wend., 9); the court of last resort in this State first announced them, and affixed to railroads their true character as public highways. It is there declared that the fact that railroad corporations may remunerate themselves by tolls and fares, ' does not destroy the public nature of the road, or convert it from a public to a private use. . . . If it is a public franchise and granted to the company for the purpose of providing a mode of public conveyance, the company, in accepting it, engages, on its part, to use it in such manner as will accomplish the object for which the legislature designed it (pages 21, 22). And in *Olcott* v. *The Supervisors* (16 Wall, 678, on page 694), the Supreme Court of the United States adjudged ' that railroads, though constructed by private corporations and owned by them, are public highways, has been the doctrine of nearly all the courts ever since such conveniences for passage and transportation have had any existence. Very early the question arose whether a State's right of eminent domain could be exercised by a private corporation created for the purpose of constructing a railroad. Clearly it could not, unless taking land for such a purpose by such an agency is taking land for public use. The right of eminent domain nowhere justifies taking property for private use. Yet it is a doctrine universally accepted, that a State legislature may authorize a private corporation to take land for the construction of such a road, making compensation to the owner. What else does this doctrine mean, if not that building a railroad, though it be built by a private corporation, is an act done for a public use? And the reason why the use has always been held a public one is that such a road is a highway, whether made by the government itself, or by the agency of corporate bodies, or even by individuals, when they obtain their power to construct it from legislative grant. . . . Whether the use of a railroad is a public or a private one, depends in no measure upon the question who constructed it or who owns it. It has never been considered a matter of any importance that the road was built by the agency of a private corporation. No matter who is the agent, the function performed is that of the State. Though the ownership is private, the use is public. . . . The owners may be private companies, but they are compellable to permit the public to use their works in the manner in which such works can be used. That all persons may not put their own cars upon the road, and use their own motive power, has no bearing upon the question whether the road is a public highway. It bears only upon the mode of use, of which the legislature is the exclusive judge.'

"All public highways are subjects of general State jurisdiction, because their uses are the common property of the public. This principle of the common law is in this State of universal application. As to the class of public highways known as railroads, the common law is fortified by the express conditions of the statutes creating or regulating or controlling them.

"The general railroad act of this State may now be regarded as the general charter of all such corporations. It authorizes the organization of corporations for 'the constructing, maintaining and operating' of railroads 'for public use,' and it imposes upon them the duty 'to furnish accommodations for all passengers and property, and to transport all persons and property on payment of fare or freight." (Laws of 1850, chap. 140, §§ 1, 36.) These words are a brief summary in respect of the duties imposed upon such corporations by all the provisions of the act. Those duties are consigned to them as public trusts, and as was said in *Messenger v. The Pennsylvania Railroad Company* (36 N. J., 407), 'although in the hands of a private corporation, they are still sovereign franchises, and must be used and treated as such ; they must be held in trust for the general good.' This relation of such a corporation to the State is forcibly expressed by Emmons, J., in *Talcott v. Township of Pine Grove* (1 Flippin, U. S. Circuit Ct. Rep., 144) : 'The road once constructed is, instanter, and by mere force of the grant and law, embodied in the governmental agencies of the State and dedicated to public use. All and singular its cars, engines, rights of way and property of every description, real, personal and mixed, are but a trust fund for the political power, like the functions of a public office. The judicial personage—the corporation created by the sovereign power expressly for this sole purpose and no other—is, in the most strict technical and unqualified sense, but its trustee. This is the primary and sole legal political motive for its creation. The incidental interest and profits of individuals are accidents, both in theory and practice.'

"The acceptance of such trusts on the part of a corporation, by the express and implied contracts already referred to, makes it an agency of the State to perform public functions which might otherwise be devolved upon public officers. The maintenance and control of most other classes of public highways are so devolved, and the performance of every official duty in respect of them may be compelled by the courts, on application of the State, while private damages may also be recoverable for individual injuries. The analogy between such officials and railroad corporations in regard to their relations to the State, is strong and clear, and so far as affects the construction and proper and efficient maintenance of their railways will be questioned by no one. It is equally clear, we think, in regard to their duty as carriers of persons and property. This springs sharply out of the exclusive nature of their right to do those things. On other public highways every person may be his own carrier; or he may hire whomsoever he will to do that service. Between him and such employee a special and personal relation exists, independent of any public duty, and in which the State has no interest. In such a case, the carrier has not contracted with the State to assume the duty as a public trust, nor taken the right and power to do it from the State by becoming the special donee and depositary of a trust. A good reason may, therefore, be assigned why the State will not by mandamus enforce the performance of his contract by such a carrier. But the reason for such a rule altogether fails when the public highway is the exclusive property of a body corporate, which alone has power to use it, in a manner which of necessity requires that all management, control and user for the purposes of carriage must be limited to itself, and which, as a condition of the franchise that grants such absolute and exclusive power over and user of a public highway, has contracted with the State to accept the duty of carrying all persons and property within the scope of its charter, as a public trust. The relation of the State to such a body is entirely different from that which it bears to the individual users of a common highway, as between whom and the State no relation of trust exists; and there is small reason for seeking analogies between them. It is the duty of the State to make and maintain public highways. That duty it performs by a scheme of laws, which set in operation the functions of its political divisions into counties, towns and other municipalities, and their officers. It can and does enforce those duties whenever necessary through its courts. It is not the duty of the State to be or become a common carrier upon its public highways; but it may, in some cases, assume that duty, and whenever it lawfully does so, the execution of the duty may be enforced against the agents or officers upon whom the law devolves it. It may grant its power to construct a public highway to a corporation or an individual and with that power its right of eminent domain in order to secure the public use ; and may make the traffic of the highway common to all on such terms as it may impose. In such case it is its duty to secure that common traffic, when refused, by the authority of its courts. (*People* v. *Collins*, 19 Wend. 56 ; *People* v. *Commissioners of Salem*, 1 Cow. 23.) Or it may grant the same powers of construction and maintenance with the exclusive enjoyment of use which the manner of use requires, and if that excludes all common travel and transportation it may impose on the corporation or person, the duty to furnish every requisite facility for carrying passengers and freight, and to carry both in such manner and at such times as public needs may require. Why is that duty, in respect of the power to compel its performance through the courts, not in the category of all others intrusted to such a body ? The writ of mandamus has been awarded to compel a company to operate its road as one continuous line (*Union Pacific R. R. Co.* v. *Hall*, 91 U. S. 343) ; to compel the running of passenger trains to the terminus of the road (*State* v. *H. and N. H. Ry. Co.*, 29 Conn. 538) ; to compel the company to make fences and cattle guards (*People ex rel. Garbutt* v. *Rochester State Line R. R. Co.*, 14 Hun, 373 ; S. C., 76 N. Y. 294) ; to compel it to build a bridge (*People ex rel. Kimball* v. *B. and A. R. R. Co.*, 70 N. Y. 569) ; to compel it to construct its road across streams, so as not to interfere with navigation (*State* v. *N. E. R. R. Co.*, 9 Richardson, 247) ; to compel it to run daily trains (*In re New Brunswick, etc., R. R.*, 1 P. & B. 667) ; to compel the delivery of grain at a particular elevator (*Chicago and Northwestern R. R. Co.* v. *People*, 56 Ill. 365) ; to compel the completion of its road (*Farmers' Loan and Trust Company* v. *Henning*, 17 Am. Law Reg. (N. S.) 266) ; to compel the grading of its track so as to make crossings convenient and useful (*People ex rel. Green* v. *D. and C. R. Co.*, 58 N. Y. 152 ; *N. Y. C. and H. R. R. R. Co.* v. *People*, 12 Hun, 195 ; S. C. 74 N. Y. 302 ; *Indianapolis R. R. Co.* v. *The State*, 37 Ind. 489) ; to compel the re-establishment of an abandoned station (*State* v. *R. R.*, 37 Conn. 154) ; to compel the replacement of a track taken up in violation of its charter (*Rex* v. *Severn and Wye Ry. Co.*, 2 Barn. & Ald. 646) ; to prevent the abandonment of a road once completed (*Talcott* v. *Pine Grove, supra*, 1 Flippin, 145) ; and to compel a company to exercise its franchise (*People* v. *A. and V. R. R. Co.*, 24 N. Y. 261). These are all express or implied obligations arising from the charters of the railroad companies, but not more so than the duty to carry freight and passengers. That duty is, indeed, the *ultima ratio* of their existence ; the great and sole public good for the attainment and accomplishment of which all the other powers and duties are given or imposed. It is strangely illogical to assert that the State, through the courts, may compel the performance of every step necessary to bring a corporation into a condition of readiness to do the very thing for which it is created, but is then powerless to compel the doing of the thing itself.

"We cannot bring our minds to entertain a doubt that a railroad corporation is compellable by mandamus to exercise its duties as a carrier of freight and passengers ; and that the power so to compel it rests equally firmly on the ground that that duty is a public trust, which having been conferred by the State and accepted by the corporation may be enforced for the public benefit ; and also upon the contract between the corporation and the State, expressed in its charter or implied by the acceptance of the franchise (*Abbott* v. *Johnstown R. R. Co.*, 80 N. Y. 31) ; and also upon the ground that the common right of all the people to travel and carry upon every public highway of the State has been changed in the special instance, by the legislature for adequate reasons into a corporate franchise, to be exercised solely by a corporate body for the public benefit, to the exclusion of all other persons, whereby it has become the duty of the State to see to it that the franchise so put in trust be faithfully administered by the trustee."

As to railroads, the legal ground on which rests this right of state control, is comparatively simple, and is easily comprehended. Railroad companies get their existence, and their property, largely under grant from the state.

But in *Munn* v. *People of Illinois*, there arose a most interesting and novel question, as to the right of the State of Illinois to fix by statute the rates of compensation to be charged by the owners of grain elevators for the use of those elevators, it being the conceded fact that the elevators were private property, owned by private individuals, acquired by ordinary private purchase. The legislature of the State of Illinois had passed a statute fixing the maximum rates to be charged for the use of the elevators in the storage and transportation of grain in transit from the interior to the seaboard, and making it an indictable misdemeanor to charge any rate above the rates so fixed. There had been an indictment and conviction in the State court below for such an overcharge ; and from the judgment on such conviction an appeal was taken to the United States Supreme Court. The position taken by the defense, which especially comes under our notice, was that the enforcement of this statutory regulation " deprived" the owners of the elevators " of their property without due process of law." It appeared in the case, though the Supreme Court appeared to give no considerable weight to the point, that a provision of the Illinois constitution (Art. XIII., sec. 5) required all railroad companies receiving and transporting grain in bulk or otherwise to deliver the same at any elevator to which it might be consigned, that could be reached by any track that was or could be used by such company, and that all railroad companies should permit connections with elevators to be made with their tracks ; so that all these elevators might be reached by the cars on their railroads. The inference was fair, that the elevators in question had been connected with different railroads by virtue of these constitutional provisions. It also appeared, that the elevators in question, with a limited number of other similar ones, had virtually the entire control of the transit of grain in bulk through the city of Chicago. The decision of the Supreme Court, sustaining the conviction in the State court, went on the ground of the public nature of the employment, that the owners of the warehouses exercised "a sort of public office," that their property, though conceded to be private property, was "devoted to a public use." To give an adequate idea of the reasoning of the court, it will be well here to give an extract from the opinion. It is as follows :(*a*)

" This brings us to inquire as to the principles upon which this

---

(*a*) *Munn* v. *People of Illinois*, 94 U. S. 113.

power of regulation rests, in order that we may determine what is
within and what without its operative effect. Looking, then, to the
common law, from whence came the right which the Constitution
protects, we find that when private property is 'affected with a
public interest, it ceases to be *juris privati* only.' This was said by
Lord Chief Justice Hale more than two hundred years ago, in his
treatise *De Portibus Maris*, 1 Harg. L. Tr., 78, and has been accepted without objection as an essential element in the law of property ever since. Property does become clothed with a public interest when used in a manner to make it of public consequence, and
affect the community at large. When, therefore, one devotes his
property to a use in which the public has an interest, he, in effect,
grants to the public an interest in that use, and must submit to be
controlled by the public for the common good, to the extent of the
interest he has thus created. He may withdraw his grant by dis-
continuing the use ; but, so long as he maintains the use, he must
submit to the control.

"Thus, as to ferries, Lord Hale says, in his treatise *De Jure
Maris*, 1 Harg. L. Tr, 6, the King has 'A right of franchise or
privilege, that no man may set up a common ferry for all passengers,
without a prescription time out of mind, or a charter from the King.
He may make a ferry for his own use or the use of his family, but
not for the common use of all the King's subjects passing that way ;
because it doth in consequence tend to a common charge, and is
become a thing of public interest and use, and every man for his
passage pays a toll, which is a common charge, and every ferry
ought to be under a public regulation, viz.: that it give attendance
at due times, keep a boat in due order, and take but reasonable toll ;
for if he fail in these he is finable.' So if one owns the soil and
landing-places on both banks of a stream, he cannot use them for
the purposes of a public ferry, except upon such terms and conditions
as the body politic may from time to time impose ; and this because
the common good requires that all public ways shall be under the
control of the public authorities. This privilege or prerogative of
the King, who in this connection only represents and gives another
name to the body politic, is not primarily for his profit, but for the
protection of the people and the promotion of the general welfare.

"And, again, as to wharves and wharfingers, Lord Hale, in his
treatise, *De Portibus Maris*, already cited, says :

"'A man, for his own private advantage, may, in a port or town, set up a wharf or crane, and may take what rates he and his customers can agree for cranage, wharfage, housellage, pesage, for he doth no more than is lawful for any man to do, viz.: makes the most of his own. . . . If the King or subject have a public wharf, unto which all persons that come to that port must come and unlade or lade their goods as for the purpose, because they are the wharfs only licensed by the Queen, . . . or because there is no other wharf in that port, as it may fall out where a port is newly erected ; in that case there cannot be taken arbitrary and excessive duties for cranage, wharfage, pesage, etc., neither can they be enhanced to an immoderate rate ; but the duties must be reasonable and moderate, though settled by the King's license or charter. For now the wharf, and crane and other conveniences are effected with a public interest, and they cease to be *juris privati* only ; as if a man set out a street in new building on his own land, it is now no longer bare private interest, but is affected by a public interest.'

" This statement of the law by Lord Hale was cited with approbation and acted upon by Lord Kenyon at the beginning of the present century, in *Bolt* v. *Stennett*, 8 T. R., 606.

" And the same has been held as to warehouses and warehousemen."

* * * * * * *

" From the same source comes the power to regulate the charges of common carriers, which was done in England as long ago as the third year of the reign of William and Mary, and continued until within a comparatively recent period. And in the first statute we find the following suggestive preamble, to wit :

" ' And whereas, divers wagoners and other carriers, by combination amongst themselves, have raised the prices of carriage of goods in many places to excessive rates, to the great injury of the trade : Be it, therefore, enacted,' etc. 3 W. & M. ch. 12, sec. 24 ; 3 Stat. at L. (Gt. Britain), 481.

" Common carriers exercise a sort of public office, and have duties to perform in which the public is interested. *N. J. Nav. Co.* v. *Merch. Bk.*, 6 How., 382.

" Their business is, therefore, ' affected with a public interest,' within the meaning of the doctrine which Lord Hale has so forcibly stated.

" But we need not go further. Enough has already been said to show that, when private property is devoted to a public use, it is subject to public regulation. It remains only to ascertain whether the warehouses of these plaintiffs in error, and the business which is carried on there, come within the operation of this principle.

"For this purpose we accept as true the statements of fact contained in the elaborate brief of one of the counsel of the plaintiffs in error. From these it appears that 'The great producing region of the West and Northwest sends its grain by water and rail to Chicago, where the greater part of it is shipped by vessel for transportation to the seaboard by the Great Lakes, and some of it is forwarded by railway to the Eastern ports. . . . Vessels, to some extent, are loaded in the Chicago harbor, and sailed through the St. Lawrence directly to Europe. . . . The quantity (of grain) received in Chicago has made it the greatest grain market in the world. This business has created a demand for means by which the immense quantity of grain can be handled or stored, and these have been found in grain warehouses, which are commonly called *elevators*, because the grain is *elevated* from the boat or car, by machinery operated by steam, into the bins prepared for its reception, and *elevated* from the bins, by a like process, into the vessel or car which is to carry it on. . . . In this way the largest traffic between the citizens of the country north and west of Chicago, and the citizens of the country lying on the Atlantic coast north of Washington is in grain which passes through the elevators of Chicago. In this way the trade in grain is carried on by the inhabitants of seven or eight of the great States of the West with four or five of the States lying on the seashore, and forms the largest part of interstate commerce in these States. The grain warehouses or elevators in Chicago are immense structures, holding from 300,000 to 1,000,000 bushels at one time, according to size. They are divided into bins of large capacity and great strength. . . . They are located with the river harbor on one side and the railway tracks on the other; and the grain is run through them from car to vessel, or boat to car, as may be demanded in the course of business. It has been found impossible to preserve each owner's grain separate, and this has given rise to a system of inspection and grading, by which the grain of different owners is mixed, and receipts issued for the number of bushels which are negotiable, and redeemable in like kind, upon demand. This mode of conducting the business was inaugurated more than twenty years ago, and has grown to immense proportions. The railways have found it impracticable to own such elevators, and public policy forbids the transaction of such business by the carrier ; the ownership has, therefore, been by private individuals, who have embarked their capital and devoted their industry to such business as a private pursuit.'

" In this connection it must also be borne in mind that, although in 1874 there were in Chicago fourteen warehouses adapted to this particular business, and owned by about thirty persons, nine business firms controlled them, and that the prices charged and received for storage were such ' as have been from year to year agreed upon and established by the different elevators or warehouses in the City of Chicago, and which rates have been annually published in one or more newspapers printed in said city, in the month of January in each year, as the established rates for the year then next ensuing such publication.' Thus it is apparent that all the elevating facilities through which these vast productions ' of seven or eight great States of the West ' must pass on the way ' to four or five of the States on the seashore ' *may* be a ' virtual ' monopoly.

" Under such circumstances it is difficult to see why, if the common carrier, or the miller, or the ferryman, or the innkeeper, or the wharfinger, or the baker, or the cartman, or the hackney-coachman, pursues a public employment and exercises ' a sort of public office,' these plaintiffs in error do not. They stand, to use again the language of their counsel, in the very ' gateway of commerce,' and take toll from all who pass. Their business most certainly ' tends to a common charge, and is become a thing of public interest and use.' Every bushel of grain for its passage ' pays a toll, which is a common charge,' and, therefore, according to Lord Hale, every such warehouseman ' ought to be under public regulation, viz.: that he . . . take but reasonable toll.' Certainly, if any business can be clothed ' with a public interest, and cease to be *juris privati* only,' this has been. It may not be made so by the operation of the Constitution of Illinois or this statute, but it is by the facts."

The warehouses in question in that case, as hereinbefore stated, were virtually part of the system of public transportation ; they had become virtually part of the public highways. This fact would seem to constitute something analogous to the dedication of a street to the use of the public, even though there had been no formal condemnation of the land, or of an easement therein ;

and to furnish a reason based on such *quasi* dedication, for holding the owners of the warehouses to public obligations resting on that ground.

In the *Munn* case there was a vigorous dissenting opinion by Mr. Justice Field, in which Mr. Justice Strong joined. But the principle decided in that case has been reaffirmed on many occasions by the Supreme Court, and is firmly established in our jurisprudence.

State control of public employments may be exercised under statutes, or in many cases by the courts without statutes. But there has been in late years a great increase in the exercise of such control by statute. It will be sufficient to give one instance of such, in a few sections of the New York statute defining the powers of the Board of Railroad Commissioners.(*a*) They are as follows :

"§ 157. *General Powers and Duties of Board.*—The board shall have power to administer oaths in all matters relating to its duties, so far as necessary to enable it to discharge such duties, shall have general supervision of all railroads, and shall examine the same and keep informed as to their condition, and the manner in which they are operated for the security and accommodation of the public and their compliance with the provisions of their charters and of law. The commissioners or either of them in the performance of their official duties may enter and remain during business hours in the cars, offices and depots, and upon the railroads of any railroad corporation within the state, or doing business therein ; and may examine the books and affairs of any such corporation and compel the production of books and papers or copies thereof, and the board may cause to be subpœnaed witnesses, and if a person duly subpœnaed fails to obey such subpœna without reasonable cause, or shall without such cause refuse to be examined, or to answer a legal or pertinent question, or to produce a book or paper which he is directed by subpœna to bring, or to subscribe his deposition after it has been correctly reduced to writing, the board may take such proceedings as are authorized by the Code of Civil Procedure upon the like failure or refusal of a witness subpœnaed to attend the trial of a civil action

---

(*a*) Laws of New York, 1892, vol. 2, p. 2129.

before a court of record or a referee appointed by such court. The board shall also take testimony upon, and have a hearing for and against any proposed change of the law relating to any railroad, or of the general railroad law, if requested to do so by the legislature, or by the committee on railroads of the senate or the assembly, or by the governor, and may take such testimony and have such a hearing when requested to do so by any railroad corporation, or incorporated organization representing agricultural or commercial interests in the state, and shall report their conclusions in writing to the legislature, committee, governor, corporation or organization making such request; and shall recommend and draft such bills as will in its judgment protect the people's interest in and upon the railroads of this state.

"§ 158. *Reports of Railroad Corporations.*—The board shall prescribe the form of the report required by the railroad law to be made by railroad corporations, and may from time to time make such changes and additions in such form, giving to the corporations six months' notice before the expiration of any fiscal year, of any changes or additions which would require any alteration in the method or form of keeping their accounts, and on or before September fifteenth in each year, shall furnish a blank form for such report. When the report of any corporation is defective, or believed to be erroneous, the board shall notify the corporation to amend the same within thirty days. The originals of the reports, subscribed and sworn to as prescribed by law, shall be preserved in the office of the board.

"§ 159. *Investigation of Accidents.*—The board shall investigate the cause of any accident on any railroad resulting in loss of life or injury to persons, which in their judgment shall require investigation, and include the result thereof in their annual report to the legislature. Before making any such examination or investigation, or any investigation or examination under this article, reasonable notice shall be given to the corporation, person or persons conducting and managing such railroad of the time and place of commencing the same. The general superintendent or manager of every railroad shall inform the board of any such accident immediately after its occurrence. If the examination of the books and affairs of the corporation, or of witnesses in its employ, shall be necessary in the course of any examination or investigation into its affairs, the board, or a commissioner thereof, shall sit for such purpose in the city or town of this state where the principal business office of the corporation is situated if requested so to do by the corporation ; but the board may require copies of books and papers, or abstracts thereof, to be sent to them to any part of this state.

"§ 160. *Recommendations of Board, where Law has been Violated.*—If, in the judgment of the board, it shall appear that any railroad corporation has violated any constitutional provision or law, or neglects in any respect to comply with the terms of the law by which it was created, or unjustly discriminates in its charges for services, or usurps any authority not granted by law, or refuses to comply with the provisions of any law, or with any recommendation of the board, it shall give notice thereof in writing to the corporation, and if the violation, neglect or refusal is continued after such notice, the board may forthwith present the matter to the attorney-general, who shall take such proceedings thereon as may be necessary for the protection of the public interests.

"§ 161. *Recommendations of Board, when Repairs or other Changes are Necessary.*—If in the judgment of the board, after a careful personal examination of the same, it shall appear that repairs are necessary upon any railroad in the state, or that any addition to the rolling stock, or any addition to or change of the station or station-houses, or that additional terminal facilities shall be afforded, or that any change of the rates of fare for transporting freight or passengers or in the mode of operating the road or conducting its business, is reasonable and expedient in order to promote the security, convenience and accommodation of the public, the board shall give notice and information in writing to the corporation of the improvements and changes which they deem to be proper, and shall give such corporation an opportunity for a full hearing thereof, and if the corporation refuses or neglects to make such repairs, improvements and changes, within a reasonable time after such information and hearing, and fails to satisfy the board that no action is required to be taken by it, the board shall fix the time within which the same shall be made, which time it may extend. It shall be the duty of the corporation, person or persons owning or operating the railroad to comply with such decisions and recommendations of the board as are just and reasonable. If it fails to do so the board shall present the facts in the case to the attorney-general for his consideration and action, and shall also report them in its annual or in a special report to the legislature.

"§ 162. *Legal Effect of Recommendations and Action of the Board.*

—No examination, request or advice of the board, nor any investigation or report made by it, shall have the effect to impair in any manner or degree the legal rights, duties or obligations of any railroad corporation, or its legal liabilities for the consequence of its acts, or of the neglect or mismanagement of any of its agents or employees. The supreme court at special term shall have power in its discretion, in all cases of decisions and recommendations by the board which are just and reasonable to compel compliance therewith by mandamus, subject to appeal to the general term and the court of appeals, and upon such appeal, the general term and the court of appeals may review and reverse upon the facts as well as the law. (Thus amended by L. 1892, chap. 676.)

"§ 163. *Corporations must Furnish Necessary Information.*— Every railroad corporation shall, on request, furnish the board any necessary information required by them concerning the rates of fare for transporting freight and passengers upon its road and other roads with which its business is connected, and the condition, management, and operation of its road, and shall, on request, furnish to the board copies of all contracts and agreements, leases or other engagements entered into by it with any person or corporation. The commissioners shall not give publicity to such information, contracts, agreements, leases or other engagements, if, in their judgment, the public interests do not require it, or the welfare and prosperity of railroad corporations of the state might be thereby injuriously affected."

Similar statutes in New York are classified under what is termed "The Transportation Corporations Law," being Chapter 566 of the Laws of 1890, as amended by Chapter 617 of the Laws of 1892. This "Transportation Corporations Law" has separate articles, which apply to ferry corporations, navigation corporations, stage-coach corporations, tramway corporations, pipe-line corporations, gas and electric light corporations, water-works corporations, telegraph and telephone corporations, turnpike, plank-road, and bridge corporations. The title of this general act seems to me extremely happy. Telephone corporations, at first glance, might not seem to concern transportation. But in their essential purpose they are common carriers, as are all the other corporations named.

So it was virtually with the warehousemen in the *Munn* case. They are all engaged in "public employments." It is clear that public control of all such employments is a necessity.

That necessity has in modern times been continually on the increase. There is every reason to believe that it will so continue.

Public control of those employments has increased in the past, and will probably increase in the future. Starting from almost nothing, it has become large and intricate.

The tendencies of the law as to these public employments, it is evident, have been directly the reverse of its tendencies in the case of private employments.

CHAPTER V.

RECENT DECISIONS AS TO CONTRACTS IN RESTRAINT OF TRADE OR COMMERCE.

Such being, and long having been, the condition of the law, there came in the year 1893 the decision of our New York Court of Appeals in *People* v. *Sheldon.*(a) It was followed by the recent decision of the United States Supreme Court in *United States* v. *The Trans-Missouri Freight Association.*(b)

These two cases hold that a mere contract, which provides that the rates or prices, for traffic or merchandise, shall be fixed by one common authority for all the contracting parties, and which thereby prevents competition between the contracting parties, there being no interference with any lawful right of any other party, unless this mere agreement be such, constitutes a crime. The New York case was decided under the provision of the New York Revised Statutes previously quoted. The United States Supreme Court case arose under a similar provision in a statute of the United States.

With all possible deference to these august tribunals, it is most respectfully submitted, that these decisions are irreconcilably in conflict with an overwhelming line of authorities, and with the fundamental principles of the English and American law.

Let us begin with a consideration of the New York case.

Before entering on that consideration, however, let us recall the positions already established. They are:

(a) *People* v. *Sheldon,* 139 N. Y. 251.
(b) *United States* v. *The Trans-Missouri Freight Association,* 166 U. S. 290.

1. Under the English common law, a mere contract, to raise or maintain prices, of the property of the parties combining, involving no interference with the legal rights of others, did not constitute a crime.

2. Such a combination did constitute a crime under certain early English statutes.

3. Those statutes never formed part of the American law.

4. Similar statutes had been passed at an early date in the State of New York, and repealed.

5. Thereafter was enacted the provision of the Revised Statutes making it a crime, for "two or more persons to conspire . . . to commit any act injurious to trade or commerce."

It was under this provision, that the Court held, that a contract of certain coal dealers in the city of Lockport, forming "The Lockport Coal Exchange," by which they agreed to sell coal at uniform rates, to be fixed from time to time for the combining parties by a five-sixths vote of the Exchange members, constituted a crime.

The question is, whether that statute, under well-established principles and rules of statutory interpretation, admits of such construction.

As to the New York common law on the subject, prior to this statute, there can hardly be said to be an open question. It was the same as the common law of England. As to what was the English common law on the subject, it is sufficient to refer to the *Mogul Steamship* case already cited. If it be said that that case is not a conclusive authority for a court of the State of New York, the answer is, that it is an authority as to the common law of England. It would seem, therefore, as already stated, that the question, what was the law of the State of New York prior to the enactment of the Revised Statutes, can hardly be said to be an open question.

To establish the position, that the English statutes as to conspiracy, and as to "Offences against Public Trade" did not form part of the law of our different States, authorities have already been cited.

But in New York the situation on this point was peculiar. The Constitution of the State of New York of April 20th, 1777, reads :

"XXXV. And this convention doth further, in the name and by the authority of the good people of this state, ORDAIN, DETERMINE, AND DECLARE, that such parts of the common law of England, and of the statute law of England and Great Britain, and of the acts of the legislature of the colony of New York, as together did form the law of the said colony on the 19th day of April, in the year of our Lord one thousand seven hundred and seventy-five, shall be and continue the law of this state, *subject to such alterations and provisions as the legislature of this state shall, from time to time, make concerning the same.* That such of the said acts as are temporary shall expire at the times limited for their duration respectively."

Thereafter the New York Legislature, pursuant to the constitutional authority then vested in it, proceeded to pass the following act :

"CHAP. XLVI.

" *An Act for the Amendment of the Law, and the better Advancement of Justice.*

" Passed 27th February, 1788.

" XXXVII. *And be it further Enacted by the Authority aforesaid,* that from and after the *first* Day of *May* next, none of the Statutes of *England,* or of *Great Britain,* shall operate or be considered as Laws of this state."(*a*)

Provisions similar to the one above quoted from the Constitution of 1777 were inserted in our later State Constitutions.

But it is not necessary to attach any special importance to the statute of 1788. It is sufficient to say, that, under the doctrine laid down by the highest courts in the differ-

(*a*) " New York Laws," Jones & Varick. Vol. II., 1787-89, p. 282.

ent States, under constitutional provisions substantially similar to that of New York, the law as to the early English statutes, as stated by Chief Justice Shaw and by Mr. Bishop, would command general assent. As to our common law, then, prior to the Revised Statutes, the position seems very simple, and somewhat ironclad.

The next question is this: In view of the position under our common law as to the crime of conspiracy, of the fact that there was a well-defined class of criminal "Offences against Trade," of the fact, that all those offences, so far as concern the present question, were statutory, and of the further fact, that those same offences had formerly been created by a New York statute which had been repealed, is it a reasonable or sound interpretation of the later provision in the Revised Statutes, to hold that that provision revived those old statutory crimes, and made criminal an act which was lawful at our common law, and which involved a violation of no legal right of any member of the entire community.

Here it becomes necessary to cite authority as to the interpretation of statutes which change the common law. Our Court of Appeals, in a leading case, held the rule to be,(*a*)

"that no such change was intended unless the statute is *explicit and clear* in that direction (1 Kent, Com. 463. *White* v. *Wager*, 32 Barb. 250 ; affirmed 25 N. Y. 328) I am persuaded that a careful analysis of the section referred to will show that no such change, so *radical and dangerous*, was either made or intended, and that the sole scope and purpose of the section was to declare in explicit terms the existing rule of the common law."

The doctrine has been laid down by Chancellor Kent as follows :(*b*)

"Statutes are likewise to be construed in reference to the principles of the common law ; for it is *not to be presumed that the legis-*

(*a*) *People* v. *Palmer*, 109 N. Y. 110, 118. See, too, *People* v. *Fanshawe*, 137 N. Y. 68, 73 ; *People* v. *Richards*, 108 N. Y. 137, 144.

(*b*) 1 Kent, Com. 464.

lature intended to make any innovation upon the common law, further than the case absolutely required. This has been the language of the courts in every age; and when we consider the constant, vehement, and exalted eulogy which the ancient sages bestowed upon the common law as the perfection of reason, and the best birthright and noblest inheritance of the subject, we cannot be surprised at the great sanction given to this rule of construction. It was observed by the judges, in the case of *Stowell* v. *Zouche*, that it was good for the expositors of a statute to *approach as near as they could to the reason of the common law;* and the resolution of the barons of the Exchequer, in *Heydon's* Case, was to this effect."

In connection with this statement of the rule, it is well for us to give from the same high authority its reason (a)

" The common law includes those principles, usages, and rules of action applicable to the government and security of person and property, which do not rest for their authority upon any express and positive declaration of the will of the legislature. According to the observation of an eminent English judge, a statute law is the will of the legislature in writing, and the common law is nothing but statutes worn out by time; and all the law began by the consent of the legislature.

" 1. *Source of the Common Law.*—This is laying down the origin of the common law too strictly. A great proportion of the rules and maxims which constitute the immense code of the common law grew into use by gradual adoption, and received, from time to time, the sanction of the courts of justice, without any legislative act or interference. It was the *application of the dictates of natural justice and of cultivated reason to particular cases.* In the just language of Sir Matthew Hale, the common law of England is, ' not the product of the wisdom of some one man, or society of men, in any one age; but of *wisdom, counsel, experience, and observation of many ages of wise and observing men.*' And his further remarks on this subject would be well worthy the consideration of those bold projectors, who can think of striking off a perfect code of law at a single essay. ' Where the subject of any law is single, the prudence of one age may go far at one essay to provide a fit law; and yet, even in the wisest provisions of that kind, experience shows us that new and un-

---

(a) 1 Kent, Com. 471.

thought-of emergencies often happen, that necessarily require new supplements, abatements, or explanations. But the body of laws that concern the common justice applicable to a great kingdom is vast and comprehensive, consists of infinite particulars, and must meet with various emergencies, and therefore requires much time and much experience, as well as much wisdom and prudence, successively to discover defects and inconveniences, and to apply apt supplements and remedies for them ; and *such are the common laws of England*, namely, *the productions of much wisdom, time, and experience.*"

In view of these declarations of a well-established principle, let us consider the language of the statutory provision in question. The statute says "act injurious to trade or commerce."

It is submitted, that the only reasonable interpretation of that phrase is, that it means an act which violates some legal right, of some individual or class of individuals, in a matter concerning trade or commerce.

Let us now see what was the construction given to it by the Court of Appeals in *People* v. *Sheldon*. And in order to be sure of giving the reasoning of the Court with accuracy, it will be well to quote from the report. The head note of the case is as follows :

" A combination between independent dealers to prevent competition between themselves in the sale of an article of prime necessity is, in the contemplation of law, an act inimical to trade or commerce, without regard to what may be done under and in pursuance of it, and although the object of such a combination was merely the due protection of the parties against ruinous rivalry, and no attempt was made to charge undue or excessive prices ; where it appears that the parties acted under the agreement an indictment for conspiracy is sustainable.

" Upon trial of an indictment for conspiracy to raise the price of coal at retail and to destroy free competition, the court charged the jury, that if the defendants entered into an organization agreement for the purpose of controlling the price and managing the business of the sale of coal, so as to prevent competition in price between the members of the organization, the agreement was illegal, and if the jury found this was their intent, and that the price was raised in pursuance of the agreement, the crime of conspiracy was established. *Held*, no error.

"The court was requested, but refused, to charge that the overt act required to be proved to sustain a conviction for conspiracy must be one which might injuriously affect the public, and that the act of defendants in raising the price of coal, was not, of itself, such an overt act. *Held*, no error."

The opinion (p. 261) says:

"The fact that the defendants subscribed the constitution and by-laws of the 'Lockport Coal Exchange,' and participated in its management, was not controverted on the trial. Nor is it denied that the object of the organization was to prevent competition in the price of coal among the retail dealers, acting as the 'Lockport Coal Exchange,' by constituting the exchange the sole authority to fix the price which should be charged by the members for coal sold by them, and there is no dispute that in pursuance of the plan the exchange did proceed to fix the price of coal, and that the parties to the agreement were thereafter governed thereby in making sales to their customers. It is not questioned that the price first established was seventy-five cents in advance of the then market price, and that there was afterward a still further advance. The defendants gave evidence tending to show (and of this there was no contradiction), that before and at the time of the organization of the exchange the excessive competition between the dealers in coal in Lockport had reduced the price below the actual cost of the coal and the expense of handling, and that the business was carried on at a loss. It was not shown that the prices of coal, fixed from time to time by the exchange, were excessive or oppressive, or were more than sufficient to afford a fair remuneration to the dealers. The trial judge submitted the case to the jury upon the proposition that if the defendants entered into the organization agreement for the purpose of controlling the price of coal and managing the business of the sale of coal, so as to prevent competition in price between the members of the exchange, the agreement was illegal, and that if the jury found that this was their intent, and that the price of coal was raised in pursuance of the agreement to effect its object, the crime of conspiracy was established. The correctness of this proposition is the main question in the case. If a combination between independent dealers, to prevent competition between themselves *in the sale of an article of prime necessity*, is, in the contemplation of the law, an act *inimical* to trade or commerce, whatever may be done under and in pursuance of it, and *although the object of the combination is merely the due protection of the parties to it against ruinous rivalry, and no attempt is made to charge undue or excessive prices, then the indictment was sustained by proof*. On the other hand, if the validity of an agreement, having for its object the prevention of competition between dealers in the same commodity, depends upon what may be done under the agreement, and it is to be adjudged valid or invalid according to the fact whether it is made the means for raising the price of a commodity beyond its normal and reasonable value, then it would be difficult to sustain this conviction, *for it affirmatively appears that the price fixed for coal by the exchange did not exceed what would afford a reasonable profit to the dealers*. The obtaining by dealers of a *fair and reasonable price* for what they sell *does not seem to contravene public policy, or to work an injury to individuals*. On the contrary, the general interests are promoted by activity in trade, which cannot permanently exist without reasonable encouragement to those engaged in it. Producers, consumers and laborers are alike benefited by healthful conditions of business."

Nevertheless the Court held, as above, that the acts proved were in contravention of the Statute, and affirmed the conviction.

This decision, it will be noted, is limited by its terms to the case of a combination to prevent competition in the sale of an article of " prime necessity." It does not, by its terms, go so far as to hold that a combination to raise prices, or to prevent competition, as to merchandise of any and all classes, is a crime.

But is it possible here to draw any sound legal distinction ?

On this point it will be well to see wherein lay the essence of the crime, according to the opinion of the Court. As to this, the Court says : " A mere agreement, followed by no act, is insufficient. The overt act charged in the indictment, and proved, was the *raising of the price of coal*."

It is almost superfluous to suggest the difficulty of satisfactorily determining what is, and what is not, an "article of prime necessity." Whose needs are to be the criterion? Nearly every article, except articles of mere luxury, is, at one time or another, one of prime necessity to some one. And shall the law undertake the function of deciding whether a particular intending buyer really needs that which he desires to purchase?

But does such a distinction rest upon any sound legal basis?

Let us consider the point first with reference to the rights of the owner, the seller. Is there any difference in his legal property rights, in the case of staple articles of food and of ordinary merchandise of other classes? Is his right to fix his own selling price, or his right to say whether he will sell at all, any different in the one case from what it is in the other? Has any individual, or the State, any greater right to limit his property rights in the one case than in the other?

On the other hand, consider the case of the would-be buyers. Is their right to compel a sale, or to fix the seller's selling price directly or indirectly, at all different in the case of staple food products from their right to do so in the case of merchandise of other classes?

To go one step further: Can any one state any sound legal principle, on which it can be held, that the legal rights of the seller of food products differ from the legal rights of the sellers of the labor which produces them? The common law is, that there is no such distinction. The wisest jurists have concluded, that any such distinction is unwise and unjust. But we are now considering it as a question of mere legal principle. Every one knows that the price of food products, as is the case with the prices of nearly all classes of merchandise, is mainly made up of the cost of labor. The cost of corn in its final market is, in the main, made up of the cost of successive sets of laborers, the farmers who have tilled the ground, planted the seed, and harvested the grain, and the carriers who have brought it to market. Now where is the ground for any sound legal distinction between the legal rights of the farmer who sells the grain when it is harvested, and those of the seller in its final market?

But it may be said, that the distinction here should be between honest, hard-working laborers who produce, and speculators who merely gamble on the needs of consumers.

But here we come on another difficulty. Every farmer, every laboring producer, tries, and tries rightly, to get for his product the highest possible price. He will hold it back from market, if he thinks that thereby he can get a higher price. He has the legal right so to do. It will be generally conceded to-day, that the merchant, or middleman, is "an article of prime necessity" in the world's commerce. Without him commerce must cease, and production by the farmer must cease. Now, how are we to draw any sound legal distinction between the right of the farmer to hold his corn for a higher price, and the same right of the merchant, who has bought the corn from the farmer, with all the property rights inherent therein? If one has the right to combine with others to hold grain for a higher price, the other has the same right.

But let us take it from a still different standpoint. In all these cases which have gone upon the theory of a necessity for protection against combinations to raise prices, there has been in reality a complete ignoring of the rights of sellers. Possible dangers to buyers have been in reality the only objects of the solicitude of the courts.

But how is it as to the rights of sellers? How is it, that the courts are under any greater obligation to protect the rights of buyers than of sellers? The one class has precisely the same right to the protection of the law with the other. Even if it were the fact, that the community were divisible into two classes, buyers and sellers, the one has the same right to the law's fullest protection for its property with the other. If the law is to protect buyers against unduly high prices, it is under an equal obligation to protect sellers against unduly low prices. As for the interest of "the public," the interest of "the public" is just as strong that sellers should make good sales as that buyers should make good purchases.

But, as matter of fact, every member of the community, who is engaged in labor of any kind, or in any kind of trade or commerce, is both a buyer and a seller. He is a seller of his own labor, or its products. He is at the same time a buyer of the labor of other men, or of its products. In either capacity, he has the same legal rights, and is entitled to the same measure of legal protection. And the interest of the community is to have men as well paid in the one capacity as in the other, and to have every man well paid in each capacity.

How is that end to be accomplished? Can it be accomplished by statute, or by indictment, or by a combination of the two?

All human experience thus far conclusively demonstrates, that the accomplishment of this end must be left to the parties interested in each separate transaction of sale, the buyer and the seller. They know, and they alone know, the facts which properly enter into the decision of all questions of price. In the decision of every question of price there are always two controlling elements: they are (1) the needs of the buyer; and (2) the needs of the seller. Those two elements determine the question of price—and determine it conclusively—in every transaction of sale. Those two elements can be justly estimated by only two persons in the whole world—the high contracting parties. They are the only persons who are in a position to weigh those two elements. It is to the interest of every one, of the buyer, of the seller, and of "the public," that the decision of these questions of value and price shall be left to the parties to the transaction, and that, in making that decision, those two parties shall have the fullest contractual freedom.

If the State has the right, or the duty, of protecting

buyers, it has the same right, and the same duty, of protecting sellers. If it undertakes to do either, it is bound to undertake both.

In all these respects, it is most respectfully submitted, there is no possible sound legal distinction as to the rights and duties, of both individuals and the State, between the sellers of labor and the sellers of merchandise, or between the sellers of merchandise of "prime necessity" and the sellers of merchandise of ordinary kinds. The law, that is, our law, under our forms of constitutional government, gives the same property rights, to both classes of citizens, and to both classes of property.

If, then, as to the matters here under consideration, no sound legal distinction is to be drawn between articles of "prime necessity" and other merchandise, it remains for us to consider the general soundness of the construction given to the New York statute by the Court of Appeals in the *People* v. *Sheldon*.

The soundness of that construction involves the consideration of the chief essential element of a crime, under the English and American law.

As to that, the proposition here submitted, and the one which lies at the foundation of this entire discussion, is this: that every "crime," under the English or American law, involves, at least in its final consummation, the violation of some legal right, of some individual, or class of individuals. Some crimes consist only in the initial stage of a violation of a legal right. Such is always the case in a conspiracy, which has not gone so far as an overt act. But no act constitutes a crime in its initial stage, unless that act, in its final consummation, constitutes a violation of some legal right, of some individual, or class of individuals.

This position is so fundamental that it will be well to give at this point what, under the circumstances, may be deemed an authoritative statement of it from Sir William Blackstone. In his consideration of "Public Wrongs" he says: (*a*)

(*a*) 4 Blackstone, Com. 5.

"In all cases the crime includes an injury; *every public offence is also a private wrong*, and somewhat more; it *affects the individual*, and it *likewise affects the community*. Thus treason in imagining the king's death involves in it *conspiracy* against an *individual*, which is *also a civil injury;* but, as this species of treason in its consequences principally tends to the dissolution of government, and the destruction thereby of the order and peace of society, this denominates it a crime of the highest magnitude. Murder is an *injury* to the life of an *individual;* but the law of society considers principally the loss which the state sustains by being deprived of a member, and the pernicious example thereby set for others to do the like. Robbery may be considered in the same view: it is an *injury* to *private property;* but were that all, a civil satisfaction in damages might atone for it; the *public* mischief is the thing, for the prevention of which our laws have made it a capital offence. In these gross and atrocious injuries the private wrong is swallowed up in the public: we seldom hear any mention made of satisfaction to the individual; the satisfaction to the community being so very great. And indeed, as the public crime is not otherwise avenged than by forfeiture of life and property, it is impossible afterwards to make any reparation for the private wrong: which can only be had from the body or goods of the aggressor. But there are crimes of an inferior nature, in which the public punishment is not so severe, but it affords room for a private compensation also; and herein the distinction of crimes from civil injuries is very apparent. For instance, in the case of battery, or beating another, the aggressor may be indicted for this at the suit of the king, for disturbing the public peace, and be punished criminally by fine and imprisonment; and the party beaten may also have his private remedy by action of trespass for the injury which he in particular sustains, and recover a civil satisfaction in damages. So also, in case of a public nuisance, as digging a ditch across a highway, this is punishable by indictment, as a common offence to the whole kingdom and all his majesty's subjects; but if any individual sustains any special damage thereby, as laming his horse, breaking his carriage, or the like, the offender may be compelled to make ample satisfaction, as well for the private injury as for the public wrong."

To the same effect is the definition of a crime given by Serjeant Stephen in his "New Commentaries on the Laws of England." He says:

" A crime is the *violation of a right*, when considered with reference to the *evil tendency* of such violation, *as regards the community at large*. The distinction of public wrongs from private, that is to say, of crimes from civil injuries, seems upon examination principally to consist in this, that private wrongs (or civil injuries) are an *infringement* or *privation* of the *civil rights* which belong to individuals, *considered merely as individuals*, while public wrongs (or crimes and misdemeanors) are a *violation of the same rights*, considered with reference to their *effect on the community in its aggregate capacity.* As if I detain a field from another man, to which the law has given him a right—this is a civil injury and not a crime ; for here only the right of the individual is concerned, and it is immaterial to the public which of us is in possession of the land. But treason, murder, and robbery are properly ranked among crimes ; since, besides the injury done to individuals, they strike at the very being of society ; which cannot possibly subsist, where acts of this sort are suffered to escape with impunity. *In all cases, crime includes an injury,* that is, *every public offence is also a private wrong,* for while it affects the individual, it affects also the community. Thus treason, in imagining the sovereign's death, involves in it a conspiracy against an individual, which is *also a civil injury ;* but as this species of treason in its consequences principally tends to the dissolution of government, and the destruction thereby of the order and peace of society—this raises it to a crime of the highest magnitude. Murder is an *injury* to the life of an *individual ;* but the law of society considers principally the loss which the State sustains by being deprived of a member, and the pernicious example thereby set for others to do the like. Robbery is an *injury* to *private* property ; but were that all, a civil satisfaction in damage might atone for it, the *public* mischief is the thing for the prevention of which our laws have made it a felonious offence."

The statement of the law here quoted needs a slight modification. There are crimes, chiefly statutory, which do not "include an injury," which are not "also a private wrong." For instance, the whole class of criminal attempts which are made crimes by statute(*a*) are often not "private wrongs," for the reason that they do not

---

(*a*) See *People* v. *Bush*, 4 Hill, 133. 2 New York Rev. Stat. 698, § 3.

get far enough on the road to accomplishment, to work the injury to the individual, which would result, if the attempt had final success. So, too, conspiracies, though crimes, may in some cases not be private wrongs, for the reason that they only reach the stage of combination or agreement, and do not result in the overt act, which, if accomplished, would be a "private wrong." Many acts are made crimes, merely because they are initial steps toward a final crime, which is a "private wrong."

But it is submitted, that Serjeant Stephen's statement is strictly accurate, with this modification, that is, that "every crime is also a private wrong, or is an initial step toward the accomplishment of a private wrong."

An apparent exception to this statement may be found in a class of crimes where the injury is commonly considered as an injury to the whole community, or, as the phrase is, to the public, such as injuries to the public health, or to the public morals. But in all these cases, it will be found that there is no injury to the public, unless there is an injury to the single individuals who compose the public.

Applying this part of our discussion to the crime of conspiracy, no agreement or combination of individuals can constitute a crime, unless the act contemplated by the combination, when accomplished, will be a legal injury to some individual, unless it will deprive some individual of some legal right. In other words, there can be no legal injury to the public, unless there will be a legal injury to some individual, or to some class of individuals, from the act which is the object of the agreement or combination.

Apply this to a combination to raise prices. In the absence of any statute fixing prices, or compelling individuals to sell at prices fixed, or to be fixed, no private individual has a legal right to have the owner of merchandise sell it to him at any fixed price, or at any price whatever. Under our system of law, with the constitutional provisions everywhere in force, it is submitted, that neither the legislature, nor any public official, or body of public officials, can fix the prices to be charged for either labor or merchandise in any private employment. For that would amount, in law, to a taking of private property for private use. No power in the state can take the property of one individual for the use of another individual, at any price whatever. Private property can be taken for public use, on making just compensation. But it cannot be taken for private use on any terms.

This point is so fundamental and essential, that it may be well to quote from the leading New York authority thereon, although it is hardly possible that any lawyer should here raise a question. The language of Mr. Justice Bronson in *Taylor* v. *Porter*(a) is as follows:

"I will not stop to enquire whether the damages must not be paid before the title will pass. The difficulty lies deeper than that. Whatever sum may be tendered, or however ample may be the provision for compensation, the question still remains, can the legislature compel any man to sell his land or his goods, or any interest in them, to his neighbor, when the property is not to be applied to public use? Or, must it be left to the owner to say, when, to whom, and upon what terms he will part with his property, or whether he will part with it at all?

"The right to take private property for *public* purposes is one of the inherent attributes of sovereignty, and exists in every independent government. Private interests must yield to public necessity. But even this right of eminent domain cannot be exercised without making just compensation to the owner of the property. (Const. Art. 7, § 6.) And thus, what would otherwise be a burden upon a single individual, has been made to fall equally upon every member of the state. But there is no provision in the constitution that just compensation shall be made to the owner when his property is taken for private purposes; and if the power exists to take the property of one man without his consent and transfer it to another, it may be exercised without any reference to the question of compensation. The power of making bargains for individuals has not been delegated to

---

(a) *Taylor* v. *Porter*, 4 Hill, 140, 143.

any branch of the government, and if the title of A. can, without his fault, be transferred to B., it may as well be done without as with a consideration. This view of the question is sufficient to put us upon the enquiry, where can the power be found to pass such a law as that under which the defendants attempt to justify their entry upon the plaintiff's land. It is not to be presumed that such a power exists, and those who set it up should tell where it may be found.

"Under our form of government the legislature is not supreme. It is only one of the organs of that absolute sovereignty which resides in the whole body of the people. Like other departments of the government, it can only exercise such powers as have been delegated to it; and when it steps beyond that boundary, its acts, like those of the most humble magistrate in the state who transcends his jurisdiction, are utterly void. Where, then, shall we find a delegation of power to the legislature to take the property of A. and give it to B., either with or without compensation? Only one clause of the constitution can be cited in support of the power, and that is the first section of the first article, where the people have declared that 'the legislative power of this state shall be vested in a senate and assembly.' It is readily admitted that the two houses, subject only to the qualified negative of the governor, possess all 'the legislative power of this state;' but the question immediately presents itself, what is that 'legislative power,' and how far does it extend? Does it reach the life, liberty or property of a citizen who is not charged with a transgression of the laws, and when the sacrifice is not demanded by a just regard for the public welfare? In Wilkinson v. Leland (2 Peters, 657), Mr. Justice Story says: 'The fundamental maxims of a free government seem to require that the rights of personal liberty and private property should be held sacred. At least, no court of justice in this country would be warranted in assuming that the power to violate and disregard them—a power so repugnant to the common principles of justice and civil liberty—lurked under any general grant of legislative authority or ought to be implied from any general expressions of the will of the people. The people ought not to be presumed to part with rights so vital to their security and well being, without very strong and direct expressions of such an intention.' He added: 'We know of no case in which a legislative act to transfer the property of A. to B. without his consent, has ever been held a constitutional exercise of legislative power in any state in the union. On the contrary, it has been constantly resisted as inconsistent with just principles, by every judicial tribunal in which it has been attempted to be enforced.' (See also 2 Kent's Com. 13,340, and cases there cited.) The security of life, liberty, and property, lies at the foundation of the social compact ; and to say that this grant of ' legislative power ' includes the right to attack private property, is equivalent to saying that the people have delegated to their servants the power of defeating one of the great ends for which the government was established. If there was not one word of qualification in the whole instrument, I should feel great difficulty in bringing myself to the conclusion that the clause under consideration had clothed the legislature with despotic power ; and such is the extent of their authority if they can take the property of A., either with or without compensation, and give it to B. ' The legislative power of this state ' does not reach to such an unwarrantable extent. Neither life, liberty nor property, except when forfeited by crime, or when the latter is taken for public use, falls within the scope of the power. Such, at least, are my present impressions."

The owner of property has the right to decide whether he will sell his property at all, and if he sells, to fix the price. That price he has the lawful right to fix, in any way he sees fit, on the exercise of his own will, or under a contract with other men. The right of every free citizen to restrict, by contract, his right to dispose of his own labor is beyond question. He may dispose of it for one year, or two, at one price, or another. He may contract to work at the bidding of another, for a longer or shorter term. His right of disposition is the same over all his other property—over his lands, or his merchandise. Some of his contracts the law may refuse to enforce. But none of them are crimes, unless they involve injury to the legal rights of other individuals. The old statutes were strictly logical, when they fixed the prices of different classes of merchandise, in that they also provided the remedy for the private individual, to compel sales to him at those prices. When, however, the old statutes did that, they really provided the legal machinery for taking the private property of one set of individuals for the private use of other individuals.

Unless that can lawfully be done, then a refusal by the owner of merchandise to sell at any price but his own, or a refusal to sell at any price whatever, violates no legal right of any other individual, and violates no legal right of that combination of individuals which we term the public.

Moreover, if every individual has the right to fix his own price by a separate act of his own will, he has a right to fix it by contract with other men ; and to precisely the same extent as he has the right to fix the price of his own labor by contract with other men. Every individual has the right to fix the price of his own labor by contract with other men, unless restrained by some constitutional statute. Every individual has precisely the same right to fix the price of his own merchandise by contract with other men. Concededly he has this right, under the ordinary contract of partnership. But where is it possible to draw a reasonable legal distinction, between his right to fix it under the contract of ordinary partnership, and under a contract of partial partnership, which covers only sale prices?

That this is the law as to combinations of laborers was decided by the Supreme Court of Massachusetts in the case of *Commonwealth* v. *Hunt*,(*a*) where the following language is used by Chief Justice Shaw :

" Without attempting to review and reconcile all the cases, we are of opinion, that as a general description, though perhaps not a precise and accurate definition, a conspiracy must be a combination of two or more persons, by some concerted action, to accomplish some *criminal or unlawful purpose, or* to accomplish some purpose, not in itself criminal or unlawful, by *criminal or unlawful means*. We use the terms criminal or unlawful, because it is manifest that many acts are unlawful, which are not punishable by indictment or other public prosecution ; and yet there is no doubt, we think, that a combination by members to do them would be an unlawful conspiracy, and punishable by indictment."

* * * * * * *

(*a*) *Comm.* v. *Hunt*, 4 Metc. 111.

"Stripped then of these introductory recitals and alleged injurious consequences, and of the qualifying epithets attached to the facts, the averment is this; that the defendants and others formed themselves into a society, and agreed not to work for any person, who should employ any journeyman or other person, not a member of such society, after notice given him to discharge such workman.

"The manifest intent of the association is, to induce all those engaged in the same occupation to become members of it. Such a purpose is not unlawful. It would give them a power which might be exerted for useful and honorable purposes, or for dangerous and pernicious ones. If the latter were the real and actual object, and susceptible of proof, it should have been specially charged. Such an association might be used to afford each other assistance in times of poverty, sickness and distress; or to raise their intellectual, moral and social condition; or to make improvement in their art; or for other proper purposes. Or the association might be designed for purposes of oppression and injustice. But in order to charge all those, who become members of an association, with the guilt of a criminal conspiracy, it must be averred and proved that the actual, if not the avowed object of the association, was criminal. An association may be formed, the declared objects of which are innocent and laudable, and yet they may have secret articles, or an agreement communicated only to the members, by which they are banded together for purposes injurious to the peace of society or the rights of its members. Such would undoubtedly be a criminal conspiracy, on proof of the fact, however meritorious and praiseworthy the declared objects might be. The law is not to be hoodwinked by colorable pretences. It looks at truth and reality, through whatever disguise it may assume. But to make such an association, ostensibly innocent, the subject of prosecution as a criminal conspiracy, the secret agreement, which makes it so, is to be averred and proved as the gist of the offence. But when an association is formed for purposes actually innocent, and afterward its powers are abused, by those who have the control and management of it, to purposes of oppression and injustice, it will be criminal in those who thus misuse it, or give consent thereto, but not in the other members of the association. In this case, no such secret agreement, varying the objects of the association from those avowed, is set forth in this count of the indictment.

"Nor can we perceive that the objects of this association, whatever they may have been, were to be attained by criminal means. The means which they proposed to employ, as averred in this count, and which, as we are now to presume, were established by the proof, were, that they would not work for a person, who, after due notice, should employ a journeyman not a member of their society. Supposing the object of the association to be laudable and lawful, or at least not unlawful, are these means criminal? The case supposes that these persons are not bound by contract, but free to work for whom they please, or not to work, if they so prefer. *In this state of things, we cannot perceive, that it is criminal for men to agree together to exercise their own acknowledged rights, in such a manner as best to subserve their own interests.* One way to test this is, to consider the effect of such an agreement, where the object of the association is acknowledged on all hands to be a laudable one. Suppose a class of workmen, impressed with the manifold evils of intemperance, should agree with each other not to work in a shop in which ardent spirit was furnished, or not to work in a shop with any one who used it, or not to work for an employer, who should, after notice, employ a journeyman who habitually used it. The consequences might be the same. A workman, who should still persist in the use of ardent spirit, would find it more difficult to get employment ; a master employing such an one might, at times, experience inconvenience in his work, in losing the services of a skilful but intemperate workman. Still it seems to us, that as the object would be lawful, and the means not unlawful, such an agreement could not be pronounced a criminal conspiracy.

" From this count in the indictment, we do not understand that the agreement was, that the defendants would refuse to work for an employer, to whom they were bound by contract for a certain time, in violation of that contract ; nor that they would insist that an employer should discharge a workman engaged by contract for a certain time, in violation of such contract. It is perfectly consistent with everything stated in this count, that the effect of the agreement was, that when they were free to act, they would not engage with an employer, or continue in his employment, if such employer, when free to act, should engage with a workman, or continue a workman in his employment, not a member of the association."

The same view was taken by the Royal Commission to inquire into the working of the Master and Servant Act,

1867, and of the Criminal Law Amendment Act (34 and 35 Vict., cap. 32) appointed March 19th, 1874, as shown by the following extract from its Report, quoted in Arnold's "Employers and Workmen" (p. 50):

"'(64) All that, as it appears to us, the law has to do, over and above any protection that may be required for classes unable to protect themselves, such as women and children, is to secure a fair field for the unrestricted exercise of industrial enterprise. It should recognize the right in the labourer to dispose of his labour, the capitalist of his capital, and the employer of his productive powers, in whatever manner each of them, *acting either individually or in association with others*, may deem for his own interest; and that *without reference to the question whether he is acting wisely for his own interest or advantageously to the public*, or the contrary. *The interest of the public will be best consulted by allowing each of these parties to do what he thinks best for himself without further interference of the law than may be necessary to protect the rights of others.*'"

All the definitions of the crime of conspiracy, that have ever been made by any competent authority, insist on the point, that the combination, or agreement, must be to do some act that is unlawful, either to compass an unlawful end, or to compass a lawful end by unlawful means. But at one point or another the combination, or agreement, must contemplate an act, which violates some legal right. If it is necessary to cite any further authority to this point, it is sufficient to refer to the decision of the United States Supreme Court in *Pettibone* v. *United States*,(a) where the following language is employed by Chief Justice Fuller in delivering the opinion of the Court:

"A conspiracy is sufficiently described as a combination of two or more persons by concerted action, to accomplish a criminal or unlawful purpose, or some purpose not in itself criminal or unlawful, by criminal or unlawful means."

Now, the mere raising of prices has never been held to be a violation of any legal right, except under those early statutes which have been referred to in the preceding

---

(a) 148 U. S. 203.

chapters of this work. Yet the raising of prices is the only act, which is in the contemplation of the agreement in *People* v. *Sheldon*, whether as means or end. There is nothing in the entire case, from its beginning to its end, so far as concerns the questions here under consideration, except an agreement to raise prices. The Court speaks of a "conspiracy." With all possible deference, the use of that term involves a begging of the whole question. The only "conspiracy" in the case consists in the agreement; and the only agreement is the agreement to raise prices. Unless, then, the raising of prices is a violation of the legal right of some one, there is in the case, either civilly or criminally, no element of the unlawful, either in means or end.

In a vague popular sense, it may be said, that the interests of the public require that trade and commerce be free, that therefore competition be free; and, consequently, that anything which restricts the freedom of competition restricts the freedom of trade and commerce, and therefore works an injury to the public.

In a vague popular sense, this may be true. But we are here dealing with legal rights, and legal injuries. My proposition is, that the public is deprived of no legal right, unless some individual is deprived of a legal right; that no individual is deprived of a legal right by the act of the owner of merchandise in selling on his own terms, or in refusing to sell on any terms, whether his act is the result of his own separate volition of the moment, or his volition of a former moment in making a contract with others. He has the full right under the law to do either, to exercise his volition in either one of the two ways, either by fixing his terms independently, or under a contract with other men.

But what is this so-called right of "the public," as to freedom of competition? Who is there, that has the legal right—that two sellers of merchandise shall compete? What individual has any such right? What combination of individuals has any such right? How does that combination of individuals which we term "the public" get any such right? When we speak of "rights" in these matters, we mean, of course, rights recognized by the law, well-defined legal rights, not vague general "public interests."

These positions, it will be found, bring us to a logical, reasonable, and just basis for the rule of the common law as to contracts of combination.

They will also be found to constitute the legal foundation on which rested the early English and American statutes, of which mention has here been made. Those early statutes, as has been shown, gave to individual citizens the legal right—to purchase labor, and to purchase merchandise, at specific statutory rates. To "inhance prices," therefore, raising them to a point beyond the statutory figure, violated a legal right.

If, however, no individual has the legal right to purchase at any figure other than that fixed by the will of the seller, then no individual suffers any legal wrong by any raising or maintaining of prices by the seller. That is the resulting legal situation, whatever be the figure fixed by the seller, whether it be reasonable or unreasonable. If, too, the would-be buyer suffers no legal wrong through the raising of prices by one man acting separately, he suffers none through the raising of prices by several men acting in concert. On the other hand, if the owner of labor, or of merchandise, has the legal right to sell or not to sell, at his own will, and to sell at his own price, he has the right to fix that price either separately or in concert with others.

But it will be said, that the effect on would-be buyers is different in case of the fixing of prices by several in concert, from the effect in the case of the fixing of prices separately by a single individual. Granted. The would-be buyer may be inconvenienced to a greater extent. He may be compelled to pay a higher price. But, unless he has the legal right to buy at a lower price, he suffers no legal wrong by being compelled to pay the higher price.

And mere loss, damage, or inconvenience, constitutes of itself no legal injury, whether it be caused by the act of one man separately, or by several men acting in concert.

The damage, in either case, comes only from the raising of prices. The legal injury, if there were one, would come only from the raising of prices. So that, in its legal aspect, in its capacity of working either damage or injury to any individual, there is no difference between the action of a single individual and of a combination. If the would-be buyer suffers no legal wrong from the one, he suffers none from the other.

It may be said, however, that every individual has the right, that all trade should have freedom, and that consequently he suffers a wrong, when several men combine to interfere with that freedom.

As to this, it is conceded, that some one suffers a legal wrong, when men combine to interfere with the freedom of others. But no other man suffers a legal wrong, when I simply put a bond on my own freedom. Bonds of that kind have been recognized as entirely lawful, under the English and American law, for centuries. Nothing that deserves to be called an authority can be cited to show that they have ever been held otherwise. The ordinary contract of hiring is such a bond, which interferes with a man's freedom, by preventing him for the time from joining in perfectly free competition in the field of labor. The ordinary contract of partnership is another such bond, which fetters a man's freedom, and prevents competition between the partners. There are cases without number where contracts which restrain the freedom of the parties contracting, which prevent competition between the parties contracting, have not only been held lawful, but have been affirmatively upheld by the courts, and even specifically enforced.

It is well at this point to consider some of those cases, with the legal grounds on which they have been decided. The case *Diamond Match Co.* v. *Roeber*(a) will first

---

(a) *Diamond Match Co.* v. *Roeber*, 106 N. Y. 473.

demand attention, being the most important of several recent cases in the New York Court of Appeals. That was a case in equity, wherein the plaintiff sought specific performance of a covenant by the defendant, whereby the defendant in a contract of sale to the plaintiff of the business of manufacturing and selling matches which defendant was carrying on in the State of New York, covenanted that he would not at any time thereafter within ninety-nine years engage in such manufacture or sale except in the service of the purchasing company " within any of the several states of the United States of America, or in the territories thereof, or within the District of Columbia, excepting and reserving, however, the right to manufacture and sell friction matches in the State of Nevada and the Territory of Montana." The point was raised that the covenant was void by reason of being in restraint of trade. The Court *held*, however, that the covenant was lawful, and sustained a decree for specific performance. The consideration of the law and the authorities was so full and so able, that it is advisable to quote from the opinion. The Court says:

" The defendant for his main defense relies upon the ancient doctrine of the common law first definitely declared, so far as I can discover, by Chief Justice Parker (Lord Macclesfield) in the leading case of *Mitchel* v. *Reynolds* (1 P. Williams, 181), and which has been repeated many times by judges in England and America, that a bond in general restraint of trade is *void*. There are several decisions in the English courts of an earlier date in which the question of the *validity* of contracts restraining the obligor from pursuing his occupation within a particular locality were considered. The cases are chronologically arranged and stated by Mr. Parsons in his work on Contracts (Vol. 2, p. 748, note). The earliest reported case, decided in the time of Henry V., was a suit on a bond given by the defendant, a dyer, not to use his craft within a certain city for the space of half a year. The judge before whom the case came indignantly denounced the plaintiff for procuring such a contract, and turned him out of court. This was followed by cases arising on contracts of a similar character, restraining the obligors from pursuing their trade within a certain place for a certain time, which apparently presented the same question which had been decided in the dyer's case, but the courts *sustained the contracts* and gave judgment for the plaintiffs ; and, before the case of *Mitchel* v. *Reynolds*, it had become settled that an obligation of this character, limited as to time and space, if reasonable under the circumstances and supported by a good consideration, was valid. *The case in the Year Books went against all contracts in restraint of trade, whether limited or general.* The other cases, prior to *Mitchel* v. *Reynolds, sustained contracts for a particular restraint*, upon special grounds, and by inference decided against the validity of general restraints. The case of *Mitchel* v. *Reynolds* was a case of partial restraint and the *contract was sustained*. It is worthy of notice that most, if not all, the English cases which assert the doctrine that all contracts in general restraint of trade are void, were cases where the contract before the court was limited or partial. The same is generally true of the American cases. The principal *cases in this State* are of that character, and in *all of them the particular contract before the court was sustained* (*Nobles* v. *Bates*, 7 Cow. 307 ; *Chappel* v. *Brockway*, 21 Wend. 157 ; *Dunlop* v. *Gregory*, 10 N. Y. 241). In *Alger* v. *Thacher* (19 Pick. 51), the case was one of general restraint, and the court, construing the rule as inflexible that all contracts in general restraint of trade are void, gave judgment for the defendant. In *Mitchel* v. *Reynolds* the court, in assigning the reasons for the distinction between a contract in general restraint of trade, and one limited to a particular place, says, ' for the former of these must be void, being of no benefit to either party and only oppressive : ' and later on, ' because in a great many instances they can be of no use to the obligee, which holds in all cases of general restraint throughout England, for what does it signify to a tradesman in London what another does in Newcastle, and surely it would be unreasonable to fix a certain loss on one side without any benefit to the other.' He refers to other reasons, viz. : The mischief which may arise (1) to the party, by the loss, by the obligor, of his livelihood and the subsistence of his family ; and (2), to the public, by depriving it of a useful member and by enabling corporations to gain control of the trade of the kingdom. It is quite obvious that some of these *reasons are much less forcible now than when Mitchel* v. *Reynolds was decided. Steam and electricity have, for the purpose of trade and commerce, almost annihilated distance, and the whole world is now a mart for the distribution of the products of indus-*

try. The great diffusion of wealth and the restless activity of mankind striving to better their condition, has greatly enlarged the field of human enterprise and created a vast number of new industries, which give scope to ingenuity and employment for capital and labor. The laws no longer favor the granting of exclusive privileges, and, to a great extent, business corporations are practically partnerships and may be organized by any persons who desire to unite their capital or skill in business, leaving a free field to all others who desire for the same or similar purposes to clothe themselves with a corporate character. The *tendency of recent adjudications is marked in the direction of relaxing the rigor of the doctrine that all contracts in general restraint of trade are void* irrespective of special circumstances. Indeed, it has of late been denied that a hard-and-fast rule of that kind has ever been the law of England (*Rousillon* v. *Rousillon*, 14 L. R., Ch. Div. 351). *The law has, for centuries, permitted contracts in partial restraint of trade, when reasonable;* and in *Horner* v. *Graves* (7 Bing. 735), Chief Justice Tindal considered a true test to be 'whether the restraint is such only as to afford a fair protection to the interests of the party in favor of whom it is given, and not so large as to interfere with the interests of the public.' When the restraint is general, but at the same time is co-extensive only with the interest to be protected, and with the benefit meant to be conferred, there seems to be no good reason why, as between the parties, the contract is not as reasonable as when the interest is partial and there is a corresponding partial restraint. And *is there any real public interest which necessarily condemns the one and not the other?* It is an encouragement to industry and to enterprise in building up a trade, that a man shall be allowed to sell the good will of the business and the fruits of his industry upon the best terms he can obtain. If his business extends over a continent, does public policy forbid his accompanying the sale with a stipulation for restraint co-extensive with the business which he sells? If such a contract is permitted, is the seller any more likely to become a burden on the public than a man who having built up a local trade only, sells it, binding himself not to carry it on in the locality? Are the opportunities for employment and for the exercise of useful talents so shut up and hemmed in that the public is likely to lose a useful member of society in the one case and not in the other? Indeed, *what public policy requires is often a vague and difficult inquiry. It is clear that public policy and the interests of society favor the utmost freedom of contract,* within the law, and *require* that business transactions should not be trammeled by unnecessary restrictions. 'If,' said Sir George Jessell, in *Printing Company v. Sampson* (19 Eq. Cas. L. R. 462), 'there is one thing more than any other which public policy requires, it is that men of full age and competent understanding shall have the *utmost liberty of contracting, and that contracts when entered into freely and voluntarily, shall be held good and shall be enforced by courts of justice.*' It has sometimes been suggested that the doctrine that contracts in general restraint of trade are void, is founded in part upon the policy of preventing monopolies, which are opposed to the liberty of the subject, and the granting of which by the king under claim of royal prerogative led to conflicts memorable in English history. But covenants of the character of the one now in question operate simply to prevent the covenantor from engaging in the business which he sells, so as to protect the purchaser in the enjoyment of what he has purchased. To the extent that the contract prevents the vendor from carrying on the particular trade, it deprives the community of any benefit it might derive from his entering into competition. But *the business is open to all others, and there is little danger that the public will suffer harm from lack of persons to engage in a profitable industry. Such contracts do not create monopolies. They confer no special or exclusive privilege. If contracts in general restraint of trade, where the trade is general, are void as tending to monopolies, contracts in partial restraint where the trade is local, are subject to the same objection, because they deprive the local community of the services of the covenantor in the particular trade or calling, and prevent his becoming a competitor with the covenantee.* We are not aware of any rule of law which makes the motive of the covenantee the test of the validity of such a contract. On the contrary we suppose a party may legally purchase the trade and business of another for the very purpose of preventing competition, and the validity of the contract, if supported by a consideration, will depend upon its reasonableness as between the parties. Combinations between producers to limit production and to enhance prices, are or may be unlawful, but they stand on a different footing.

* * * * * * *

" In the present state of the authorities we think it cannot be said that the early doctrine that contracts in general restraint of trade are void, without regard to circumstances, has been abrogated. But it is manifest that it has been much weakened, and that the foundation upon which it was originally placed has, to a considerable extent at least, by the change of circumstances, been removed."

It will be noted that the Court says: "The law has, for centuries, permitted contracts in partial restraint of trade, when reasonable." But in this case, in accordance with well-established principles, the Court went beyond mere permission, and carried its ruling to the point of affirmative enforcement.

This case, which was decided in 1887, was followed soon thereafter by *Leslie* v. *Lorillard*,(a) decided in October, 1888. That was the case of a stockholder seeking to enjoin and to recover payments by the corporation in which he was a member under a contract between that corporation and a second, the contract and the payments thereunder being made to prevent competition between the two contracting parties in the traffic between the City of New York and certain ports in the State of Virginia. One of the grounds on which the injunction and the recovery were sought was that the contract was against public policy, and therefore illegal, as being "prejudicial to some public interest." Here, too, the reasoning of the Court is so sound as to make it desirable to give the following extract from the opinion :(b)

"Testing by these rules the case made by plaintiff in his complaint, we find, in considering that pleading, that the only respect in which the contracts in question could be viewed as prejudicial to public interests, and, therefore, become the subject of judicial condemnation, as being against public policy, would be that they were in restraint of competition and tended to create a monopoly. The tendency of modern thought and of the decisions, however, has been no longer to uphold in its strictness the doctrine which formerly prevailed in respect of agreements in restraint of trade. The severity with which such agreements were at first treated became more and more relaxed by exceptions and qualifications. This change was gradual, and may be considered, perhaps, as due mainly to the growth and spread of the industrial activities of the world, and to enlarged

---

(a) *Leslie* v. *Lorillard*, 110 N. Y. 519.   (b) *Ibid.*, 532.

commercial facilities, which render such agreements less dangerous as tending to create monopolies. The earlier doctrine, of course, obtained in respect of agreements between individuals. The limitation which became imposed was, that the agreement should operate as to a locality and not as to the whole land. In later times the danger in such agreements seems only really to exist when corporations are parties to them, for their means and strength would better enable them to buy off rivalry and to create monopolies.

"The object of government, as interpreted by the judges, was not to interfere with the free right of man to dispose of his property or of his labor ; it was to guard society, of which he was a member, from the injurious consequences of his agreement ; whether they would arise from his own improvidence in bargaining away his means of gaining a livelihood, or in the deprivation to society of the advantages of competition in skilled labor. At the present day there is not that danger, or at least it does not seem to exist to an appreciable extent, except, possibly, as suggested in the case of corporations. In their supervision and in their restriction within the limits of their chartered powers, the government and the public are directly interested. Corporations are great engines for the promotion of the public convenience, and for the development of public wealth, and, so long as they are conducted for the purposes for which organized, they are a public benefit ; but if allowed to engage, without supervision, in subjects of enterprise foreign to their charters, or if permitted unrestrainedly to control and monopolize the avenues to that industry in which they are engaged, they become a public menace ; against which public policy and statutes design protection.

"When, therefore, the provisions of agreements in restraint of competition tend beyond measures for self protection and threaten the public good in a distinctly appreciable manner, they should not be sustained. The apprehension of danger to the public interests, however, should rest on evident grounds, and courts should refrain from the exercise of their equitable powers in interfering with and restraining the conduct of the affairs of individuals or of corporations, unless their conduct, in some tangible form, threatens the welfare of the public. The doctrine relating to contracts in restraint of trade has been elaborately discussed in a careful opinion of Andrews, J., in the recent case of the *Diamond Match Company* v. *Roeber* (106 N. Y. 473). Under the authority of that case, it may be said that no contracts are void as being in general restraint of trade, where they operate simply to prevent a party from engaging or competing in the same business. It is there said (p. 483) : ' To the extent that the contract prevents the vendor from carrying on the particular trade, it deprives the community of any benefit it might derive from his entering into competition. But the business is open to all others and there is little danger that the public will suffer harm from lack of persons to engage in a profitable industry. Such contracts do not create monopolies. They confer no special or exclusive privileges.'

"Under the doctrine of that case, it is difficult to see how the contracts, which are complained of here, are open to the objection suggested by counsel. Regarded only in the light of what they tended to effect, these agreements removed a business rival, whose competition may have been deemed dangerous to the success or maintenance of the business of the Old Dominion Company. They could not, of course, exclude all competition in the business, but would in that particular case.

"How, then, is the result different from the simpler case of the sale by an individual of his business and his right to conduct it in a particular part of the land? The doctrine held by this Court in *Diamond Match Company* v. *Roeber* (*supra*) should control in the case at bar, and these contracts, therefore, cannot be considered objectionable on the ground that they restrained competition. Whether competition in this particular business would be a public benefaction, or its restraint a source of prejudice, we are unable, of course, to judge. I do not think that competition is invariably a public benefaction; for it may be carried on to such a degree as to become a general evil."

Next came *Tode* v. *Gross*,(a) which upheld an agreement which bound the defendant not to engage in the business of manufacturing a certain kind of cheeses, without limitation as to time or place, and allowed the recovery of five thousand dollars as liquidated damages for its breach. The Court cited the cases just mentioned with the remark, " Recent cases make it very clear that such an agreement is *not opposed to public policy*, even if the restriction was unlimited as to both time and territory."

In *Matthews* v. *Associated Press of the State of New*

(a) *Tode* v. *Gross*, 127 N. Y. 480.

York, (a) a by-law prohibiting members of the defendant, a news association, from receiving or publishing "the regular news despatches of any other news association covering a like territory and organized for a like purpose" was held to be lawful; and the Court said :

"The latest decisions of courts in this country and in England show a strong *tendency to very greatly circumscribe and narrow the doctrine of avoiding contracts in restraint of trade*. The courts do not go to the length of saying that contracts which they now would say are in restraint of trade are, nevertheless, valid contracts, and to be enforced; they do, however, now hold many contracts not open to the objection that they are in restraint of trade which a few years back would have been avoided on that sole ground, both here and in England. The cases in this court which are the latest manifestations of the *turn in the tide* are cited in the opinion in this case at General Term, and are *Diamond Match Co.* v. *Roeber* (106 N. Y. 473); *Hodge* v. *Neill* (107 *id.* 244); *Leslie* v. *Lorillard* (110 *id.* 519).

"So that when we agree that a by-law which is in restraint of trade is void, we are still brought back to the question what is a restraint of trade in the modern definition of that term? The authority to make by-laws must also be limited by the scope and purpose of the association. I think this by-law is thus limited and that it is not in restraint of trade as the courts now interpret that phrase. Some of the grounds showing the reasonableness of the by-laws are well and clearly set forth in the opinion delivered by the learned judge at the General Term. Here are a number of persons who are owners of or interested in various newspapers in the State outside of the city of New York. They enter into business relations with each other, to a certain extent, through the form of an organization known as a corporation, and for the purpose, among others, of collecting and supplying themselves with telegraphic news. The greater the number belonging to the organization the larger will be its income and the greater amount it will be able to spend for making the collection of news and the more efficient and valuable such collection will be. *To suppress competition in such chosen field among themselves and to thus enhance the value of the property and the conveniences arising from the extended use of the means and opportunities of the*

(a) *Matthews* v. *Associated Press of the State of New York*, 136 N. Y. 333, 340.

association, it would seem most appropriate to provide that the members of such association should not take news from any other. The division of the business among two or more associations tends directly toward the making of the membership in each less valuable than it otherwise would be, and the membership being less valuable the association itself would tend to decrease in members and to grow less efficient in service and less capable of fulfilling promptly one of the great objects of its existence, the procuring and supplying of news to its members. Thus a by-law of the nature complained of would have a tendency to strengthen the association and to render it more capable of filling the duty it was incorporated to perform. A business partnership could provide that none of its members should attend to any business other than that of the partnership, and that each partner who came in must agree not to do any other business, and must give up all such business as he had theretofore done. Such an agreement would not be in restraint of trade, although its direct effect might be to restrain to some extent the trade which had been done.

" It seems to me this by-law is a natural and reasonable restraint upon the members of the association, appropriately regulating their conduct as members thereof with respect to the business which the association was specially organized and incorporated to transact. Its success must greatly depend upon the number of its members, and that in its turn must depend upon the efficiency, reliability, and promptness with which it collects and distributes its news.

" This by-law, I think, plainly tends to aid the association in the accomplishment of this object."

These decisions all get additional light from the course taken by the Court of Appeals in the case *People* v. *North River Sugar Refining Company.*(a) That was an action to dissolve the defendant corporation for an abuse and disuse of its corporate powers, such abuse and disuse consisting in a consolidation of the defendant with other corporations, for the purpose of placing their properties and businesses under one common management, with a view to the prevention of competition, and the acquiring of complete control in the United States of the business of refining sugar. The Court below had affirmed a judg-

---

(a) *People* v. *North River Sugar Refining Company*, 121 N. Y. 582.

ment of dissolution. That affirmance was rested on the ground, among others, that the consolidation in question was a combination

"for an unlawful purpose, detrimental and injurious to the public; instead of manufacturing its product and disposing of it to the public on what might be fair competitive prices, it had become a party to a combination, in part, at least, designed to create a monopoly, and exact from the public prices which could not otherwise be obtained."(*a*)

In another passage of the opinion the Court said, that "the agreement, association, combination or arrangement, or whatever else it may be called, having for its object the removal of competition and the advancement of prices of necessaries of life, is subject to the condemnation of the law, by which it is denounced as a criminal enterprise. The law at this time, as it has for many years in this State, has made it a misdemeanor for two or more persons to conspire ' to commit any act injurious to the public health, to public morals, or to trade or commerce, or for the perversion or obstruction of justice, or of the due administration of the law. ' "(*b*)

The Court of Appeals, however, avoided an approval of this position, and rested its affirmance of the judgment on the ground that the surrender by the corporation, its stockholders and officers, of the control of the corporate property and business constituted a violation of its charter, and a failure in the performance of its corporate duties; and that such violation and failure justified a judgment of dissolution. At that time, the Court had apparently not reached the view of the law laid down in *People* v. *Sheldon*.

Most significant, too, is some of the language of the Court in the still later case of *Lough* v. *Outerbridge*,(*c*) where the contention of the plaintiff was that the defendants, the owners of a line of steamships, had been guilty of an unreasonable discrimination in rates against the plaintiffs, with a view to preventing the plaintiffs from shipping by another line. The Court used this language :(*d*)

(*a*) *People* v. *North River Sugar Refining Company*, 54 Hun, 354, 386.
(*b*) *Ibid.*, p. 380.
(*c*) *Lough* v. *Outerbridge*, 143 N. Y. 271.   (*d*) P. 282.

"The significance which the learned counsel for the plaintiffs seems to give to it in his argument is that it conclusively shows the purpose of the defendants to compel the plaintiffs to withdraw their patronage from the other line, to *suppress competition in the s' ness*, and *to retain a monopoly for their own benefit*. Conceding that such was the *purpose*, it is not apparent how any *obligation that the defendants owed to the public was disregarded.*"

Thereupon the Court cites with approval the *Mogul Steamship* case, and quotes from its opinion.

As a question of legal principle, how is it possible to reconcile the decision in *People* v. *Sheldon*, even with its limitation as to articles "of prime necessity," with the long line of authorities in which, as has been shown, our courts have not only upheld, but have enforced, contracts "in restraint of trade"? The Court of Appeals, on its equity side, in suits between the parties, enforces contracts in restraint of trade, of which almost the only purpose is the prevention of competition, while on its criminal side it indicts and punishes those same parties for making the contracts which it enforces.

In the multiplicity of cases which are presented before our courts of highest jurisdiction it is an impossibility that every case should receive the full degree of consideration which is its due. Counsel sometimes fail in making a full presentation of the legal principles on which a case should be decided. And the Courts, it must be conceded, do in some instances make oversights and errors.

It is most respectfully submitted, that the case of *People* v. *Sheldon* is the case of such an oversight and error.

We come next to the consideration of the case in the United States Supreme Court.(*a*)

In its most important aspect, this case decides the same point with *People* v. *Sheldon*, that is, that a mere contract, providing for the fixing by one common authority of the rates to be charged by the contracting parties, of itself constitutes a crime.

(*a*) *The United States* v. *The Trans-Missouri Freight Association*, 166 U. S. 290.

Bearing in mind the primary distinction heretofore made, and here throughout maintained, between public and private employments, bearing also in mind the unquestioned power of Congress to regulate interstate commerce, and its unquestioned lack of power to make laws as to trade and commerce in their mere ordinary relations to individuals and the State, let us first examine the two acts of Congress considered by the Supreme Court in its opinion in the Freight Association Case. The following summaries will suffice to present the features of those acts which bear upon the present discussion:

The *Inter-State Commerce Act*(a) begins by defining the application of its provisions " to any common carrier or carriers engaged in the transportation of passengers or property wholly by railroad or partly by railroad and partly by water when both are used under a common control, management, or arrangement for a continuous carriage" from one State to another or from or to any place in the United States to or from or through any foreign country; the Act next defines the term "railroad," and then provides that "All charges made for any service rendered or to be rendered in the transportation of passengers or property as aforesaid, or in connection therewith, . . . shall be reasonable and just; and every unjust and unreasonable charge for such service is prohibited and declared to be unlawful." Section 2 prohibits the making of special rates and rebates to particular shippers. Section 3 prohibits the giving of undue preference or advantage to particular persons or localities, and requires equal facilities to be given to connecting lines without discrimination of rates.

Section 4 is the "long and short haul" clause. Section 5 prohibits pooling agreements or combinations of competing lines to divide earnings, and provides a penalty for the maintaining of such agreements.

(a) Laws of 1887, ch. 104 ; 24 U. S. Stat. at Large, 379.

Section 6 requires carriers to post schedules of their freight and passenger rates, and provides for a notice of ten days before any advance in such rates ; it also requires the filing of copies of such schedules with the commissioners appointed by the Act, defines the powers of the commissioners with respect to the same, and provides remedies by mandamus, contempt proceedings, and injunction for a failure to comply with such requirements.

Section 7 makes it unlawful for carriers by combination or agreement to prevent continuous carriage of freights.

Section 8 makes carriers liable for damages to persons injured by a violation of any of the clauses of the Act.

Section 9 provides for complaints to the commission or, in the alternative, suits for the recovery of damages, by persons injured.

Section 10 makes violations of the Act misdemeanors and prescribes a penalty.

Sections 11–21 provide for the creation of the commission and define its powers, duties, and procedure.

Section 22 makes certain exceptions to the "discrimination" and "undue preference" provisions of the Act, and continues existing common law and statute remedies.

The Act of July 2d, 1890, entitled " *An act to protect trade and commerce against unlawful restraints and monopolies*"(a) provided that :

" § 1. Every contract, combination in the form of trust or otherwise, or conspiracy, in restraint of trade or commerce among the several States or with foreign nations, is hereby declared to be illegal." Engaging in such a combination is to be deemed a misdemeanor and punishable by fine or imprisonment.

" § 2. Every person who shall monopolize, or attempt to monopolize, or combine or conspire with any other person or persons, to monopolize any part of the trade or commerce among the several States or with foreign na-

---

(a) 26 U. S. Stat. at Large 209, chap. 647.

tions, shall be deemed guilty of a misdemeanor," and shall be punished by fine or imprisonment.

§ 3 prohibited under like penalties contracts in restraint of trade in any Territory.

§§ 4 and 5 conferred jurisdiction on the circuit courts in the cases covered by the Act and regulated the procedure.

§ 6 provided that "any property owned under any contract or by any combination, or pursuant to any conspiracy (and being the subject thereof) mentioned in section one of this Act, and being in the course of transportation from one State to another" shall be forfeited to the United States.

§ 7 gives a right of action to any person injured in his business or property by any other person by reason of anything forbidden by the Act.

Here then are two statutes on their face relating to two quite distinct subjects—one to common carriers, the other to the trade relations of ordinary individuals.

As to the Interstate Commerce Act, it would seem evident from its general scope, and all its provisions, that the intention of Congress was to comprise in that act, with any subsequent amendments that might be made thereto, the entire body of the regulations, which it intended to make as to common carriers, and their performance of their duties to the public—especially in the matter of rates and charges. No lawyer will question the power of Congress to regulate the rates to be charged by railroad companies engaged in interstate commerce.

But in what act, or series of acts, would such regulations be found?

Manifestly such regulations properly belong, and would naturally be looked for, in the general act of Congress governing the specific subject of Interstate Commerce. It was found, however, that, while that Act did, as we have seen, expressly (1) require that rates shall be reasonable and provide machinery for the enforcement of that requirement, and (2) prohibit the making of agreements for the "pooling" of charges between competing carriers, it did not in terms or impliedly prohibit the making of agreements for the fixing of rates, whether reasonable or unreasonable.

On the other hand, the Trust Act did not in terms refer to the business of carriers in any shape or connection. By its terms it purported to deal with "trusts," "monopolies," and "conspiracies in restraint of trade." Against those particular objects of its reprobation the provisions of the Act were strong and comprehensive. Not content with dealing in general terms with "trusts" and "conspiracies" in restraint of trade, it actually made a criminal of "*every person* who shall monopolize or *attempt to monopolize* . . . *any part* of the trade or commerce among the several States or with foreign nations." On reflection, it is difficult to imagine a merchant above the grade of a retail dealer who is not within the condemnation of this language of the statute.

The Supreme Court had held, however, in the case, *United States* v. *E. C. Knight Company*,(a) that this statute applied to monopolies in restraint of interstate or international trade or commerce, and not to monopolies in the *manufacture* even of a necessary of life; that the intent to manufacture or export a manufactured article to foreign nations or to send it to another State did not determine the time when the article or product passed from the control of the State and belonged to commerce; and that, accordingly, the Act did not apply to a company engaged in one State in the refining of sugar under the circumstances detailed in that case, because the refining of sugar under those circumstances bore no distinct relation to commerce between the States or with foreign nations.

Such is the statement of the doctrine of that case given by Mr. Justice Peckham in the course of his opinion in the *U. S.* v. *Trans-Missouri Freight Association*. The

---

(a) 156 U. S. 1.

following extracts from the opinion of Mr. Chief Justice
Fuller will serve to make the position still more clear,
besides throwing some light on the general subject under
discussion :

"The fundamental question is whether, conceding that the existence of a monopoly in manufacture is established by the evidence, that monopoly can be directly suppressed under the Act of Congress in the mode attempted by this bill. . . . The argument is that the power to control the manufacture of refined sugar is a monopoly over a necessary of life, to the enjoyment of which by a large population of the United States interstate commerce is indispensable, and that therefore the general government in the exercise of the power to regulate commerce may repress such monopoly directly and set aside the instruments which have created it. But this argument cannot be confined to the necessaries of life merely, and must include all articles of general consumption.

*   *   *   *   *   *   *

"It was in the light of well-settled principles that the Act of July 2, 1890, was framed. Congress did not attempt thereby to assert the power to deal with monopoly directly *as such ;* or to limit and restrict the rights of corporations created by the states or the citizens of the states, in the acquisition, control, or disposition of property ; or to regulate or prescribe the price or prices at which such property or the products thereof should be sold ; or to make criminal the acts of persons in the acquisition and control of property which the states of their residence or creation sanctioned or permitted. Aside from the provisions applicable where Congress might exercise municipal power, what the law struck at was combinations, contracts, and conspiracies to monopolize trade and commerce among the several states or with foreign nations ; but the contracts and acts of the defendants related exclusively to the acquisition of the Philadelphia refineries and the business of sugar refining in Pennsylvania, and bore no direct relation to commerce between the states or with foreign nations. The object was manifestly private gain in the manufacture of the commodity, but not through the control of interstate or foreign commerce. It is true that the bill alleged that the products of these refineries were sold and distributed among the several states, and that all the companies were engaged in trade or commerce with the several states and with foreign nations ; but this was no more than to say that trade and commerce served manufacture to fulfil its function. Sugar was refined for sale, and sales were probably made at Philadelphia for consumption, and undoubtedly for resale by the first purchasers throughout Pennsylvania and other states, and refined sugar was also forwarded by the companies to other states for sale. Nevertheless it does not follow that an attempt to monopolize, or the actual monopoly of, the manufacture was an attempt, whether executory or consummate, to monopolize commerce, even though, in order to dispose of the product, the instrumentality of commerce was necessarily invoked."

Having thus rendered nugatory the provisions of the Act, for most of the purposes obviously within its scope, the court held, when the *Freight Association* case came before it, that the statute did apply to agreements by common carriers of the nature of the agreement there before it. As said by *Peckham, J.*, in the opinion of the court :(*a*)

"To exclude such agreements would leave little for the act to take effect upon."

It was urged against the applicability of the Act, that such a construction involved a repeal by implication of the provisions of the Interstate Commerce Act. But in answer to this argument the learned Justice pointed out that the Interstate Commerce Act contained no provision either authorizing or prohibiting such agreements, and held, therefore, that there was no case of repeal by implication and no inconsistency between the two statutes. It is most respectfully submitted that in reaching this conclusion the court lost sight of the undisputed legal position that such an agreement needs no statutory authority to make it lawful. In the absence of a statute expressly prohibiting it, it is lawful and always has been lawful. Consequently when the Interstate Commerce Act, though prohibiting certain acts and agreements of a kindred nature, yet left untouched the common-law right of the carrier to enter into an agreement for the fixing of reasonable rates for its services, it did in so far expressly

---

(*a*) 166 U. S. p. 313.

continue the authority for the making of such agreements.

The decision, however, was otherwise. By construction based upon previous decisions under other acts, it was further held that the terms "trade and commerce" in the Trust Act included the business of transportation by common carriers between the States.

It is now apparent that in the view of the case taken by the Supreme Court the validity of the agreement was not necessarily affected by the circumstance that the contracting parties were common carriers; except in so far as their business of interstate carriage brought them within the scope of the term "trade and commerce between the states." The decision was not rested upon the conceded right of government to control public employments. A similar agreement for the fixing of prices between parties engaged in any other business, public or private, would have fallen under the condemnation of the Court, provided the business were within the description of interstate commerce.

In this aspect, the decision of the court is covered, it is respectfully submitted, by the line of historical statement, and legal argument which is the main burden of this treatise. It is as a mere "contract or combination in restraint of trade" that the agreement in question was treated by the court. As a violation of the legal obligation of a common carrier to charge only rates that were reasonable, there might of course have been a ground for criminal jurisdiction. If, on the other hand, either of the combining companies had charged rates above those fixed under the authority of the Interstate Commerce Commission, then their action would have had another criminal aspect. But it was conceded on the record, that the rates charged had been reasonable. And it was not contended that there had been any violation of the act regulating interstate commerce.

The case therefore resolves itself into one where the mere act of combining—not to accomplish any unlawful purpose, or to use any unlawful means for the accomplishment of a lawful purpose—was held criminal, under a statute not expressly prohibiting the particular act in question, and not in terms referring to the particular parties or class of parties proceeded against. So regarded, it is submitted that the considerations urged against the case *People* v. *Sheldon* apply with at least equal force here.

Each of these two cases holds that a mere contract, to fix rates or prices of the property of the parties contracting, which interferes in no respect with the freedom of action of all the rest of the world beside, which therefore violates no legal right of any member of the entire community, constitutes a crime.

It is most respectfully submitted, that therein these cases are irreconcilably in conflict with the fundamental principles of the English and American law, as established by a long line of authorities, the soundness of which has never been called in question.

CHAPTER VI.

SOME GENERAL CONSIDERATIONS.

This discussion on these questions of law really involves a question of economics. That question is this: Do these combinations, formed to prevent competition among the combining parties, or to raise prices, work any substantial damage to " the public" ?

To this question the answer is to be found in the facts of history.

The answer is, that the experience of both the English and American peoples, an experience long and exhaustive, shows that such combinations work no substantial damage to any but the parties combining. Such combinations have been known in England for centuries. They have existed in this country ever since the operations of trade and commerce acquired large proportions. No instance can be cited, where such a combination has been able to raise or maintain prices, of either labor or merchandise, above a reasonable figure, for any considerable time. That is the real reason, why those early statutes were not enforced, why there is an almost entire absence in the English reports of prosecutions for their violation. No one was seriously damaged. No one had any sense of injury. Such combinations have been formed without number in the history of English and American trade, to raise and maintain the prices of all the necessaries of life, of wheat, corn, lard, pork, coal, of substantially all the staples of commerce. No such combination has ever had any substantial result, other than to make a slight rise in prices, in some local market, for a very short time. The only substantial result, to others than the parties combining, has been the wreck of a few speculators. These combinations to raise prices have been made, not only in the staples of commerce, of which the supply, especially in these modern times, is always large and unknown, but in stocks and securities, of which the supply is limited and exactly ascertainable. The result has been invariably the same, in cases of both classes; only a temporary "flurry in the market." The reason is not hard to find. The combinations always come to an end from their own inherent necessities. The advance of prices is only their primary purpose; their ultimate purpose is the making of sales at the prices so advanced. If the prices are advanced too high, sales cease, and prices soon fall to a figure that is warranted by the existing supply and demand. The unfailing protection of the community at large is always to be found in the interest account. Large amounts of merchandise cannot be carried without large amounts of money, involving in one form or another the payment of large amounts of interest. Meantime, in the case of all staples, all "articles of prime necessity," the streams of supply continue to pour in. Sooner or later, and always soon, the growth of the interest account, with the impending danger of a falling market, compels sales; and the sales, when made, must be made at prices which buyers are willing to pay. If the combinations are small, then it is easy to buy from other sellers. If the combinations are large, then it is a virtual certainty, that some of the combining parties will soon break away from the combination, or prices will be the sooner reduced by the increase in the interest account.

Many men in modern times have been alarmed by the mere magnitude of the masses of capital employed in the great modern so-called "trusts." But this alarm has no sound foundation. It is in that very magnitude, that "the public," and every individual member of it, has the surest protection. The reason is, that where capital is invested in special industries in such large masses, the magnitude of the investments, and of the expenditures, with the necessity of paying interest and dividends, compels the investors to put prices down to figures which will bring buyers, and bring them quickly. Moreover, the investment of large amounts of capital in single enterprises invariably leads to large economies. The reason is, that the amount of waste reaches larger figures, and therefore makes a larger impression on the minds of managers. In addition to that fact, the larger the number of men there are employed in a single business, the greater is the certainty that some of them will find new materials, and devise new processes, to be used in that business. The uniform experience, therefore, has been that the modern methods, of consolidation, and concentration of large masses of capital in single industries, have caused large decreases in price, and have thus prevented the very results which have so long been dreaded as likely to be their outcome.

But we get still more light on this branch of our examination from the course of prices in the instances of genuine "monopolies," which exist in large numbers under our law, and are fostered by it. Every patent is a "monopoly." Every author's copyright is a "monopoly." Every railroad company has, to a certain extent, a "monopoly"—that is, it has a property which is sole and exclusive, and is made such by law. In all these cases it has invariably proved an impossibility in practice, for the owners of patents to keep up the prices of their patented articles, or for the owners of copyrights to keep up the prices of their books, above what is reasonable, in other words, above what buyers are willing to pay. If a buyer is not willing to pay the price of the seller, he simply declines to buy. He buys something else. Or he goes without. In that course the buyer has always found adequate protection. Suppose that some individual today had a strict legal "monopoly" in wheat, and then made the attempt to raise the price of wheat unduly. The immediate result would be that people would use other kinds of food. To "corner" wheat successfully, a man must be able to "corner" corn, rye, rice, oatmeal, peas and beans, with other kinds of food products too numerous to mention. He might as well try to "corner" the ocean. Every article of trade and commerce, staple or other, has to compete with many other articles, which, though not precisely identical, can be made to serve substantially the same uses. In this way, even railroads, in effect, compete with other railroads, although their control of their own traffic seems at first sight to be without limitation. Take the case of any railroad leading into one of our large cities. In effect, it has to compete with other roads which tap other territory. If its rates are higher than those of other roads, for passengers or merchandise, people will move away and live on other lines. Aside from that, however, every owner of a railroad, of a patent, of a book, or of property of any kind, finds that he makes more money by putting prices down to figures that are reasonable, that is, to figures which correspond to the values of the things sold to the buyers, than by keeping them up beyond those figures.

Prices must be left to that kind of regulation. They need no other. No other can be just. All attempts to regulate prices by the arm of the law, directly or indirectly, by direct legislation, or by criminal indictment, have resulted in failure. Experience shows, that there is no way practicable for the right fixing of prices, except by competition of one kind, that is, competition between buyers and sellers. That kind of competition will always exist, and will always be found effectual to fix prices at figures which are reasonable, and therefore just. That is all that we have the right to ask. It is all that we can get.

Many economists, and many jurists and legislators, in their consideration of these questions, have had an especial fear of the large modern combinations of capital in the hands of corporations. Corporations, in this respect, have seemed more dangerous than individuals. This is a point which calls for some attention.

SOME GENERAL CONSIDERATIONS. 183

In my opinion, this is an unsound position. On the contrary, it will appear, that the interests of the community, and especially of that portion of the community which some men term the laboring classes, will be best served by giving the largest possible facilities for the formation of corporations, and by ensuring the fullest degree of freedom and protection to their property and business. The well being of the laborer, and most of us are laborers, depends especially on a combination of three conditions: they are, large variety of employment, high and stable rates of wages, low and stable prices of all kinds of merchandise which he needs to use. These three conditions can be obtained, only by giving every facility, and every protection, to the employment of capital in large masses, under continuous and stable management. Such employment of large masses of capital can be had only through the agency of large corporations. By such agencies, in the main, has come the great reduction in the prices of nearly all manufactured products, including articles of food, which has been the distinguishing feature in the history of modern industry. This decrease in the prices of manufactured products has at the same time been accompanied by a decrease in the profits of capital, and an increase in the rates of wages. These results, it is evident, can be had only under modern methods, by the employment of large masses of capital, under continuous management, which will ensure large business experience in the men at the head, with a continuous steady supply of new men in each separate department, to take the places of old men as they die and retire. It is evident, too, that these large businesses, under stable control, such as is possible only in large and rich corporations, furnish the best practicable security that every workman will be able to find his own level, with steady employment at stable wages fitted to the quality of his work. At times we hear laments over the disappearance of the independent individual proprietor, resulting from the increase in the number of these large corporate industries. These laments lose sight of the fact, that comparatively few men have the soundness of judgment, and the business capacity, which fits them to be independent employers. It is not an advantage, either to the individual or to " the public," that the individual should waste his energies in work of independent superintendence, when he is unfit for such work. The large majority of men in the great armies of industry are fit only for the positions of subordinates. It is for the advantage of no one, that time and money should be wasted in their fruitless efforts to fill the places of superiors. Let them fall into the ranks, or into positions of subordinate leadership, into the places which they are fit to fill. The interests of all are best served by having our industrial armies led by the natural leaders, who are sure to find the places at the head, if they have an open field—and time. These conditions are to be had only when industries are organized on a large scale, and under conditions of permanence. That is a possibility only by the agency of large and rich corporations.

But some men look at capital in the large modern community as a separate single mass, under a separate single control, handled in a sole interest antagonistic to the interests of the community in general, and especially of the laboring classes. That is an error. Capital never has been under one control, and it never can be. To-day it is more impossible than ever before, by reason of its magnitude. The ownership of capital is, and always must be, diverse. Its interests are diverse. Between all those diverse interests there is never-ending competition. That cannot be avoided, or prevented. Any consolidation, of its interests, or of its control in single hands, is an economic impossibility.

The increase in the size of the modern masses of capital is only in keeping with the increase in wealth throughout the entire community. These masses of capital have the same increase in all directions. Even if this increase were confined to a single industry, there would be no solid danger therefrom. For any attempt on its part to secure undue advantages would at once arouse a combination of other industries and other financial interests in self-defence against its aggressions. But, as matter of fact, the increase of masses of capital takes place in industries of all kinds, and thereby insures the diversity of interests which constitutes the protection of the community against the possible encroachments of any one.

If it be said, that the increase of these masses of capital constitutes a menace to labor, the answer is that labor can, and does, consolidate, and concentrate, as well as capital. Thus far consolidated labor has had decidedly the best of the contest between the two. And there seems no reason to apprehend any different result in the future. Since the great increase in the quantity of machinery used in modern industries, an increase which it was at first supposed would displace labor, and thereby decrease wages, the actual result has been an increase in wages, and a decrease in the rates of interest. At the same time there has been a remarkable increase in the quantity and quality of the articles which the laborer can procure with his wages. No doubt, there has been an increase in the number, and the size, of the great fortunes. But at the same time there has been a great increase in the rates of wages of the industrial classes, and a great improvement in their general condition. Experience shows that, in its contest with capital, labor is well able to take care of itself. We need have no fears for its future.

Whichever way we consider it, we shall find, that the immense increase in the modern masses of capital is only comparative—that it is not out of proportion with the growth of society, and of its means for keeping capital in its proper position of involuntary servitude. Capital must be employed ; else it is fruitless. It must employ labor ; else it has no employment for itself. Labor can get on without capital better than capital can get on without labor. Each must use the other. Neither will, in the long run, get more than its just dues. Each can well take care of itself. Each is fully protected by the industrial laws.

It is time that these large combinations of capital, these great agencies of modern civilization, should be looked at in their true light. It is always to be assumed, that their owners will handle their large properties with a view to their own interests, and their own profit ; that their management will be selfish. But the inevitable and inexorable laws of trade and commerce compel the owners of capital, whether they will it or not, to be public servants. Take the case of any of our most powerful and prosperous railroads. They are all managed on selfish business principles, with a view to the profit of their owners. Yet they are compelled, whether they will it or not, to be great public charities. The reason is, that the successful management of such great properties imperatively demands the employment of large armies of men who are honest, capable, and industrious. Such men command employment, at good wages, at all times and places. These great railroad companies cannot get such men, unless they pay them well. Moreover, their employees must be men of experience, each one used to his own work, and all used to working together. In other words, these employees must be kept in the service permanently. So that the practical result is, that these great corporations are compelled, whether they wish it or not, to give permanent employment, at reasonable wages, to honest and industrious men. They become public charities, of the best kind. So it is with all large industries.

But these large masses of capital can be had, and used to the best effect, only if capital is secure. Capital is proverbially timid. Give it security, throw around it every protection possible under the law, and we shall draw it in large amounts, adequate to our largest needs, from all quarters of the globe. Thereby the laborer will secure the fullest variety of employment. Bring it here in the largest masses possible. Give it the fullest liberty possible. In that way alone can we secure the amplest supply of it for the prosecution of every form of industry that man can make profitable. Labor will thereby secure its fullest possibilities of a diversity of profitable employment. But those conditions can be secured only through the agency of large rich corporations. The more there are of them, the more keen will be the competition of capital for the highest grades of labor.

It is, therefore, unnecessary, to make the attempt by statutes or by any provisions of the civil or criminal law, to protect the public against the raising of prices by large combinations of capitalists. The protection against such efforts is to be found in the natural laws of trade and commerce. That protection has always been found adequate.

But if such protection were not adequate, the history of the attempts to get it from statutes, and from the criminal law, shows that it is not to be found in that direction. Those attempts have uniformly had one result—failure. They have also had another result, the annoyance of that portion of the community who honestly try to obey the law. Moreover they are directly in opposition to the tendencies of modern industrial development. Those tendencies are in the line of consolidation, concentration, and organization. In a less degree, those tendencies were apparent in the mediæval guilds. But at the present day the growth of trades unions, of exchanges, and industrial associations of all kinds, for the protection of the interests of their members is more marked than ever before. It is one of the ordinary features of such organizations to have regulations of the rates and wages of their members.

Now, in principle, where is there any reasonable legal basis for a distinction between the right of the sellers of labor to agree on the price of their own labor, and the right of the sellers of merchandise to agree on the price of their own merchandise? None can be given. The seller of one has the same legal rights with the seller of the other, no greater and no less. So it was under the

English common law. So it was under the English statutes. So it was under our law, it is respectfully submitted, until the decision in *People* v. *Sheldon*, followed by the decision in the *Freight Association* case, with others in the same line.

Our law duly recognizes, in manifold ways, the obligation resting on the State to make adequate provision for the poor and needy who are unable to help themselves, in the matter of food, clothing, and shelter. In the discharge of that obligation, the State is bound to purchase many "articles of prime necessity." But it has not the right, to compel a sale of such articles, by their owners, to persons who may need them, either directly or indirectly, by statute or indictment. For the due discharge of that obligation, the State, in times of stress, may find it necessary to take private property for public use. There might easily arise instances, in a time of war, in the midst of actual military operations, when a military commander would find himself compelled to supply the population of a city, or of a district, with food, and would be compelled, in order to do so, to seize large quantities of food supplies. But our law recognizes no right vested in the State, in the discharge of its ordinary legal obligations, to transfer the property of one person to another. Yet that is what it really assumes to do, as shown in *Taylor* v. *Porter*, when it undertakes to fix prices by statute. That is, too, what it really tries to do—indirectly—when it attempts to keep down prices by indictment.

Let us now consider the positions which we have reached.

Certain propositions, it is submitted, are well established.

I. The only possible loss, or damage, to any individual, or to that combination of individuals which we term the community, resulting from combinations of the kind here under consideration, consists in a slight temporary raising or enhancing of prices. No loss or damage to any one, to any individual, or to the community, can come from the mere act of combination, or agreement; and this raising or enhancing of prices works precisely the same loss or damage, whether it result from the act of one individual separately, or of several individuals in combination.

II. The existence of a standard of prices fixed by law is the sole legal foundation on which can rest the unlawful or criminal quality of the mere act of raising prices, or preventing competition between the parties combining.

If prices are fixed by statute, then every buyer has the right in law to buy at the prices so fixed; and he suffers a legal injury if any seller raises prices to a figure above the ones so fixed. In such a case, the raising of prices above the statutory figure is an act in violation of the legal rights of buyers, and may be a crime. Its criminal quality is the same, whether such raising be the act of one individual separately, or of several individuals in combination. If, on the contrary, prices are not fixed by statute, then no one has the legal right to buy at any fixed price; then, too, no one suffers a legal injury from any raising of prices. It follows, then, in that case, that a combination to raise prices is not a combination to do an act that is unlawful. It is, therefore, not a crime.

III. The early English Statutes went on that idea. They fixed prices by statute. Thereby they gave buyers certain definite legal rights. Thereby they made it a violation of those rights to raise prices above the rates so fixed. And such raising of prices was equally unlawful, whether done by a single individual separately, or by more than one in combination.

IV. The crimes arising under this branch of the law were well known, in the English law, under the general classification of "Offences against Public Trade;" and under definite legal terms, "forestalling," "engrossing," and "regrating."

V. The raising of prices was also made a crime under some of our early statutes, under a scheme of legislation of the same nature with that of the early English statutes. The crimes created by those early statutes had assigned to them the old well-recognized English names.

VI. Those early State statutes were either repealed, or became obsolete.

VII. Thereafter, until recent interpretations by some of our courts of mere general phrases, which made crimes of combinations to do "acts injurious to trade or commerce," no authority exists, which has come under my observation, which holds that a mere agreement, to raise or maintain prices, of the property of the parties combining, or for the mere regulation of the action of the parties combining, constitutes a crime.

VIII. On the contrary, there was a large class of combinations, which, from a very early period in the English law, were held to be indictable conspiracies. Such were all combinations "to injure individuals," that is, to deprive other individuals than the parties combining of recognized legal rights. Such combinations, especially combinations by a number of individuals to injure another in his business or trade, were manifold in form. So far as I have been able to discover, such combinations became criminal under no statute. If any acts can be considered crimes at common law, those acts are such. Here then was a large class of crimes which were "acts injurious to trade and commerce," and which came properly under no other classification.

In view of these positions, how should our courts interpret statutes which make it an indictable conspiracy for persons to combine to do acts "injurious to trade or commerce"?

It is respectfully submitted, that they should follow the common law, and that long line of authorities in our tribunals of the highest weight, which hold, with an unvarying tenor, that the essence of a crime is an "injury," that is, the violation of some legal right, and which hold especially, as to the crime of conspiracy, that an agreement, or combination, which is to be criminal, must contemplate the doing of some act that is unlawful, either as means or end. A mere agreement to do an act is only the initial stage of that act. With all possible deference to our two most august tribunals, it appears to be an error in legal reasoning, to hold that the mere agreement, the mere initial stage of an act, can constitute a crime, when the act itself, when consummated, will violate no legal right. And it is further submitted, as before stated, that the correct legal interpretation of the phrase an "act injurious to trade or commerce" is, that it means an act which violates some legal right in connection with trade or commerce.

One further consideration may be added. The United States Supreme Court has laid down the following as one of the guiding principles in the interpretation of statutes :(a)

" Even in construing the terms of a statute, courts must take notice of the history of legislation, and out of different possible constructions, select and apply the one that *best comports with the genius of our institutions* and is therefore most likely to have been the construction intended by the law-making power."

" The history of legislation," as set forth in the preceding pages, seems to make it clear, that attempts to control the contractual freedom of persons engaged in trade and commerce have been found unwise and pernicious. The "genius of our institutions" is overwhelmingly in favor of emancipation from all restrictions on complete contractual freedom—in private employments.

In public employments—wise jurists and wise legislators are well agreed, that the individual citizen must have all needful protection at the hands of the State.

But what are we to say of the latest attempt at State control of trade and commerce, in private employments?

(a) *Texas & Pac. R. Co.* v. *Interstate Commerce Commission*, 162 U. S. 197, 218.

In a recent issue of our daily press we find the following statement :(a)

"ANTI TRUST AMENDMENT.

"WASHINGTON, June 29.—The Republican members of the Judiciary Committee at a meeting this morning agreed upon the following form of an amendment to the Tariff Bill :

"'Every person, firm, or corporation who shall monopolize or engross, or attempt to monopolize or engross, or who shall combine or conspire with any other person, firm, or corporation to monopolize or engross the *trade or commerce in any article*, among the several States or with foreign nations, for the purpose of unduly *enhancing the price of such article*, shall be deemed guilty of a misdemeanor, and on conviction thereof shall be punished by a fine of not less than $500 nor more than $10,000, and by imprisonment at hard labor not less than six months nor more than two years ; and in case of a corporation found guilty of said offence the jury shall also ascertain and find what officers of the corporation caused or directed the corporation to commit such offence, and such officers, on being found guilty of causing or directing the corporation to commit the offence of which it is found guilty, shall be liable to the punishment aforesaid. It shall be a sufficient pleading, in the indictment, to describe the offence in the language of this law ; and the fact that a manufacturer or dealer refuses to sell to the public in interstate or foreign trade otherwise than through special factors or agents shall be deemed *prima facie* evidence of monopolizing or attempting to monopolize the trade among the several States or with foreign nations.

"'The several circuit courts of the United States are hereby invested with jurisdiction to prevent and restrain violations of this law ; and it shall be the duty of the several District Attorneys of the United States in their respective districts, under the direction of the Attorney-General, to institute proceedings in equity to prevent and restrain such violations. Such proceedings may be by the way of a petition setting forth the case and praying that such violation shall be enjoined or otherwise prohibited. When the parties complained of shall have been duly notified of such petition the court shall proceed, as soon as may be, to the hearing and determination of the

---

(a) New York *Sun*, June 30, 1897.

case, and pending such petition and before final decree the court may at any time make such temporary restraining order or prohibition as shall be deemed just in the premises.'"

What shall we have next in the course of the present anarchistic crusade against capital and property?

And at such a time, where shall we find the two courts which have heretofore been the bulwarks on which we could always depend—for the protection of life, liberty, and property?

GENERAL INDEX.

APPRENTICESHIP, 33, 34.
"ANTI-TRUST" ACT, 172.
    considered in connection with Interstate Commerce Act, 173.
    provisions of, as to monopolies, 174.
    U. S. v. *E. C. Knight Company*, 174.
    effect of this decision upon, 176.
    held not inconsistent with Interstate Commerce Act, 176.
BLACKSTONE,
    definition of offences against public trade, 91.
    definition of conspiracy, 90.
    definition of crime, 147.
BUYERS AND SELLERS,
    respective rights of, in matter of control of prices, 143.
    buyers have been objects of law's solicitude, 144.
    sellers are entitled to equal protection, 144.
    the "public interest," 145.
    in fact all are both buyers and sellers, 145.
    the "public interest" must be left to the parties, 145.
    duty of the State to afford equal rights and protection, 146.
    no distinction between sellers of labor and of merchandise, 146.
    or between sellers of "articles of necessity" and others, 146.
CAPITAL,
    effects of concentration of, 181.
    corporations the best agency to handle, 184.
    ownership of, always diverse, 184.
    increase of, proportionate to increase in wealth, 184.
    relations of, to labor, 185.
    necessity for security of, 186.
COLONIAL LAW,
    entire absence at first of attempts to fix prices, 3.
    congressional action during revolution, 4.
    very soon repealed, 4.
COMBINATIONS TO FIX PRICES
    made criminal conspiracies by early English Statutes, 43.
    previous law as to conspiracy, 44.
    essence of such crime the fixing prices *contrary to law*, 46.
    such statutes only one feature of attempts to control prices, etc., 82.
    statute a dead letter as to prices of merchandise, 46, 47, 49.

only one case as to prices of labor, 46, 47, 49.
later statutes recognize workmen's right to combine, 47.
English law as finally established, 49
permits such combinations provided no legal injury to others, 49.
Mogul S. S. Co. v. *McGregor*, 50.
of merchandise and of labor on same footing, 83.
(See " Conspiracies to commit acts injurious to trade or commerce.")
classified by Blackstone under " Monopolies," 92.
and so considered in recent decisions, 94.
but not with legal accuracy to be so regarded, 94.
English statutes as to, never part of our law, 96, 137.
Commonwealth v. *Hunt*, 96.
Commonwealth v. *Carlisle*, 97.
departure from the law in recent cases, 135.
People v. *Sheldon*, 135, 140.
U. S. v. *Trans-Missouri Freight Assn.*, 135, 170.
definition of conspiracy applied to such combinations, 149.
no legal right to buy at any price in absence of statute fixing price, 149.
no legal injury by refusal to sell, 153, 158.
decision as to, in *Freight Assn.* case same as in *People* v. *Sheldon*, 170.
this point explained, 177.
reasonableness of prices fixed not a consideration, 177.
decision of the two cases summarized, 178.
economic aspects of, 179.
experience shows no damage done by, 179.
reason is found in the interest account, 180.

COMMON CARRIERS,
English statute law as to, 86-88.
great increase in control of, 117.
large number of American statutes regulating, 117.
also cases of intervention by courts, 118.
People v. *New York Central, etc. R. R. Co.*, 118.
Railroad Commissioners of New York, statute, 130.
Transportation Corporations Law of New York, 133.
Lough v. *Outerbridge*, 169.

COMPETITION,
contracts to restrict between parties combining, not a crime in England, 82.
though such contracts may not be enforced, 82.
such a contract held criminal in New York in *People* v. *Sheldon*, 135.
and by Supreme Court in *Trans-Missouri F. A.* case, 135.
these decisions irreconcilable with previous authorities, 135.
" public interest " in freedom of, 157.
contracts to prevent, enforced in New York, 159.

GENERAL INDEX. 197

CONSPIRACY,
   Hawkins' definition of, 44.
   Blackstone's definition of, 90.
   definition of crime as applied to, 149.
   of workmen to raise price of labor, 153.
   definition of, 156.
   Pettibone v. *United States*, 156.
   none in *People* v. *Sheldon*, 157.
   the true doctrine, 190, 191.
"CONSPIRACIES TO COMMIT ACTS INJURIOUS TO TRADE OR COMMERCE,"
   combinations to raise prices so classified, 89.
   Blackstone's definition of conspiracy, 90, 190.
   no mention of conspiracies in restraint of trade, 90.
   such combinations not indictable conspiracies at common law, 91.
   English statutes as to, never part of our law, 96, 137.
   New York statute of conspiracy, 109, 110.
   People v. *Fisher*, 110.
   the source of later heresies in the law, 110.
   but sound as to the point decided, 112.
   not an authority that mere combination to raise wages is a crime, 112, 190.
   interference with legal rights of others essential to the crime, 113.
   amendment of 1870, 114.
   did not change the common law, 115.
   departure from the law in *People* v. *Sheldon*, 135.
   unsound interpretation of the statute in that case, 138.
   meaning of the phrase "act injurious to trade," 140.
   the construction given to it in *People* v. *Sheldon*, 140.
   People v. *North River Sugar Refy. Co.*, contrasted, 169.
CORPORATIONS,
   the best means of employing large capital, 183.
   the advantages of, to society, 186.
CRIME,
   essentials of, 146.
   involves violation of legal right, 146.
   attempts to commit, 146.
   Blackstone's definition, 147.
   Stephen's definition, 148.
   modification of the latter, 149.
   apparent exception, 149.
   definition applied to conspiracy, 149.
DEMAND AND SUPPLY, LAW OF, 5.
   makes legislative interference with prices needless, 5.
ECONOMIC ASPECTS, 179.
ENGLISH LAW,
   to-day favors freedom of owner's rights to fix prices, 3.
   many early statutes restricting that right, 9.

GENERAL INDEX.

ENGROSSING,
    of butter and cheese, prohibited ; penalty therefor, 38.
    (See Forestalling, etc.)
FOOD,
    prices of to be reasonable, 12.
FORESTALLING, REGRATING AND ENGROSSING, 37.
    made crimes by early statutes, 38.
    exceptions, 40.
    forestalling defined, 39.
    regrating defined, 39, 40.
    engrossing defined, 40.
    attempt to raise prices constituted the crime, 40.
    no distinction between acts of individuals and of combinations, 40.
    examples of statutes against, 38, 39, 41.
    effect of such statutes, to abolish middlemen, 41.
    statutes repealed, 1772, 48.
    intent to abolish offenses also, 48.
    but *Rex* v. *Waddington, contra*, 48.
    offenses expressly abolished, 1844, 48.
    enumerated by Blackstone as " Offences against Public Trade," 91, 92.
    English statutes as to, never part of American law, 96-98.
    never crimes here except under certain Revolutionary statutes, 98, 189.
    early Massachusetts statute against, 108.
FREEDOM OF CONTRACT, 152.
HANDICRAFTSMEN,
    to use but one trade or " mystery," 22.
    goldsmiths' work regulated, 23.
    clothiers' work regulated, 24.
INDICTMENT,
    for combinations to raise prices, very few, 3, 46, 49.
    under New York statute of conspiracy, 110.
    People v. *Fisher*, 110.
INTERPRETATION,
    of statutes changing the common law, 138.
    Tex. & Pac. R. R. Co. v. *Interstate Commerce Comn.*, 191.
INTERSTATE COMMERCE,
    Act examined, 171.
    considered in connection with " Anti-Trust" Act, 173.
LABOR,
    right to fix prices of one's own, 153.
    and to combine for that purpose, 153.
    Commonwealth v. *Hunt*, 153.
LABORERS, STATUTES OF, 9, 15.
    every person bound to serve when required, 10, 27, 28, 29.
    wages fixed, 11, 16.

penalty for taking more than lawful wage, 11, 13, 19.
penalty for giving to beggars, 12.
found inadequate and superseded, 24, 27.
hours of labor fixed, 29.
certain laborers not to abandon work until completed, 30.

MANUFACTURES,
of cloths, length, breadth and quality regulated, 35.
of worsteds, inspectors to ordain rules respecting, 36, 37.

MONOPOLIES,
enumerated by Blackstone among "Offences against Public Trade," 92.
and said by him to include combinations to raise prices, 92, 94.
but not so with accuracy, 94, 95.
defined, 95.
not unlawful until 21 Jac. I., 95.
early Massachusetts statutes against, 101, 108.
a ground for decision below in "Sugar Trust case," 169.
but not approved in Court of Appeals, 169.
provisions of "Anti-Trust" Act as to, 174.
effects of, on prices, 181.
proposed amendment to Tariff Act of 1897, as to, 192.

NECESSITY, ARTICLES OF,
basis of attempted distinction in *People* v. *Sheldon*, 142.
difficulty of determining what are, 143.
no sound legal basis for such distinction, 143, 146.

OFFENCES AGAINST PUBLIC TRADE,
Blackstone's enumeration of, 91–93.
legal injury involved was the "enhancing prices," 94, 189.
this offence same whether by individual or by combination, 94.
English statutes as to, never part of our law, 96.
but were in minds of drafters of our early statutes, 109.
(See " Prices.")
no conviction reported in this country under those statutes, 109.

PRICES,
statutory regulation of, in early statutes, 2, 4, 9.
raising of, by individuals or combinations, a crime, 2.
conspiracies to raise, 2.
statutes fixing, examples of, 10, 12, 16, 21, 24.
enhancing, by engrossing merchandise, forbidden, 21.
abandonment of attempts to fix definite prices by statute, 26.
but authority given to justices of peace, etc., to fix prices of labor, 26, 30, 31.
of merchandise, legislation to prevent raising of, 37.
attempts to ra'se, constituted crimes of engrossing, etc., 40.
the same whether act of individual or combination, 40, 83.
statutes to keep prices up, examples of, 42.
combinations to raise, made criminal by early statutes, 43.

(See combinations to raise prices.)
right of owner to fix his own price fully established in England, 83.
combinations to raise, never criminal at common law, 83.
though such an agreement might not be enforced, 83.
English statutes fixing, never part of our law, 96.
early American attempts to control, by statute, 98.
Resolutions of Congress of Nov. 22, 1777, 98.
New York statute pursuant to the above, 100.
repealed the same year, 100.
similar experience in New England, 100.
Providence resolutions of Dec. 25, 1776, 101.
Massachusetts statutes pursuant to above, 101-107.
logical in that they gave the public the right to buy, 105.
difficulty of enforcing recognized, 107.
repealed for their futility, 108.
contract to fix held a crime in *People* v. *Sheldon*, 135.
of " articles of prime necessity," 142.
seller's right to fix his own, 143, 152.
no distinction between seller of labor and of merchandise, 143.
no legal right to buy at any price in absence of a statute fixing, 149.
such a statute would be unconstitutional, 150.
Taylor v. *Porter*, 150.
unless State can fix, there is no legal injury in owner's fixing his own, 153, 189.
either by his own will or by combination with others, 153.
no legal wrong in buyer having to pay higher, 158, 188.
effects of monopolies on, 181.
the proper regulation of, 182.
statutory control unnecessary, 187.
and inadequate, 187.

PROPERTY,
no right to take for private use, 150.
the old statutes fixing prices practically did this, 152.
suspension of this rule in times of stress, 188.

PUBLIC AND PRIVATE EMPLOYMENTS,
distinction between, in regard to State control, 6.
opposite tendencies of the law, 7.
control of public employments a necessity, 7.
its province increasing, 7.

PUBLIC EMPLOYMENTS,
right of State control now fully established, 84.
distinction between, and private employments, 84.
Munn v. *People*, 84.
number of, at first small, 85.
chiefly incident to use of public highways, 85.
innkeepers, 85.

carriers, 85.
English statutes as to carriers, 86–88.
course of English law as to, reverse of course as to private employments, 88.
same with American law, 117.
great increase in control of, 117.
due to increase in number of, 117.
and because property acquired by eminent domain, 117.
large number of statutes regulating railroads, 117.
also cases of intervention of courts by mandamus, 118.
People v. *New York Central, etc. R. R. Co.*, 118.
Munn v. *People*, 124.
warehouses there in question virtually part of the highways, 129.
New York statute creating Railroad Commissioners, 130.

RAILROADS,
(See "Common Carriers; Public Employments").

REGRATING,
(See "Forestalling," etc.).

RESTRAINT OF TRADE,
English law as to contracts in, 50.
may not be enforced, 49, 82.
but not criminal, 49, 82.
and not violations of legal rights of others, 49, 83.
Mogul S. S. Co. v. *McGregor*, 50.
American courts have even enforced such contracts, 159.
Diamond Match Co. v. *Roeber*, 160.
Leslie v. *Lorillard*, 164.
Tode v. *Gross*, 166.
Matthews v. *Associated Press*, 167.
People v. *North River Sugar Ref'g Co.*, 168.

ROYAL COMMISSION ON MASTER AND SERVANT ACT,
extract from report, 156.

SERVANTS,
diet and apparel of, regulated, 23.
unmarried under thirty, must serve when required, 28.
not to be put away except for reasonable cause, 28.
nor without one quarter's warning, 28.
women, wages and service of, to be fixed by justices, etc., 33.

STEPHEN, SERJEANT,
definition of crime, 148.
modification thereof, 149.

TRUSTS AND MONOPOLIES,
recent revival of ancient fears respecting, 4.
modern legislation on same line with ancient, 37, 192.
provisions of "Anti-Trust" Act as to, 174.
no basis for alarm on account of, 180.
proposed amendment to Tariff Act of 1897, as to, 192.

WAGES,
> To be fixed by certain officers, 30, 31.
> penalties for giving or receiving higher than lawful, 32.
> exceptions of day laborers in harvest, 32.
> authority of officers to fix wages extended, 35.
> as a result of inefficiency of previous statute, 35.
> these statutes not repealed until 1875, 35.
> combinations to raise or reduce, not a crime at common law, 97.
> *Commonwealth* v. *Hunt*, 96.
> *Commonwealth* v. *Carlisle*, 97.
> *Bishop's Criminal Law*, 97.
> New York Statute as to conspiracy and decisions thereunder, 109, 110.
> (See " Conspiracy.")

WHOLE NUMBER OF PAGES 218.

www.ingramcontent.com/pod-product-compliance
Lightning Source LLC
Chambersburg PA
CBHW031830230426
43669CB00009B/1296